ARTHUR SAMUEL PEAKE 1865 - 1929

Arthur Samuel Peake
A BIOGRAPHY

JOHN T. WILKINSON

Arthur Samuel Peake

A BIOGRAPHY

WIPF & STOCK · Eugene, Oregon

Wipf and Stock Publishers
199 W 8th Ave, Suite 3
Eugene, OR 97401

Arthur Samuel Peake
A Biography
By Wilkinson, John T.
Copyright©1971 Methodist Publishing - Epworth Press
ISBN 13: 978-1-5326-0534-5
Publication date 8/19/2016
Previously published by Epworth Press, 1971

Every effort has been made to trace the current copyright owner of this publication but without success. If you have any information or interest in the copyright, please contact the publishers.

To the memory of
ELSIE CANN

ACKNOWLEDGEMENTS

Thanks are due to the following for permission to reprint selections from Peake's writings:

Messrs Hodder and Stoughton; Messrs Thomas Nelson & Sons Ltd; Epworth Press; the John Rylands Library; Manchester University Press; the *Methodist Recorder*; the *Primitive Methodist Leader*; *The Times Literary Supplement*; the National Free Church Federal Council.

CONTENTS

Preface		ix
Table of Events		xi
1.	Formative Years: 1865–1883	1
2.	Oxford: 1883–1892	18
3.	Hartley College, Manchester	45
4.	The University of Manchester	68
5.	The Interpreter of the Bible	85
6.	The Editor	124
7.	The Preacher	138
8.	Movements towards Reform	144
9.	The Ecumenical Churchman	156
10.	The Man and his Achievement	173
Appendix		
	Select Bibliography	198
Index		208

ABBREVIATIONS

P.M.Q.R.	*Primitive Methodist Quarterly Review*
P.M.L.	*Primitive Methodist Leader*
H.R.	*Holborn Review*
M.R.	*Methodist Recorder*
J.R.L.B.	*John Rylands Library Bulletin*
E.G.T.	*Expositor's Greek Testament*
Memoir	Leslie S. Peake, *Arthur Samuel Peake: A Memoir*
Essays in Commemoration	(ed.) J. T. Wilkinson, *Arthur Samuel Peake (1865–1929): Essays in Commemoration*

PREFACE

I AM greatly honoured by the invitation of the Trustees to deliver the A. S. Peake Memorial Lecture during the Methodist Conference in the city of Birmingham in 1969. I am the more so because this is the second time this honour has been conferred upon me. The earlier occasion was in 1960, when the subject was *Principles of Biblical Interpretation*, in which I sought to indicate the main stress of Peake's teaching, recognizing that the things for which he stood were still in need of renewed emphasis. This year, 1969, is the fortieth anniversary of Peake's death, and, in this time of biblical and theological uncertainty, it seemed a fitting thing to present the same emphasis again, but to do so on the background of his life and times.

Twice during the earlier years I have been approached with the request that I should undertake the wider work, but, largely from a sense of personal inadequacy, I refused to commit myself to the responsibility of so important an enterprise. However, in an endeavour to meet these requests at least half-way, in 1956 I did consent to edit a volume of tributes to Peake's life and work, which was published under the title *Arthur Samuel Peake : 1865-1929 : Essays in Commemoration*; included in the volume were representative excerpts from Peake's own writings. When, however, it was again suggested to me that the occasion was ripe for the larger study, after much careful and prolonged thought, and under the pressure of a number of friends whose judgement I could not easily set aside, I reluctantly agreed. In 1930, the Rev. Leslie S. Peake M.A., B.LITT. published a biography of his father entitled *Arthur Samuel Peake: A Memoir*. It was his unhesitating approval which finally brought me to a decision to undertake the present work. I should like at once to acknowledge my grateful indebtedness to Mr Peake's volume, much of which is directly or indirectly embodied in my own book.

Two things were important factors in my ultimate decision.

Many years ago, the late Miss Elsie Cann, who had been Peake's private secretary for some twenty-five years, asked me whether, following her decease, I would accept the responsibility of dealing with her numerous papers. I was then unaware of either the content or extent of the material involved, but when these papers eventually came into my temporary possession, I discovered that they were almost entirely Peake's own papers, comprising thousands of letters, manuscripts, reviews and printed material. When I was asked to undertake the present new biography, I could not deny that this amazing collection of papers did provide the primary material for the undertaking.

Furthermore, the issue of a revised edition of *Peake's Commentary on the Bible* in 1962, which though entirely re-written still bears the original title, was at once an indication of the far-reaching influence of his creative work still existing, and was in itself a tribute to his greatness.

In the light of these things it did seem fitting that some picture of Peake's life and work was both reasonable and required, as a final memorial of his unique labours.

I am most grateful for the encouragement and help of many friends, amongst whom I must name the following: the Rev. Gordon S. Wakefield, M.A., B.LITT., who first urged upon me that the book should be written, and whose unfailing interest and friendship I greatly value; the Rev. J. Y. Muckle, B.A., my friend and former colleague at Hartley Victoria College, Manchester, with whom I have discussed many matters; Mr James Muckle, M.A., who has willingly given me help with a quantity of Peake's correspondence; the Rev. Henry Rack, M.A., Librarian of Hartley Victoria College; and to my younger son, the Rev. Alan B. Wilkinson, M.A., Ph.D., with whom I have discussed the whole structure and content of the book. By no means least do I owe much to my wife for her constant encouragement and unfailing patience.

I have been growingly aware that those who still regard themselves as 'Peake's men', although gradually diminishing in number, owe an incalculable debt not only to his teaching but to his friendship, and none more than myself. I trust that this volume may, in some small measure, indicate and acknowledge that unspeakable debt.

Knighton,　　　　　　　　　　　　　　　　　　　　　　JOHN T. WILKINSON
Radnorshire

TABLE OF EVENTS

1865 Born at Leek, Staffordshire, 24 November.
1874 Entered Ludlow Grammar School.
1876 Entered Grammar School, Stratford-on-Avon.
1877 Entered King Henry VIII School, Coventry.
1883 Went to Oxford with a Close Scholarship from St John's College and a School Exhibition from Coventry.
1884 Became a local preacher on the Oxford Circuit.
1885 Gained a Third Class in Classical Moderations.
1887 Elected Casberd Scholar at St John's College.
Gained a First Class in the Honours School of Theology.
1889 Elected Denyer and Johnson Scholar by Oxford University.
1890 Gained University Prize for Ellerton Essay.
Accepted Lectureship at Mansfield College, Oxford.
Elected to Theological Fellowship at Merton College.
1891 Spent two months at Heidelberg.
1892 Appointed tutor at Hartley College, Manchester.
Married Harriet Mary Sillman, of Oxford, on 29 June.
1895 Accepted Lectureship at Lancashire Independent College, Manchester.
1897 Published *A Guide to Biblical Study*.
1899 Spent two months in Switzerland and Italy.
Appointed one of the original members of the Council of Governors for the John Rylands Library, Manchester.
1900 Birth of eldest son, Leslie Sillman, 4 April.
1902 Published *Commentary on Hebrews* in 'The Century Bible'.
Underwent first operation.
1903 Birth of second son, Arnold Arthur, 16 March.
Published *Commentary on Colossians* in 'Expositor's Greek Testament'.
1904 Became Professor of Biblical Criticism and Exegesis at Manchester University.
Appointed Dean of the Faculty of Theology.
Published *The Problem of Suffering in the Old Testament*.
Accepted Lectureship at United Methodist College, Manchester.
Engaged Miss Elsie Cann as private secretary.
1905 Birth of third son, Clive Talbot, 20 May.
Published *Commentary on Job* in 'The Century Bible'.

1905	Appointed Chairman of the Book Committee of the John Rylands Library. Became a Director for the newly-created *Primitive Methodist Leader*. Edited *Inaugural Lectures* for the Faculty of Theology, Manchester University.
1906	Received Honorary Degree of Bachelor of Divinity at Manchester University. Published *Reform in Sunday School Teaching*.
1907	Received Honorary Degree of Doctor of Divinity from Aberdeen University.
1908	Published *The Religion of Israel, The Christian Race, Election and Service, Faded Myths, Christianity: its Nature and Truth*.
1909	Published *A Critical Introduction to the New Testament*.
1910	Published *Heroes and Martyrs of Faith*, and first volume of *Commentary on Jeremiah* in 'The Century Bible'.
1912	Undertook extra work at Manchester University and resigned lectureships at Lancashire Independent and United Methodist Colleges. Removed to Freshfield, near Southport. Published the second volume of *Commentary on Jeremiah*.
1913	Published *The Bible: Its Origin, its Significance and its Abiding Worth*.
1914	Majority Celebrations at Hartley College.
1917	Attended Committees on Army and Religion Enquiry.
1918	Elected President of the Manchester Classical Association. Became Member of Methodist Union Committee. Published *Prisoners of Hope*.
1919	Published *The Revelation of John* (Hartley Lecture). Edited *Peake's Commentary on the Bible*. Appointed Editor of the *Holborn Review*.
1920	Returned to Manchester. Received Honorary Degree of Doctor of Divinity at the University of Oxford.
1921	Elected Vice-Chairman of the Council of John Rylands Library.
1922	Published *The Nature of Scripture*. Began to attend Lambeth Conferences on Reunion.
1923	Published *Brotherhood in the Old Testament* (John Clifford Lecture).
1924	Elected President of the Society for Old Testament Study. Invited to deliver the Cole Lectures for 1926 at Vanderbilt University, Tennessee. Subsequently forbidden under medical advice.
1925	Edited *The People and the Book*. Edited (along with Dr R. G. Parsons) *An Outline of Christianity*. Appointed Pro-Vice-Chancellor of Manchester University.
1926	Published *Life of Sir William P. Hartley*.
1927	Elected Chairman by the Council of John Rylands Library. Attended Lausanne Conference.
1928	Became President of the National Free Church Council.
1929	Went on tour to Egypt and Palestine. Died following an operation, 19 August.

CHAPTER ONE

FORMATIVE YEARS: 1865–1883

I

IN A surviving fragment of autobiography the subject of this book records the story of his early days.

I was born at Leek, in Staffordshire, on 24 November 1865, about ten minutes to seven in the morning. My father, Samuel Peake, was a Primitive Methodist minister: my mother, Rosabella Peake, was the daughter of John Smith, a farmer who farmed his own land at Newton, near Cwm, in Herefordshire. Her parents were old-fashioned Church of England people, but their daughter, Rosabella, was converted under the preaching of the Primitive Methodists, and had to endure opposition from some members of her family. My father was stationed in the Cwm Circuit, and in that way made the acquaintance of my mother. They were married towards the end of 1860.

My father's family were Primitive Methodists. His father, Benjamin Peake, was a local preacher and for several years conducted a night school, which proved of great value to a good many who had grown up with scarcely the rudiments of education. My great-grandmother on my father's side lived at Madeley in Shropshire. She was a god-daughter of the famous John Fletcher, Vicar of Madeley—Wesley's designated successor—and was a member of Mrs Fletcher's class. As we should expect, her god-father took his responsibility very seriously. The Methodist preachers used to stay at her home, so that my father's family had been in connexion with Methodism from the days of John Wesley.

My uncle, George Peake, was an elder brother of my father. He entered the Primitive Methodist ministry some years earlier. The two brothers were very different in temperament and appearance. My uncle was a man of sweet and gentle disposition. He broke down in health comparatively early in life, and I remember him only as an old gentleman with grey hair, a long white beard and a benevolent face. My grandfather had a knack of rhyming which he turned to account in the composition of numerous hymns, which had a certain vogue for a time in the district to which he belonged, although they had not the faintest trace of poetic quality. My uncle George wrote comparatively little, but was the author of the hymn, 'I'll sing of Jesus crucified', now almost entirely forgotten, but the chorus of which was well-known throughout the Primitive Methodist Church:

Above the rest this note shall swell,
My Jesus hath done all things well!

He was also a temperance advocate, and designed two trees, one the tree of misery and death, exhibiting the roots of intemperance and the multitudinous evils which it produced, and the tree of health and happiness, showing the fruits in health, character, and fortune of total abstinence. The pictures hung on the walls of many a cottage and did not a little to foster temperance sentiment.

Of his father, the Rev. Samuel Peake, who was born at Wheaton Ashton, Staffordshire, on 12 December 1830 and who died on 25 October 1914, in his eighty-fourth year,[1] Peake writes in some detail.

He had a naturally strong constitution and great vitality, though the reckless energy which he had thrown into his work in earlier years had told its tale, and left him with all too little strength for the much-loved work, as old age came upon him. For the greater part of his ministry he had been afflicted by deafness, which largely shut him out from social intercourse and greatly hindered his work. He was by nature a moral rather than religious temperament. After his conversion he was a deeply religious man, reverent, devout, given to prayer and meditation, concerned for his own salvation and the salvation of others: but primarily religion for him rested on morality. He gave himself to God because it was his duty. His experience in conversion, however, and in his Christian life, kindled the morality with an intense glow, and charged it with a more thrilling emotion. Hence he found himself at home in the torrential evangelism of his earlier period, though he was always alert in his distrust of mere feelings, and inflexible in applying the ethical test. He had great gifts as an evangelist. He accepted with unquestioning conviction the old-fashioned evangelicalism; his message was never paralysed by the modern misgivings or attenuated by modern sentiment. In his late years he perhaps yielded something to the time-spirit, but not so as to weaken the affirmations on which his ministry had rested. He had a passionate earnestness, deep pity for the unconverted, unfaltering faith in Christ's power to save the worst, a faith abundantly verified in the course of his ministry. He had in a remarkable degree the faculty of appeal, an appeal sometimes of tremendous force. The sense of urgency was especially notable. But he was never a mere revivalist: he laid much emphasis on the fruits of the Spirit. As one who claimed to have received 'the second blessing' he was in full sympathy with the holiness movement, and often preached the doctrine and pressed home the privilege of entire sanctification. As a preacher he was plain, practical and direct. He was no scholar or theologian, at least in the technical sense, but he knew the answer to the question: 'What shall I do to be saved?' The common people heard him gladly, and if he knew little theology, except of the Methodist type, he had at least studied that.

His children honour him for the integrity of his character; they are grateful for the self-sacrifice for their welfare. He was stern and even severe in the training he gave them, but the sternness masked a real depth of affection and was the expression of his concern for their highest good. And now within the veil he rests in God, in whom indeed he had rested long before.[2]

---

[1] He was buried at Birtley, in the Leintwardine Circuit, Herefordshire, by the side of his first wife who had died in 1875.

[2] Cf. 'The Rev. Samuel Peake: An Appreciation' (*P.M.L.* 5 November 1914) 'He lived in vital correspondence with Christ.'

It is more than probable that Arthur inherited from his father his noble sense of duty, his quality of rectitude and his strong loyalty to what he believed to be the truth.

For his mother, who died when he was but ten years of age, Arthur always cherished a deep affection, and spoke of her with the utmost reverence. Many years afterwards his eldest son recorded that the only time he ever saw his father moved to tears in public was when Peake mentioned her name at the celebrations in honour of his twenty-one years of service at Hartley College.[1] When very young she and her sister Margaretta had become members of the Newton Society, and despite the fact that in the neighbourhood Methodism was frowned upon, they still held fast to their profession. She possessed a deepening experience of Christ, and one who knew her from her youth speaks of her many years afterwards as one who 'seemed to live on the borders of the better world'![2] As late as 1924 one who had known her during the days of ministry at Leintwardine, and who had been Arthur's first schoolmaster in the village school, wrote to her son: 'I often visited Leintwardine; it will please you to know that the fragrance of your dear mother's memory endures there, and will so long as any remain who knew her.'[3] From her early years she had been a diligent student of the Bible, and until he was seven years of age Arthur's education was almost entirely in her hands, and it was from her that he was largely disciplined in the reading of the Scriptures, much of which he learnt by heart.[4]

Those who knew her say that Arthur inherited from her not only his brilliant gifts, but the gracious and lovable nature which was an outstanding mark of his character and disposition.

The mother of six children and an eager fellow-labourer at the churches where her husband ministered, she toiled beyond her strength. In the autumn of 1875 she was taken seriously ill, and on 7 October 1875, she died amidst universal sorrow.

The Peake family consisted of four brothers and two sisters.[5] Arthur's eldest brother, George Newton, was a boy of fine character and he found in him a noble example. Many surviving letters reveal the quality of his

---

[1] Leslie S. Peake, *Arthur Samuel Peake: A Memoir* (1930) p. 27.

[2] J. Farr: 'Reminiscences' (*P.M.L.* 26 December 1912).

[3] Letter from Rev. E. E. Ingham, of Knutsford, dated 19 January 1924.

[4] An amusing reference to his early days is recorded by Peake in a letter to the Rev. Thomas Hacking, one of his former students, dated 1 June 1924: 'About the time when I was six years old I was very eager to become a missionary. My mother said to me: "But suppose you were to be in a desert country, where there was nothing to eat or drink, what would you do then?" I was rather shocked at what I took to be her want of faith, and said: "But don't you know the promise: 'Thy bread shall be given and thy butter shall be sure'?"' We are tempted to suggest that this was Peake's first incursion into the field of textual emendation!

[5] George Newton, b. at Weobley, 20 October 1861; Rosabella Alice, b. at Leintwardine, 20 December 1863; Arthur Samuel, b. at Leek, 24 November 1865; Emily Margaret, b. at Hadnall, 15 September 1867; Albert Edwin, b. at Hadnall, who died in infancy; Ernest Vincent, b. at Bromsgrove, 4 October 1871, who died in Johannesburg. William Oliver, b. 11 March 1879 was the son of a second marriage.

inspiration and the depth of his wise counsel. In a letter[1] following George's death in 1916, Peake paid a fine tribute to his influence:

... He was a fine character, very unselfish, exceptionally considerate, charitable in his judgment of others, very sympathetic, helpful to those in trouble, and without any parade. He was very upright in his dealings, energetic, hard-working, with careful attention to detail, gracious and sound in judgment. He seemed not to have a trace or speck of jealousy in his disposition. He rejoiced heartily in the success and welfare of others. He endeared himself to all. He and I were greatly attached to each other. He was my oldest link with the past. He was four years older than I was, so that in childhood he was less my playmate than my sister who was less than two years younger.

Of his elder sister, Rosabella Alice, Arthur writes with great tenderness.[2]

She took her first name from my mother. She was a child of extraordinary precocity, and very lovable disposition. At the age of three she was taken ill suddenly one evening, and died during the night when my father was away from home. My father had scarce learned the tragic news when he was called away to bury the child of another man, and I have heard him speak of the sharpness of pain which he experienced in performing in such circumstances the duty of his vocation. The loss of Alice was irretrievable to us. Probably it affected my younger sister more seriously than any of us, partly because she had only brothers and no sister, partly because too heavy a burden of responsibility was thrown too early upon her. But it was a great loss to my eldest brother, and it was similarly, though perhaps not in so great a degree, a loss to myself. My mother felt the loss of Alice very keenly, and dedicated a touching poem to her memory.

In the case of a child who died when she was a little over three years old, it may seem strange to speak of her knowledge, and of goodness in one so immature. But she had a knowledge of the Bible much beyond her years. When she and my brother were catechised by my father, George complained that Alice gave him no chance owing to the eagerness of her replies. The sweetness of her disposition and her unselfishness were a cherished tradition in our family. Her piety would now be regarded as unnatural and even morbid, for her mind dwelt constantly on the thought of heaven, so much so indeed that my mother's apprehensions were often aroused that we should soon lose her.

The example of Alice, of which within the family there was constant remembrance, left a deep impression upon Arthur even as a boy, and he always cherished the memory of her in after years.

Arthur's youngest sister Emily Margaret stood nearest to him in time, and till he left home when he was eight years old they were almost inseparable. He taught her her letters, and when he was grown up he would laughingly say that she was his first pupil. In a tiny poem which he wrote he reveals the fact that to some measure she had taken upon herself the responsibility for the motherless family:

[1] A.S.P. to the Rev. H. J. Pickett, 27 October 1916.
[2] MS. Autobiography.

> *When I'd been climbing o'er the crags*
> *And torn my trousers all to rags,*
> *Who was it darned those tender bags?*
> *My sister!*

II

In his brief autobiography Peake has left a clear picture of the domestic background:

I need not say that we were poor. A Primitive Methodist minister at that time would rarely have any private means, and neither my father nor my mother had any. The salaries were very small. During the four years of probation the ministers had to remain unmarried, and the salaries met only the bare necessities. At the end of probation a minister usually married, and was entitled to a furnished house – a small house and very plainly furnished. My father's salary at the time when he married was £13 a quarter. There were some allowances for children and some provision for superannuation to which ministers themselves contributed. From the same source a tiny income was provided for the widows of ministers. In later years his salary was usually £22 a quarter. If the manse was in the country, the garden contributed a good deal to the wants of the household. But our means were of course very straightened, and prolonged sickness made various inroads into them. No doubt all this had a really moral value for us. We were brought up in great simplicity, plain food, plain clothes and no luxuries. We could afford but little help in the house and were trained to make ourselves useful. We had no pocket money. If money was given to us we were not allowed to spend it, but had to save it. The application of the principle was undoubtedly pushed too far, and I wished, looking back, that a little more wise elasticity had been displayed. My father had very little sympathy with a boy's sensitiveness, and I was unfortunately endowed with too much, and suffered not a little shame and misery in consequence. This would not have been altogether avoided, but it might have remained less acute. Extravagant we could never have been in the nature of the case, but literally not to know where one could get a penny from, however one might need it, was a source of no little unhappiness.

A letter from his father written years later,[1] when both Arthur and his brother George had achieved considerable success in their respective spheres, emphasizes the stress of the earlier days:

... Your mother and I were deeply anxious for all of you; it was our pleasure to make sacrifice. We did not deal in those days in luxuries; at the same time, by your mother's good management, we had plenty of good wholesome food, and I did not think that any one of us suffered in the least. I had used to walk long journeys and your mother would often be up on washing days at four or five o'clock in the morning to get the washing done before our younger branches

[1] S. Peake to A.S.P., (?) 11 February 1902.

were about. Ministers' salaries were little in those days, and without this self-denial it would have been impossible for us to have given George and you the chance to succeed....

I may truly say that the results of our early acts gives me very great joy and satisfaction at all times. If otherwise my family had turned out like some it would have destroyed my comfort and shortened my life. You are all kind to me, but that is but little to the satisfaction your upright lives and the work you have done gives me.

The religious background is given at length in Peake's own narrative.

Religion was the dominant interest in our home. The atmosphere in which we lived was that of a rather narrow evangelicalism. Fortunately it was not Calvinistic, so life was never shadowed by doubts as to our election, or the possibility of a fixed decree of reprobation from which we could not escape. The universality of sin was counteracted by the universality of redemption and the universal offer of salvation which all were free to accept. But a very sharp line was drawn between the converted and the unconverted, and the eternal destiny of both classes was regarded as fixed at death. The state of the lost was regarded as inconceivably terrible, a state of hopelessness and unending agony both physical and moral. The unquestioned conviction gave tremendous urgency to the evangelical appeal proclaimed both in the open-air and in the little chapels, especially on Sunday nights. The Sunday night service was followed by a prayer-meeting which had for one of its primary objects the appeal to the sinner to turn from his evil way and live. The appeal to fear was prominent, but also the appeal to love and gratitude for the grace which had been displayed in redemption. Personally I have no criticism to make on the appeal to fear, once the premises on which the appeal rested are granted, for if the fate of the unconverted was so appalling as was firmly believed it was legitimate to bring home with all the passion the preacher could command how terrible the consequences were which, through all eternity, the sinner must endure. The fault or defect lay in the premises themselves. The inspiration of the Bible was accepted without misgiving. To question it was one of the marks of an infidel. Whether this would have been generally defined as verbal inspiration I could hardly say. I was accustomed to the noun without any adjective. The difficulties presented by the Old Testament were removed by an appeal to the differences between the two dispensations, so that what was permitted under the old dispensation might not satisfy the demands of the enlightened Christian conscience. The Bible was taken as it stood, and difficulties about the canon were not commonly recognised: 'canonical' and 'inspired' would have been regarded as practically convertible terms. In this connection I have always been very interested to remember that my mother, who had a very exceptional knowledge of scripture, once said to my father in my hearing when I was a little boy that she did not believe that *Ecclesiastes* was inspired. Anything in the nature of Biblical Criticism as we understand the term today would have been repudiated. Probably the news of this had penetrated but very little into our circle. The name which would have been most familiar would, I think, have been that of Colenso. It was taken for granted that his views could not be true, and it was assumed that the replies to him, as to Tom Paine's *Age of Reason*, were conclusive. Similarly the conflict between *Genesis* and Science was thought to have been settled in favour of *Genesis*. The story of the tree of knowledge of good and evil was regarded as literal history, and as involving the fall of the whole of mankind in its first parents. The doctrine of the atonement was the firm foundation on which all evangelical effort of the Church depended. It was almost universally interpreted as substitutionary.

In these theological matters the Primitive Methodists were in no sense unusual in their beliefs, which were in general almost universally accepted by all orthodox churches at that time. They were more strongly convinced, however, that, if their scheme of salvation was sound, then they should be unsparing in their efforts to rescue those who through their negligence might become irretrievably lost. Conversion was therefore regarded as the most crucial and critical of all experiences and that the difference between the old life and the new should be vivid, that conversion normally should be catastrophic, and that the solution of the crisis would commonly be a sense of rapture and release. It is not surprising that the experience sometimes found extreme and even frenzied expression.

The Christian life was to be nurtured by simple means of grace, which might be private, such as prayer, meditation, the reading of the Bible and religious literature; or communal, such as the class meeting and prayer-meeting and the chapel services of worship. The religious life of the individual and the Church did not centre around the sacraments. Parents were expected to bring their infant children for baptism, but any notion of change from an unregenerate into a regenerate nature would have been repudiated, and the suggestion that unbaptized children would be eternally lost would have been instantly rejected. The sacrament of the Lord's Supper was observed, but not frequently, and was regarded as a commemorative rite in obedience to the command of Christ, and as such touching the deepest springs of gratitude and love, as bringing vividly to the mind the meaning of Christ's sacrifice, and as searching the conscience of the recipient with a call to renewed loyalty to Christ. Its observance was probably too infrequent, in many places once a quarter being regarded as sufficient.

Peake recalls his experience of that special Methodist institution, the class-meeting, as a means of grace.

In the old-fashioned class-meeting as I knew it it was necessary for the leader of the class to go round to each member in turn and ask him for his experience. When this had been given the leader made such reply as seemed to him appropriate. Much depended of course on the wisdom of the leader and his competence for that particular work. The ideal was that the individual related his experience and received his counsel, encouragement and admonition for the benefit both of himself and of his comrades, and no doubt in many cases this aim was realised. But the defects, as I remember them, were rather serious. The experiences were of much too general a character. The individual conflicts, temptations, lapses and triumphs were not brought out in any concrete detail. In the nature of the case this would have been largely impossible and in many cases quite undesirable. But the helpfulness of very general statements such as might be made by any member of the class was very slight. Not only did members stick to generalities but these were clothed in very conventional language. There was a particular language of Canaan which found copious expression. In the case of a quite considerable number of the members it was possible to predict with considerable confidence precisely what they would say. In view of these limitations it is not surprising that the old-fashioned class-meeting has been radically transformed.

Continuing his autobiographical recollections Peake gives us some account of his own religious training in these early years.

The Bible naturally played a large part in my religious education. When we could read at all we often had to read at family prayers, my father's deafness making the performance something of a trial. My mother gave me a New Testament quite early, and reading this to her was a regular part of my lessons. Later when I was about eight years old she gave me a Bible.

I was also sent at an early age to Sunday School, and I still remember that when I was about three years old and had recited a piece my mother had written for me, in the afternoon of a Sunday School Anniversary a deputation of teachers came to ask that I might be permitted to repeat the performance at night. Oddly enough, although I can remember the incident itself quite well, I cannot be quite sure of the sequel, but my strong impression is that my mother was firm and wisely sent me to bed.

The teaching given in the Sunday School which I attended was often very crude, though it is only fair to say that my later experiences were of a different kind, but in my early childhood my teachers were earnest and well-meaning but had little other equipment for the task. . . .

There were hymns in the hymn-book about Hell but they were not often much sung in the Sunday Schools, though more frequently in the Sunday night services. In the Sunday School, hymns about heaven were more common. But these were also favourite hymns with grown-up people, and I am struck as I look back with the prominence given to the idea of rest. The people who sang them worked long hours for a small wage, and they found inexpressible comfort as they sung hymns which struck this note:

> *Though often here we're weary*
> *There is sweet rest above!*

III

Peake's early years were marked by physical frailty, yet there was early evidence of outstanding mental ability and the possession of a remarkable power of memory. He writes:

During my infancy I was very delicate and scarcely expected to live. When my father returned home and my mother told him of the death of Alice he understood her to mean that it was I who was dead. Alice had been in good health when he left home shortly before, whereas my death at any time would have occasioned no surprise. Fortunately my early life was spent in villages or small country towns. I did not go to school till I was nearly seven, and the open-air life did a great deal for me. Whooping-cough and measles left no evil effects behind. I suffered a great deal from toothache and from chilblains, but these ailments, though they created much misery, did not seriously affect my general health. I had, however, little physical strength. When I was eight years old, one of the masters at a school to which I was sent told a friend that it quite went to his heart when he took hold of my arm. My four limbs he said would have made up a good one.

Till I was nearly seven my education was carried on by my mother. I could read moderately well when I was four, and quite well by the time I was six. Spelling also came quite easily to me. My father offered me a prize if I knew my tables by the time I was six. He meant the multiplication table, but I had learnt the money table as well. On the day before my birthday he examined me very thoroughly on the multiplication table, not hearing it in order but asking every detail of it, and pencilling a tick against each as I answered it until the whole had been exhausted, and I had answered without a single mistake. Curiously enough my mother taught me no arithmetic. The consequence was that when I went to school and was given an addition sum to do, I managed quite well till I came to a nought. This baffled me, so I turned to the little girl next to me and asked her what I was to do with it, and she instructed me to leave it out. It was a great help to me when I came to multiplication that I had been so thoroughly drilled in my tables. My writing was inconceivably bad. The letters were ill-formed, the whole appearance of the script clumsy and ugly, and disfigured with blots.

Early in July 1870, the family moved from Hadnall, near Shrewsbury, and, in the brief interval before entering the new circuit at Bromsgrove, they spent a short holiday in the home of relations at Birkenhead. Arthur records that on this holiday he saw the sea for the first time. 'I remember a visit to New Brighton, and our walk upon the sands; a visit to the museum in Liverpool—where I was especially struck with the recumbent figures of ancient monarchs—and a visit to St George's Hall.'

From Birkenhead they came to reside at Bromsgrove and here Arthur found interest in watching the local nail-makers at work in the little forges attached to their houses. After a stay of two years Mr Peake accepted an invitation to the Church Stretton Circuit, and the family came to live next to the small chapel at Little Stretton.

It was a small damp house and my health gave my father and mother some anxiety. My chilblains were specially bad, and I had to lie on a sofa for about three weeks as I could not walk owing to the broken chilblains on my feet. Our brief stay at Stretton is specially memorable to me because my school days began here. There were no facilities for education in the village, but there was a National School at Acton Scott from a mile and a half to two miles away from my home. The name of the master was Williamson. I had been pretty well grounded in reading, spelling and the tables; my writing was of course atrocious, but I am inclined to think that this was partially due to the condition of my hands, which were badly scarred with chaps which would last right on into May, as well as being tormented and swollen with chilblains. But partly no doubt it was due to the same defect which made me a complete failure so far as drawing was concerned. Years afterwards my position in this subject was normally a couple of forms at least below my general status. Perhaps connected with this was my indifferent success in the study of geography. Probably the subject was very badly taught in those days too. But I have never been gifted with a strong sense of locality nor with any talent for apprehending the lie of the land. Maps mean much less to me than they do to many of my friends. This has been a real drawback to me in my later work.

As I was eager to learn and fairly quick I did fairly well during my year at Acton Scott. I used to go and see the master when I revisited the place, and have kindly remembrances of him.[1]

Much of my time was of course spent in lessons and in play but I read a good deal. A friend of our family who lived near Stretton told us in later years that when I was physically too tired to sit any longer I would go down on my knees and put the book in the chair.

Arthur was far too young to understand what books his father possessed. A small book, however, which made a great impression while he was still at Bromsgrove was entitled *Learning Better than Houses or Lands*. 'I do not remember with any distinction the lines along which the story went, but its main lesson was at a very early age firmly fixed in my mind.' From the Sunday School at Stretton he received as a prize a copy of *The Pilgrim's Progress*. Years later he recorded its impression along with that of other of Bunyan's writings:

When I was barely seven I had the *Pilgrim's Progress* for a Sunday School prize and I read it over and over again. In a house where fiction was pretty rigidly excluded, it was a very valuable element in one's education to have a work of imagination by a genius of the first rank in these impressionable years. Not long after I had *The Holy War*, also a Sunday School Prize. It was not till later that I read *The Life and Death of Mr Badman*, and that wonderful autobiography, so full of interest to students of the psychology of religion, *Grace Abounding to the Chief of Sinners*. I cannot claim to have read all his other work systematically, though I have frequently dipped into it.[2]

Somewhat later, however, the scope of Arthur's reading in the field of imaginative literature widened, for, when he was at another school and living away from home, *Robinson Crusoe* and *It's Never Too Late to Mend* came into his hands; indeed books by R. M. Ballantyne, *The Coral Island* and *The Gorilla Hunters*, found their way into his home, being lent to his mother who took a rather more liberal attitude than did his father.[3]

There were other benefits also belonging to the brief sojourn at Stretton.

---

[1] In 1924, with his family, when passing along the road from Shrewsbury to Hereford, Peake turned aside to revisit the old school. 'We found the children just assembled for afternoon school and the mistress kindly allowed us to see the room where I had sat when I was six years old more than half a century earlier.'

[2] *H.R.* October 1928.

[3] Leslie S. Peake: *Memoir*, p. 44.

The country life was beneficial to me. The long walk to school and back again was my salvation, not only for the exercise, but because it took me out of our damp house. I scarcely ever went up the Long Mynd, but Ragleth was on the other side of the railway immediately behind our house, and it was good for me then—and for years afterwards—to be in the lovely scenery of Shropshire and Herefordshire.

But as we have noted the sojourn in Stretton was brief, for the circuit did not suit the health of his father.

He was a robust man, with considerable physical strength, but a specialist in Shrewsbury told him that the climbing involved in reaching some of the more distant places on his circuit was affecting him unfavourably and that he ought to leave. When towards the end of his ministry he returned to Stretton some of these places had been given up, and he had a pony which he could ride or drive. We left Stretton accordingly at the end of a year, when I was seven. My father had accepted an invitation to Leintwardine.

Leintwardine is a village in Shropshire, about nine miles from Ludlow, situated in pleasant country. The Primitive Methodist society there was at that time fairly strong, and several wealthy farmers were associated with it. The period here opened a new chapter in Arthur's experience, of which he writes in some detail.

My brother George was sent to Ludlow Grammar School in September 1873. I was too young as no boy was admitted till he was eight. It so happened that the Congregational minister, Mr Ingham, had a small school at Leintwardine which met in the vestry of the Church, and to this I was sent till December. In January 1874, the age disqualification having lapsed, I entered Ludlow Grammar School.

My brother and I had to leave home, but of course my father could not pay the fees required for boarding. We lodged accordingly with one, Miss Susan Bishop. She did not board us. My brother had the responsibility of buying our food under the strict and vigilant oversight of the expenditure by my father. Exact accounts had to be kept and sent in for very critical scrutiny. The money we had to spend was supplemented by occasional hampers from home. We had, it is needless to say, no luxuries, and the diet was rather capriciously selected, though of course we had some guidance from home and some definite instructions. In those days little account was taken against the protests of nature against an article of food in which great virtue was supposed to reside. One of the forms of food forced upon me was porridge. It is not simply the sliminess and slitheriness of porridge which is an abomination to me, but I detest the taste of oatmeal in every shape or form. Nor do I doubt that Nature, who is much wiser than old-fashioned parents, was giving her emphatic warning that porridge was an unsuitable diet for me. On the other hand it was a real advantage that we could to a considerable extent study our preferments in the selection of our diet. Our slender resources were an effective check on any tendency to extravagance.

In another respect this additional liberty was valuable. When in later years I lived at home as a school-boy my half-holidays were systematically spoilt by the principle that work must precede play. Homework was heavy, and my Wednesday and Saturday afternoons were commonly lost because work had the first claim on my time. At Ludlow we were able to get the full benefit of our half-holidays. The Castle grounds and Whitcliffe, with the River Teme running at the foot of it, gave us ideal opportunities for playing, and our absence from home enabled us to take full advantage of them.

Thus young Arthur and his brother had a great deal of happiness in their life at Ludlow, and one or two interesting episodes are included in his own account.

I vividly recollect that when I went to Ludlow Grammar School at the age of eight, it was the custom of the headmaster, Dr Sparrow, to have the copybooks of the preparatory form sent up to him. He was an adept, as most schoolmasters were, in the use of the cane, and the other boys told me that he caned even for a single blot. Every page of my books was disfigured with blots, and I looked forward to his visit with terror. When he brought the books back, and my turn came, he simply held the book open in front of the class, and said: 'This is small Peake's book.' It was a great relief to be let off so lightly. I did not mind the public exhibition of my disgrace, as my writing was fairly notorious.[1]

I think it was my writing that must have accounted for another curious fact. I was high up in the preparatory, and expected to be promoted when the end of the school year came. This, however, did not happen, and the reason given in my case, as in that of some others, was bad spelling. This was a surprise to me as my spelling was really good. This was proved later at a 'Spelling Bee',[2] which was arranged for the Grammar School boys and was held in the Assembly Hall at Ludlow. There were four prizes and I remained in till our numbers were reduced to six. Not only had all the other preparatory boys gone long before, but most of the other forms as well. We had a large audience and there was considerable interest in the problem whether I should be able to hold out till I secured one of the prizes. The words naturally grew more difficult. I spelt 'cygnet' correctly and came down with 'hectacomb'. The word was of course entirely unfamiliar to me at that age. Another boy fell in the same round, so we left the four prize-winners in. In the next round one of these fell, so that had I survived a little longer I should have shared the honours with three of the boys at the head of the school.[3] The audience gave me an ovation which was renewed at the end of the proceedings when the headmaster made a special reference to me and one of the bigger boys took me up and held me so that all the audience could see me.

It was decided some time later to hold a consolation 'Spelling Bee' at the Grammar School itself, and I was looking with some confidence to securing a prize, but I by no means covered myself with glory on that occasion, for I came down when I was asked to spell 'apparel'. Many people find the problem of

---

[1] Amongst the Peake papers there are many notes in manuscript which are entirely legible. In particular are his notes in an interleaved copy of the Hebrew text of *Job* the writing is not only infinitesimal in size, but perfectly easy to read.

[2] These open spelling competitions, which were known by the name 'Spelling Bees' at this time had become a widespread craze, and were sweeping through the whole country.

[3] One of these was G. B. Matthews, the Captain of the School, who later became Senior Wrangler.

single or double consonants difficult, and I believe that what added to my undoing was the intrusion of the word 'parallel' into my head. Anyhow I bungled it, probably to my moral advantage, for my performance in the Assembly Hall had made me a little conceited about my spelling. I think however it did prove that it could not have been my spelling which robbed me of my promotion from the preparatory, and I cannot think of anything but the execrable character of my writing to account for the misjudgment.

Although Arthur remained at the Ludlow Grammar School less than three years he steadily progressed in his studies. In particular under the Headmaster, Dr Sparrow, he secured a good drilling in Latin declensions and conjugations in which he acquired a readiness which stood him in good stead later on. When he moved into the upper school he began to learn Greek, which he might have begun a year earlier but for the unfortunate blunder which kept him, though second in his form, a year too long in the preparatory.[1]

The period of his father's ministry in Leintwardine proved to be valuable to Arthur in another respect. It brought him into three friendships which were to last all through the ensuing years. Arthur's parents had formed a firm friendship with three families of the name of Nott, and with the children of one of them the Peake children were playmates. In later years they frequently were to enjoy the hospitality of this particular home. Humphrey Nott became Arthur's special friend and the association continued unbroken through many years.

Another family with which Arthur formed a close friendship was the Merediths, and one son, William, two years older than Arthur, became a fellow pupil at Ludlow, to which place the family eventually moved. In their early years these two bound themselves to each other by a covenant of rules for self-improvement. This friendship lasted for forty years and was maintained by a long and intimate correspondence, which did not cease even when Meredith, who had gained an honours degree at London University, went out to South Africa as a schoolmaster in 1887. A small portion only of this correspondence has survived but sufficient to reveal how unfortunate it was that, after Meredith's death more than twenty years later, all Peake's letters to him were destroyed along with others by Mrs Meredith.

Another lasting friendship was with one Thomas Dyke, who lived in the tiny hamlet of Bucton, near Leintwardine, and to whom Arthur acted as an early mentor in the study of Shakespeare. Thomas became a devotee of Henry George, and much of the correspondence was concerned with discussion about the tenets of socialism, as well as upon theological questions. In 1889 Dyke emigrated to America and after a period in teaching school, entered the ministry of the Methodist Episcopal Church. In 1920 on a visit to the homeland he stayed with Peake in Manchester—

---

[1] In 1917 Peake returned to the School as the distinguished guest on the Annual Speech Day; the School still possesses an enlarged portrait of him.

'It has given me much pleasure to see you in your appropriate environment'. He was a diligent student of Peake's writings—'I enjoy the *Holborn Review*, and your part in it specially appeals to me'—and, writing on his return voyage, he makes an interesting reference to his mother's admiration of Peake: 'Mother is still a loyal Primitive, and she follows you almost blindly.'

The constancy and long endurance of these friendships illustrates the influence of the early contacts of Peake in these formative years of his childhood and youth.

Whilst still at Leintwardine, in the autumn of 1875, the family suffered the immeasurable loss of Mrs Peake.

In the following year they moved to Stratford-upon-Avon. Here, in September, at the age of eleven, Arthur entered the Grammar School—where Shakespeare had been a pupil three hundred years before. Arthur remained only a year, of which little record has survived.

In 1877 the family moved to Coventry, and for the next six years Arthur was a pupil at the King Henry VIII Grammar School. These years proved to be crucial in his academic and spiritual development, though, through a sense of loneliness, his school life was not altogether happy. Writing, towards the end of his time at Coventry, to his brother George in Manchester, he declares:[1]

I am glad you are well and happy in your apartments and have a congenial companion. I feel very much inclined to envy you, for I have nobody to associate with who in any way is particularly a congenial companion; so there you see you have me on the hip, as Shakespeare says ...

I am doing a Greek play by myself, with Mr Escott—three times a week, at the rate of a hundred lines each time; that is in addition to the other work which the sixth kids do. Those fellows never do a Greek lesson till I have done it over to them, so they can't be very congenial companions. Their conversation seldom rises higher than cricket, football, politics etc. I shall write as often as possible; but now it is growing very late and I am very tired.

Yet in spite of his loneliness these years proved a continuing and mounting success. In 1880 he was placed in the Second Class in the Oxford Local Examinations; in 1882 he gained a Second Class in the Cambridge Local Examinations, with distinction in Latin and Greek, and was awarded the school Prizes both in Divinity and History, together with the Prize of the Cambridge Local Examination Committee. In addition, early in 1883, he sat for the second stage of the South Kensington Science and Art Examination and obtained a First Class in Mathematics. He now faced an Oxford Scholarship examination, early in June 1883. He writes to his brother:[2]

The examination begins a fortnight today, so I suppose I shall go to Oxford a

---

[1] A.S.P. to George Peake, 17 February 1883.
[2] A.S.P. to George Peake, 29 May 1883.

week next Monday. It's rather sooner than I expected, but sooner come, sooner gone. I hope most heartily I shall get it this year. I shall have to do a piece of Latin Unseen and a piece of Greek Unseen, Latin Prose and Greek Prose. Critical Paper and History Paper, General Questions Paper. I feel funkiest about the Greek Prose and the Critical Paper. I don't care much for the rest.

A later letter declares his success:[1]

... This morning I heard about the scholarship examination. *I've got it*, Hallelujah!—as the Salvation Army would say!

So he had gained a Close Scholarship to St John's College, Oxford, consisting of £100 a year for five years. He was also awarded an Exhibition of £55 a year for four years from his school at Coventry.

This is a fitting point at which to notice a further aspect of Arthur's time at Coventry.

It would appear that associated with the Ford Street Primitive Methodist society there was a 'Mutual Improvement Society', of which he had undertaken the duties of secretary. He tells of this in a letter to his brother:[2]

I am glad you have a 'Mutual' to attend. Are the Secretary's duties arduous? I believe I sent you one of our programmes. Next Saturday is business night. I shall try and revive the old affair with Mr Wilkinson's help. We shall throw up our offices both of us. I believe the old machine might be made to work, but it wants thorough cleaning and repairing and refitting. Mr W. and I struck out a scheme or rather some part of one, some time ago, but we must get it finished as next Saturday night I want to raise a good thunderstorm to clear the atmosphere and liven us up again.

In a further letter some two months later he refers to the matter again in a way that discloses some of the difficulties involved:[3]

I congratulate you on your thriving 'mutual', wishing that you might be able to congratulate me, as you might have a few weeks ago. The thing's rotten. Why, do you know, I merely proposed a discussion on everlasting punishment, but I was obliged to let it drop, for I saw probably a preliminary paper might be needed to inform them that the New Testament wasn't originally written in English! You can conceive what a heap of ignoramuses they must be, the only chance of a good discussion they have had for some time to throw it away like that!

This incident reveals not only the power of his intense convictions, but also an early expression of that passion which never departed from him, namely the concern to communicate religious truth and intellectual betterment to those who were ignorant of these issues. This attempt, it will be noted, was made whilst he himself was involved in his own critical academic studies.

[1] A.S.P. to George Peake, 25 June 1883.
[2] A.S.P. to George Peake, 17 February 1883.
[3] A.S.P. to George Peake, 14 April 1883.

One further incident is associated with these Coventry days. During this period he came under the influence of one Mr Charles Stringer, who was his Sunday School teacher. Fifty years later he wrote a moving tribute in memory of what he owed to him.

I was eleven when I came under his influence and seventeen when I left Coventry for Oxford. He was held in warm regard by the members of his own society and throughout the circuit, alike for his character and his gifts. His judgment was trusted; his intellectual qualities were highly esteemed.... I do not know that I learnt much of the biblical story, or of the actual text of Scripture from him; with these I was already familiar. But on the other side of a teacher's ministry he exercised a real influence over me in those critical years.

One special form of kindness stands out in my memory. It happened that the *Cambridge Bible* was then in its early days. Mr Stringer procured some of them as they appeared. I am grateful that he allowed me to order them for him, and get them from the booksellers when they arrived and have them in my hands to read. I think, in particular, of Plumptre's *Ecclesiastes* to which I owed my first acquaintance with Fitzgerald's 'Omar Khayyam' . . . I cherish a keen sense of his work and desire to place my modest wreath on his grave.

These years at Coventry had been of great strain upon Arthur's constitution. He writes again to his brother:

I am fairly well, Father is morbidly anxious about my health, and I have to take that confounded cod-liver oil, Cadbury's cocoa essence, Peruvian Bark, Nicholl's Food of Health, oatmeal, exercise etc. etc. Laws! isn't it enough to frighten a fellow almost out of his senses!

But his father's concern was not without some foundation. In September 1883 the family moved from Coventry to the Peaton Strand circuit, in Shropshire, and shortly afterwards Arthur had a severe attack of pleurisy and inflammation of the lungs. Under medical care he made eventual recovery, but the experience indicated physical weakness which had manifested itself under the stress and strain.

Towards the end of September 1883 Arthur went up to Oxford to pass Responsions and to make necessary arrangements for his residence. He records the occasion in a further letter to his brother.[1]

I like Oxford very well. I have chosen my rooms, bedroom and sitting-room. I think they will be comfortable. I went to see Mr Crompton[2] on the Friday after I arrived. He took me to see several places on Monday. We went on the river on Tuesday morning. I went to the Bodleian Library in the afternoon. My viva-voce was on Wednesday. It lasted about ten minutes. I had a piece of translation from one of my Greek books, and then the fellow asked me some questions and all was over.

In the same letter there is a paragraph relating to what seems to have been

---

[1] A.S.P. to George Peake, 5 October 1883.
[2] The Rev. J. Crompton, who proved to be both guide and friend to Arthur, was the superintendent of the Oxford Primitive Methodist Circuit.

understood as the conditions attaching to the Exhibition which had been awarded him by the school. It is somewhat revealing as to young Peake's own convictions.

> The Exhibition from the Grammar School is only given to those who intend to take Holy Orders, so eventually I shall become a Church clergyman, and I hope in a soon-to-be-disestablished Church. I think one can do a great deal of good in the Church against the Ritualists, by going to work in the right way. I hate ritualism, and there is far too much of it in Oxford. Keble College has been endowed by the High Church party, in memory of Keble, the friend and co-worker with Pusey, for the express purpose of training up men to follow in their steps, and Romanize the Church. As a Methodist one can do little or nothing against the Romanizing party in the Church, but as a church-clergyman one may do much to stem the tide. There are two churches in Oxford, I believe, at which the service is so ritualistic as to differ hardly at all from a Roman Catholic chapel. So perhaps it may be well in the end.
>
> I have ordered a gown and surplice. I don't have one of those miserable little affairs, the undergraduates gown, but a nice long scholar's gown.

So at length through much toil and not a little anxiety an important milestone had been reached. On Friday, 5 October, Arthur came up to the University of Oxford as a scholar of St John's College.

CHAPTER TWO

OXFORD: 1883–1892

IN THE last quarter of the nineteenth century Oxford was at least outwardly much the same as it had been for generations, even centuries. The High Church Party was still the leading group of Anglicanism in the University, though the Evangelicals, who had Wycliffe Hall as a seminary for Evangelical students in training for the ministry, were not without influence. Politically, the University remained on the whole fairly Tory, for though the Liberals had their societies, most of the students came up from family backgrounds that were Conservative.

Nevertheless the breath of change had begun to stir in the thought and life of the University. An important decision had been taken in 1871 when the doors of the University were thrown open to those who were not members of the Anglican Church. New impulses of social concern were also beginning to work, as illustrated in the founding of the Toynbee Hall Settlement in the East End of London. Further, in the realm of theology, the first springs of a critical approach to the understanding of the Bible were beginning to cause concern. An Oxford scholar has described the situation:

Strauss and Renan, like Ewald and Wellhausen were regarded with horror as laying the axe at the root of religious belief. Robertson Smith was equally dangerous in Scotland. There was no one in Oxford corresponding to the Cambridge trio of Westcott, Lightfoot and Hort. Theology was bound up with patristics. Grave divines still shook troubled heads over the memories of *Essays and Reviews*; and even the cautious opinions of Samuel Driver and William Sanday were looked upon, by High Churchmen and Evangelicals alike, with misgiving and dread. Nor was the resentment at the conclusions of the critics mere obscurantism. As traditional authorships were questioned, and traditional interpretations discredited, there was a sense of personal loss. Like the orthodox struggling with the Arians in the fourth century, perturbed but earnest Christians cried with a real sinking of the heart: 'They have taken away my Lord'. . . .

The High Church party enjoyed the intellectual prestige, and its members feared the influence of the Evangelicals less than most of them feared the influence of the philosophers. After a hard struggle, led by T. H. Green, what had been the reigning system of J. S. Mill and Herbert Spencer had been vanquished, and Plato and Aristotle were interpreted as leading on to Kant and Hegel. The orthodoxy of Green himself, one of the most selfless and devoted men whom Oxford had known, was gravely suspected, but the influence which he exercised over the ablest of his students was at one time almost unbounded, and both High Churchmen and Evangelicals regarded it as something of a triumph when a young scholar could go through a course of German philosophy and yet not jettison his faith. Happily for them, neither the students nor their tutors as yet gave a thought to the still (in Oxford) unknown Karl Marx. But Cardinal Newman, whose passing over to Rome had caused a wave of consternation, was now the idol of the High Churchmen.[1]

Such, then, was the religious and intellectual climate of the Oxford which young Arthur at the age of barely eighteen, found when he came up to the University in October, 1883.

I

Of his early life in Oxford little direct or detailed account has survived, though it is clear that he came to the new situation armed with the highest resolves. A letter from his former school-friend, William Meredith[2] who was two years older than himself, sets forth a long code of rules for the purpose of their mutual self-improvement and the cultivation of the Christian life. It reveals a fine idealism, and it was with such spiritual assurance that Arthur entered college life a few months later. This correspondence reveals the older youth's deep concern for Arthur's welfare.

From his brother George, Arthur also received counsel as he took up his new responsibilities. A short while before his departure he had the following letter:[3]

Dear Arthur,
... You will require to exercise great care in the method you adopt, with reference to living, exercise, study and sleep, now that you are about to go to College. They are each and all requisite to success, and you will find it impossible to obtain that power of concentration, that vigour of mind, that strength of body, that firm nerve and clear brain, all so necessary in grappling with your studies, without you give the other three their proper place. I would recommend you to become *methodical*: have method in everything you do. Have a certain time for rising, a certain time for going to bed, fixed times for study, set times to take your exercise, certain hours in the day for writing letters or doing other odd jobs. In fact I think you would find it a good thing to draw up a plan to regulate your daily life. When once you had got into this mode of using your time, I do not think you would deviate from it, but rather prize it as being of

---

[1] W. F. Lofthouse, in *Oxford Days* Ch. 2, in *Arthur Samuel Peake, 1865–1929; Essays in Commemoration* (edited by J. T. Wilkinson, 1958).
[2] W. Meredith to A.S.P., 28 April 1883.
[3] George Peake to A.S.P., 2 October 1883.

considerable assistance in making your college life not only successful but agreeable. You will of course join our people in Oxford. I believe Mr Crompton, the minister, is a very good man.

A further letter[1] reached Arthur not long after he arrived in Oxford.

... I am glad that you are now safely at Oxford and making preparation for a useful if not a brilliant career, either as a minister, schoolmaster or barrister, or may be some other profession, in any of which you may decide to take up. I wish you unequalled success ... I am pleased that you are thinking of joining this society called 'The Wesley Guild': at the same time you must bear in mind that you are a Primitive Methodist, and not become a proselyte to the Wesleyan Connexion. Be very careful in your choice of companions; endeavour to acquaint yourself with those who are older and better than yourself and from whom you may gain experience and sound advice.

It is not surprising that a number of early letters from Mr Peake, Arthur's father, express a deep concern with regard to the maintenance of his son's health, as the weight of his studies increased, and inevitably he became more and more involved in the life of the College. From Presteign he writes:[2]

... I must remind you about your health. You must be more particular to observe which way the wind blows than how the sun shines. It is the easterly winds that will have a bad effect on you.... Get out when the wind is in the south and west. It will do you a lot of good then, but if it is anywhere about the east keep inside as much as possible.

Again![3]

... There are three things you have fully to attend to. 1st. your studies: 2nd. your health: 3rd. serving God faithfully, constantly and fully—this is the most important of all.... But your health is more important than your studies, and you must fully attend to its claims. Take walking exercise every day when it does not rain. Keep out of the back streets and filthy places, and do not be out more than you can help when it is foggy. Take plenty of Cadbury's Essence of Cocoa daily and a raw egg. Scott's oatmeal would be a good thing for you. Do not walk beyond your strength; get up in good time and do not sit up late at night. Attend to private devotion; ask the Lord to help you and serve and glorify him in everything.

And yet again[4]

... I would say, mind these points: 1st. Take plenty of outdoor exercise. 2nd. Have plenty of nourishing food and the books you really need. 3rd. Be in soon at night, and if you are to win get up soon. 4th. Stick well to your studies. 5th. Above all serve God faithfully.... Count position, office or honour *loss* if they interfere with your studies.

---

[1] George Peake to A.S.P., 27 October 1883.
[2] Samuel Peake to A.S.P., 14 April 1885.
[3] Samuel Peake to A.S.P., 26　?　1885.
[4] Samuel Peake to A.S.P., 9 November 1885.

I feel persuaded that you will succeed if you will mind what you do and stick to it at College, and in the vacation. It is of great importance that you should succeed; therefore deny yourself—of the injurious indulgence of *lying in bed* but *be up and at it*. It will require courage and fixed determined notion—but surely you can conquer. Pray! Pray! and that will mean First Class!

Mr Peake's concern was not unfounded, for during the first two years at Oxford Arthur's health was far from complete, and this certainly had its effect on his studies. During these years he devoted himself to the study of the classics, not however with great success, taking only a Third in Classical Moderations. This was largely due to the reason just stated. The fact that he had entered the course when so young in age had also some effect, a fact of which Mr Escott, his former headmaster at Coventry had reminded him at the beginning of his work, though hoping that he might secure a second-class.[1] Another factor may have been his labours in teaching and preaching during this period. Despite his father's insistence that he should not involve himself in work extraneous to his academic studies his service in these ways had been considerable.

On his return to Oxford after the vacation he received news that the College authorities had decided not to renew his scholarship because he had not succeeded in fulfilling the requirements of securing at least a second-class. It was the more unfortunate because it presented a financial problem in which his father was unable to offer much help. To his brother George he wrote:[2]

The dons have not thought well to extend my scholarship, which I much regret as it prevents me from sending you a present this year. That is a straw to show you how the wind of economy blows. I believe the dons will grant me an exhibition for one year. So that I shall be compelled to read Pass Greats, and take my degree probably next year. This however will be decided on Wednesday next. For myself I am resigned but scarcely satisfied. I should prefer to have read Theology and kept my scholarship. I have no doubt it is all for the best.

With characteristic generosity his brother at once offered financial aid, the acceptance of which, however, Arthur delayed, pending the decision of the dons in the matter of the exhibition. Later he wrote to his brother:

I hear today that the dons have given me an exhibition of £20. They will deduct it from my next term's battels. I suppose after that I must keep myself.[3]

In the meantime, after consultation with his tutor, Peake had decided to enter the Honours School of Theology. In so doing he opened the door to what was to be his future vocation.

During these early years at Oxford he was a pupil of Mr T. C. Snow,

---

[1] W. Escott to A.S.P., 18 August 1885.
[2] A.S.P. to George Peake, 19 October 1885.
[3] A.S.P. to George Peake, 3 November 1885.

tutor in Classics at St John's College, who made a profound and lasting impression on him. He wrote:[1]

In some subjects I learnt, I am afraid, a very little, simply because I was too fundamentally ignorant to profit by his teaching. The course of lectures I specially valued was on the *Odessey*. It was my first introduction to criticism, and I have always been glad that I had my earliest insight into critical principles in connection with a non-biblical text.

Many years afterwards, at the time of Snow's death he penned a revealing appreciation of his former tutor.

I was his pupil for two years, at the end of that time passing from Classics to Theology. As a teacher he was fettered by an unfortunate stammer, and it was a pity to waste talents so brilliant on unappreciative pass-men. His gentle manner and halting delivery were ill-fitted to impress undergraduates who despised learning in comparison to sport. But his honours students, meeting him alone or in small classes, quickly came to recognise his exceptional gifts and as they got to know him better, admiration deepened into reverence.... His own subject was Greek, and he was a considerable authority on Comparative Philology. But among his many interests theology won a prominent place. In his theological position he had been greatly influenced by Coleridge and his followers, and he was devoted to Browning.[2]

I happened to be the only student of theology in the Essay Society, and this created a new link with Mr Snow that grew into an intimate friendship. His father had been a Church of England clergyman, and he was a member of the Church of England himself. His mother was of Methodist origin, his uncle being a well-known Methodist minister. He had thus a sympathetic insight into the Methodist point of view, which was not at that time very common in Oxford. He invited me to his home, a very rare privilege, and I gained more from this less formal relationship than from his lectures. In later years I generally went to see him when I was in Oxford.... The last time I saw him was when I went to give my Presidential Address to the Society of Historical Theology....

He had a very high standard of excellence... and amazing range of erudition, deep sympathy with whatever was best and highest in literature and in life, penetrating insight, exceptional felicity and brilliance of expression.[3]

From the above we are now able to discern something of the early

---

[1] *H.R.* January 1922. Peake adds a further interesting recollection. 'I remember with amusement how, having spent some time over Gladstone's *Juventus Mundi*, I retailed the results of my reading in an examination paper, which was returned to me with the caustic but thoroughly deserved criticism that I had been writing a good deal of nonsense on a subject of which I was entirely ignorant.'

[2] It is interesting to note that in a letter to his brother George (28 January 1885) Peake wrote: 'Coleridge's *Table Talk* is consistently fresh and invigorating. Of course Coleridge had his prejudices, but I do reverence his wonderful mind.' Also the manuscript of an essay on Browning written by Peake is extant, and on more than one occasion this was the subject of his literary lectures.

[3] *H.R.* January 1927. In January 1922 in the *H.R.* Peake printed a brilliant paper by Mr Snow on 'The Birth of the Nineteenth Century in England', which had been read at the Essay Society in 1886.

stimulus by which Peake's steps were directed into the field of Theology, a transition which was certainly the most significant thing during this period at Oxford. For him it was a discovery which was to determine his whole future career.

This discovery was greatly strengthened by his participation in the meetings of the St John's Essay Society, of which eventually he became President.[1] Of his association with this Society Peake afterwards declared:

It so happened that all the papers I read for the Essay Society were theological. I began with Gnosticism and went on to Manicheism, then to Paulinism, and then to the thorny problem of Paul's relation to the Jewish Christians. It was, curiously enough, the work I did for the College Essay Society which determined my own interests much more than my proper work as a student, though naturally all these subjects fell within it.[2]

It was after the reading of the essay on Manicheism that he wrote to his friend, William Meredith:

I had rather a select audience and was much complimented. All which means I am gaining sure ground and a wider outlook in Theology. It was for Theology I was born, and I am learning to walk and feel my feet. There are few things which give more perfect pleasure than the consciousness of increasing power.[3]

Peake also found similar stimulus in the reading of theological papers to the St Hilary Society, of which also he became President. He writes to his brother of his preparation of a paper on 'The Theology of the Epistle to the Hebrews' and another paper on 'The Development of Paulinism' in which are discernible the main features which were set out later in *The Quintessence of Paulinism* (1917). Clearly throughout these early years at Oxford Peake was laying the solid foundations for his future work.

These biblical and theological studies received further stimulus by a visit to Oxford of Archdeacon Farrar who was Bampton Lecturer in 1885, and whose subject was the Bible. Peake attended his lectures, and although up to this time his attitude to the Bible had been somewhat conservative and the lectures were in no sense extreme, these courses moved Peake a little further from the more rigid position in which he had been brought up.[4]

It was toward the end of the same year that Principal Henry Drummond delivered a series of lectures which made a strong impression on Peake. He wrote of these to his brother:

---

[1] Of this Essay Society Peake makes the following record (*H.R.* January 1922). 'We were nearly all undergraduates, but we owed much to the presence of two of our teachers, Mr Sidney Ball, who was our President, and to Mr Snow. I once made the jesting proposal that we should call ourselves "The Snowball Society". The reading of essays was never followed by set speeches but by free conversation: and for the success and profit of this we were always much indebted to the stimulus which Mr Snow gave us.'
[2] *H.R.* January 1927.
[3] A.S.P. to William Meredith, February 1887.
[4] A.S.P. to George Peake, 6 March 1885.

Professor Drummond, the author of *Natural Law in the Spiritual World* has been in Oxford lately. Last night and the Sunday night previous he was giving an address on the relation between science and religion, showing how the same laws held in both. The first night he spoke on 'Evolution and Evolution in Religion'; last night on 'The Survival of the Fittest', showing how that held in religion too. He is wonderfully fertile in illustrations, which are well-nigh perfect.[1]

II

It is at this point that we must note the more direct influence of those eminent scholars in Oxford who were his theological teachers, and from whom he discerned the extreme value of the historical method applied to the interpretation of the Bible. He writes:

When I began the study of theology in Oxford, the University was adorned by three Biblical scholars of the first rank. The Oxford Triumvirate consisted of Driver, Cheyne and Sanday. Hatch was there also, but his main subject was Church History, though he was of course an accomplished biblical scholar. Fairbairn came somewhat later.[2]

Of T. K. Cheyne, who was Oriel Professor—and of whom Dr Abrahams said he knew the Hebrew Bible by heart—Peake writes:[3]

Of the three scholars I have bracketed together Cheyne was the most interesting —in the sense that he excited a livelier interest than his colleagues. . . . With Cheyne we anticipated surprises. Each new book was carefully examined to discover what new theories he had formulated. . . . One could always count on interesting self-revelation, fascinating bits of autobiography, *obiter dicta* and side-lights, indeed a wealth of suggestion and information not always strictly relevant to the subject it might be, but none the less welcome for that. If he was annotating a text the student could reckon on freshness of suggestion, of felicitous expression, on insight into its meaning. . . . His output was astonishing, especially when we remember his frailty and the grave limitations of eyesight from which he suffered.[4]

Samuel R. Driver, then Regius Professor of Hebrew in the University, is usually regarded chiefly as an Old Testament critic, holding however a considerably conservative position, but for Peake he was essentially a

---

[1] A.S.P. to George Peake, 2 November 1885.
[2] *H.R.* April 1920.
[3] Ibid.
[4] In later days, as is well-known, Cheyne's critical development became one of the tragedies in the history of scholarship. He framed his 'Jerahmeelite' theory as the key to all problems of the Old Testament and this aberration permeated and vitiated all his later work. Nevertheless Dr Sanday spoke of him as 'a genius as well as a scholar'. Peake wrote an account of him in *The Expository Times* (November 1894) and in the *Dictionary of National Biography, 1912–21,* pp. 119f.

philologist.[1] Peake's estimate at the time of Driver's death seems unconsciously to reflect his own position as a critic and theologian—in itself a strong suggestion of the power of Driver's influence upon him during his Oxford days.

Clearly he had no love of novelty for its own sake; if he moved forward it would be because he was driven by the sheer weight of evidence. His type of mind resembled Lightfoot's and it had a peculiar attraction to English students. His positions were supported by hard facts and black and white reasons, admirably marshalled, lucidly expressed, judicially stated. With subjective incommunicable impressions he had little to do; he always turned by instinctive preference to arguments that would appeal to the common sense of the average cultured reader. Above all he was endeared to the English mind by his moderation. Temperamentally cautious and distrustful of extremes, he studied both sides of his case, prepared to recognise what was good in each, to hold the scales evenly and register the verdict with the impartiality of a judge.[2]

In the field of New Testament study and interpretation Peake owed a great debt in his Oxford days to William Sanday, Lady Margaret Professor of Divinity, not only as a teacher but also as an intimate personal friend. In 1921 Peake wrote of him:

I had known him for a third of a century and received much kindness from him and much encouragement and appreciation. I greatly admired his wide learning, his exact scholarship and his critical, balanced sagacity. It was in this last quality that I think he specially shone.... His critical gift was, I think, a keener and more finely tempered instrument than Lightfoot's, and he recognised the strength of his opponent's case more fully than Westcott. And there was such a poise and balance in his judgment, unhurried patience and self-restraint in the study of the evidence, so resolute a refusal to let the issues be confused, or his decision biased by irrelevant considerations, that when the verdict was finally given the greatest weight was attached to it. His gift lay rather in criticism and history than in philology, theology or interpretation.[3]

The intimacy between them is revealed by the following sentence penned after Sanday's death:

The close here on earth of so long an intimate friendship with one to whom I owe so much brings with it a sense of irreparable loss, but the sadness is relieved by happy memories and lit by a radiant hope.

[1] Driver's *Introduction to the Literature of the Old Testament* (1891) became the standard work for some thirty years and went through nine editions, and by it probably secured, as no one else did, the triumph of the critical cause in England. His work as a philologist is evidenced in *The Use of the Tenses in Hebrew* (1874); *Notes on the Hebrew Text of the Books of Samuel* (1890) and his contribution to the *Oxford Hebrew Lexicon* (1891–1905).

[2] At the time of Driver's death in 1914 Peake wrote appreciations in *The Expositor* and in the *Journal of the Manchester Egyptian and Oriental Society*. Cf. H.R. April 1920: 'He did a work in England for the critical cause which no one else, not Cheyne, nor A. B. Davidson, or even Robertson Smith could do quite in the same way, and which none of them could probably have done so efficiently.'

[3] *H.R.* January 1921. Also art. 'Dr William Sanday' in *The Expositor*, vol. xx. 1920.

It was through Sanday's teaching that Peake saw that revelation was a process in history—an approach to the interpretation of the Scriptures; through the after years that was to become the central principle in his own teaching. A letter written to his brother expresses Sanday's estimate of Peake during his time at Oxford.

... Prof. Sanday was much pleased with my Romans work and has complimented me on it. He has asked me if I would mind editing the Roman sheets. It will involve a good deal of work and some responsibility. However I am much gratified by it, and of course it showed his confidence in me. I shall have largely the work of the Seminar in my hand, as Headlam, who has managed it till now, will be going down for a year or so.[1]

Peake also came under the influence of Edwin Hatch, Reader in Ecclesiastical History in the University, who died prematurely in 1889 before Peake left Oxford. His estimate of Hatch is best expressed in a letter which he wrote to Miss Sillman, dated 8 January 1891.

His early death was one of the saddest things I have known, a great blow to the progress of sound theological science. He has left no one behind him to take his place. He was a man of stupendous learning, of large and liberal mind, of splendid and well-disciplined intellect, of great originality and genuine piety. He was a great example to all of us of impartial search for truth without being bound by the prejudices of one sect or theology. Though a member of the Anglican Church he was in sympathy with all denominations that were zealous for goodness and progress. He seemed to us to be free from the bigotry which members of our community often feel towards those of another. At the same time he held his convictions with great tenacity and defended them with conspicuous success. It is very sad to think what quite lately we have lost by death: Dr Hatch, Bishop Lightfoot, Aubrey Moore, Browning, Delitzch, Döllinger, Cardinal Newman, Canon Liddon, Dean Church and many more. The call of each to us is to be up and doing, and carrying on the great work at which they laboured. I feel ashamed of myself that at twenty-five I have done so little.[2]

One further name amongst those teachers who so profoundly influenced Peake in his Oxford years remains to be mentioned. His debt to Andrew Martin Fairbairn, Principal of Mansfield College, whom Peake met in the second year of his theological course was beyond measure. In a memorial article Peake recalls this personal relationship:

I met him shortly after he came to Oxford in the autumn of 1886. During his first year at Oxford I often heard his Sunday evening lectures and I missed no opportunity of hearing him preach. I saw something of him also in his home and on walks. From 1887–1891 I attended his lectures at Mansfield College, though I was not a student of the College. At the end of the time he invited me to join

---

[1] *The International Critical Commentary* on *Romans* by Sanday & Headlam was published in 1895. Cf. W. Sanday to A.S.P., 4 March 1912: 'I seem to be always in a state of undischarged indebtedness to you ... I always admire anything you write.'

[2] I am indebted for this letter to L. S. Peake, *Memoir*, p. 79.

the staff of the College. I was his colleague for two years only, since, with his warm approval, though to our mutual sorrow, I came to serve my own Church in Manchester in 1892. For several years after this time, however, I was a good deal in Oxford and saw much of him.[1]

It was with singular pleasure that in 1908, when as Dean of the Faculty of Theology, Peake presented Fairbairn for the first degree of Doctor of Divinity to be conferred in the University of Manchester. Peake was profoundly impressed with Fairbairn as a theologian who possessed a strong philosophical approach and who was an unflinching Free Churchman.

He was an expert who had mastered the whole history of philosophy; he had studied with minute care the various religions of mankind. He was a master in historical and constructive theology. He was widely read, moreover, in history and in literature. And he had a singular power of fusing all the various subjects of his investigation into a unity and seeing them as parts of a great whole. He thus always spoke not simply out of a fulness of knowledge, but of knowledge digested and co-ordinated into a systematic scheme of the universe....

I came more closely into contact with him after I had taken my degree. I remained in Oxford, and for three years attended his lectures. Especially in Comparative Religion and above all in Systematic Theology I found his lectures the most stimulating and instructive I ever had the privilege of attending. I have no doubt that I should have got much more out of them had I been able to devote more time to them, and had I been a quicker writer. But I had a certain amount of teaching to do, and in addition to this, I was working for university scholarships and prizes.... But even when allowances were made for that, I regard his lectures as the most powerful formative influence which I received from any of my teachers.

I am especially grateful to him for the apologetic value of his teaching. It was a wonderfully steadying thing that a man who knew the whole range of theological and philosophical literature, who had thoroughly sounded the worst that could be said against Christianity by its ablest opponents, nevertheless believed wholeheartedly and with intensity of conviction in the truth of Christianity. It was the reasons for faith which he stated with a lucidity and cogency that carried the judgment as well as the feeling along with it. Moreover, his interpretation of religion, and in particular our own religion, was to myself very valuable. It was fundamentally loyal but in a sense narrow. His words were measured and responsible, scrupulously balanced and carefully weighed. One had always the impression of a teacher who had thought the whole subject through and through down to its depth, who had settled convictions and whom no question could find unprepared to meet it.

Another debt which I owed to him was that he rooted and grounded me in Free Church principles. Here it was less his lectures than his writings which helped me, but they were writings which he put into my hand. Oxford was not a favourable climate for our principles. I can only recall with gratitude the way in which he taught me that we were the true High Churchmen, and anchored me firmly by the Free Church position. He was quite clear that research into the primitive history of Christianity had not helped the sacerdotalist position.

---

[1] *The Expositor*, 1912.

On the contrary he believed that the position taken up and successfully vindicated by the early Puritans had been endorsed and strengthened by modern investigation, and what he held on historical grounds he held also on theological.[1]

Through the years that followed, their correspondence was frequent and, significantly, Fairbairn wrote in one letter:[2]

It is one of the pleasures of my life to be able to think of you as having been for a brief session my colleague, and for a longer period still, a dear personal friend.

During these Oxford years Peake's range and quantity of reading, especially in the field of German criticism and theology,[3] was tremendous, but in the area of Old Testament studies he notes in particular the important influence of the writing of Robertson Smith (1846–1894), Scottish theologian and Semitic scholar, as being in some measure the determinative influence in his interest in the Old Testament. Writing of *The Religion of the Semites* (1889) he declares:[4]

My own debt to the book goes back to a rather earlier period. I had been fortunate enough to discover the *Prophets of Israel* (1882), when I was beginning my theological studies. It was later that I took up his *Old Testament in the Jewish Church* (1881), and I got more from it in the second and enlarged edition than I did from the first, in particular from his discussion of the Protestant doctrine of the Scripture. *The Religion of the Semites* I met with soon after its publication in 1889. It opened a new epoch for me, not only to the study of Semitic religion but to anthropology, and in particular to the study of totemism and taboo.

Peake was also impressed by 'the stress' Robertson Smith laid 'upon History as the vehicle of Divine revelation; not of course that he originated the idea, but he had grasped it thus early with unusual firmness and decision. To those who regarded revelation as a mere dictation from on

---

[1] *Aldersgate Magazine*, 1912: art. 'Some Reminiscences of Dr Fairbairn'.
[2] A. M. Fairbairn to A.S.P., 15 June 1904.
[3] Early in his Oxford career Peake recognized the indispensibility of a knowledge of German scholars, and the following letter to Dr Vincent Taylor (24 June 1926), prophetic in its content, reveals this:
  ... The people who are sniffy about the Germans have either no first-hand knowledge of their work or at any rate very little, or they seem to be afflicted with a kind of judicial blindness. And that is why, since you consult me, I should urge you to learn German. You have I hope a long and distinguished career before you but I feel sure that you will be sadly hampered if you cannot read German. A great deal of the best work is never translated, and this is above all true of the specialist literature, which was considered too small a sale for publication to be risked.... Hewlett Johnson, the Dean of Manchester, confessed his indebtedness to me for having forced him to learn German. He had put himself under my guidance for some work he was going to do for his D.D., which was very successfully accomplished, and I told him that for the work he was contemplating a knowledge of German was vital.
[4] *H.R.* January 1928. Peake was writing an account of Dr Stanley Cook's new edition (3rd edition) of *The Religion of the Semites* and spoke of the book as for himself 'revealing a new world to be explored' after his reading of it in 1894.

high of truths about God and man, he replied that this would be revelation in a heathen not a Christian sense.'[1]

It is clear that during these years at Oxford Peake was steadily finding his way to a decision as to his final vocation in life. As we have noted as early as 1883 the issues had been tentatively raised in connexion with the terms of his Exhibition from the school at Coventry, and he himself believed that from within the Church of England as a clergyman he could the better challenge the ritualism which he so disliked. 'As a Methodist one can do little or nothing against the Romanising party.'[2] The issue seems to have been raised again the following year in his correspondence with his former schoolfriend William Meredith, for the latter wrote a reply, tactfully urging postponement of any decision on the matter:[3]

For though it is a good desire ... yet I think it may be doubted whether as yet we have sufficient experience to guide in such a close mapping out of the future. I think the length to which you had proceeded is as far as you should venture on at present, viz; that you will be a clergyman. For the present I should say restrict yourself to that and do your best to qualify yourself to be a thoroughly noble one. Circumstances over which you have no control will probably settle your career (providing you hold yourself ready for work in whatever form it may turn up), more definitely; in other words I believe that, to the man who is ready and waiting to do God's will, that will shall be plainly shown when the right time comes.... You, though younger than myself, have at all events definitely settled your position: and if God wills you will take it.

For some time Peake's father had considered whether his son should enter the Primitive Methodist ministry, but had set aside the idea on two grounds: first that his delicate health would probably prove unequal to the exacting demands of circuit life; secondly, on the notion, though probably falsely, that there was a rather widespread feeling of prejudice against the entry of ministers' sons into the work.[4]

In a letter to his cousin Annetta Peake,[5] Peake refers to his strong conviction, born out of a reading of *The Bitter Cry of Outcast London*,[6] that he should undertake social work amongst the poor, a work he could better fulfil as an Anglican clergyman.

All this I tell you *confidentially*: no one of our family knows so much of my intentions as you. Please do not mention this to anyone else.... You may have

---

[1] A.S.P. in art., 'Robertson Smith' in *P.M.L.*, 18 July 1912.
[2] A.S.P. to George Peake, October 1883.
[3] William Meredith to A.S.P., 4 May 1884.
[4] Samuel Peake to A.S.P., 25 June 1890, in which he records his views of the matter some years earlier.
[5] A.S.P. to Annetta Peake, 18 July 1884; quoted in L. S. Peake's *Memoir*, to which I am indebted.
[6] This tract was written by three young Congregationalists in 1883 and was given immense publicity by W. T. Stead. A similar disclosure of the abysmal conditions in the slums was also given by William Booth of the Salvation Army in his *Darkest England and the Way Out* (1890), in collaboration with W. T. Stead.

already surmised that it is not my intention to become a Primitive Methodist minister. I intend to enter the Church of England.

He proceeds to give several reasons for his decision; in the light of his delicate health, fearing his years might be few; the probationary period would prevent his early entry into the work; he might not be appointed to a London area; as an Anglican he would have more freedom, unhindered by the severity of rule to which a Primitive Methodist minister must submit. Writing further in the same letter he refers to the challenge he has felt presented in the closing verse of Isaac Watts's hymn 'When I survey the wondrous cross', and underlines the words 'my life, my all', wherein he feels the Divine demand is upon him. He writes with moving conviction:

You will not then think anything too much for Him: health and strength and every other selfish conviction will be thrown to the winds. I am thankful that in some measure this has been accomplished in me, but I long to rise to the height of self-devotion, to lose entirely the thoughts of self and have my affections and whole being concentrated on the Saviour. My success would then be assured me; if I could but reach that pitch of self-annihilation in which I should no longer be myself, but lose my own identity in Christ, swallowed up in Him.

Written only a few months after his arrival in Oxford this fine, youthful idealism seems to have been a great spur to his intent, but the wise counsel of his friend William Meredith exercised a determinative influence. Clearly Peake was feeling deeply the need for certainty in the matter of his future vocation, for in the summer of 1889 he wrote to his friend:

It is nobler to lay the foundations in the dark than to place a fine spire on your building: I should like to have something to do with the laying the foundations of men's belief and character.[1]

Thus far had he come—and it was a long way on the road.

The passing of time brought a change of mind, for, as we have already noted, Peake's loyalty to Free Church principles was strengthened through his contact with Dr Fairbairn. In 1889 we find him writing to his brother:

... Don't mention it to any one, not even at home just now, but I think that I shall very probably enter Mansfield with a view to the Congregational ministry. I am not at all fascinated by the idea of taking orders in the Church of England. But I have not made any decisions as yet, and would have liked to talk about it with you. I have spoken to Fairbairn, but he thinks it is a matter a man must decide for himself. I have no doubt they would give me a scholarship, and if at the end of the time I didn't care to take a church, I should have a good chance of a Fellowship.... I dare say I may talk the matter over with Father. I think that the Governors at Coventry would not make hard terms about the Exhibition, considering I have I think a better record than any Coventry boy, and school Exhibitions are given with a tacit recognition that a man's University course is a very testing and trying time, and it is impossible to bind his future convictions.

[1] A.S.P. to William Meredith, 1889. Quoted in L. S. Peake's *Memoir* p. 93.

Peake did not become a Congregational minister: indeed he was never ordained; the door opened to final decision in 1890 as to his future when he accepted an invitation from Fairbairn to become a member of the staff of Mansfield College. Many times in after years he declared that his decision to remain a layman had been a wise one in every respect. He had at last found his true vocation.

III

As is well known, for Peake the Oxford years were marked by many academic achievements.

We have already noted that in 1885 the College authorities decided to withhold his scholarship because he had not fulfilled the college regulation of taking at least a second class in Classical Moderations. This involved him in financial strain, as his father was unable to render much assistance. On his return to Oxford in October 1885, however, he turned from Classics to Theology and in so doing he opened the door to his life's work. The College authorities awarded him an Exhibition of £20 which slightly eased the financial situation. In January 1886 he sat for the Casberd Scholarship, but although the award went to one who had been at work two years longer in Theology, Peake was told that his papers showed promise for the Schools.

In January 1887 Peake sat again and secured the Casberd, in value £100. He sent a note to his brother: 'Rejoice with me for I have found the sheep which I lost. In other words I have been elected scholar.' He received many congratulations including a 'hearty note' from his former headmaster, Mr Escott, who promised a school holiday for Coventry in recognition of Peake's success. From his former classical tutor, Mr Snow, he received this word: 'I must congratulate you and the College has done you slow justice.'

In June of the same year Peake took a First Class in the Honours School of Theology. On October 27, 1887 he took his B.A. degree. 'The ceremony had nothing noteworthy about it; one of the feeblest things I ever knew!'[1]

The Denyer and Johnson Scholarship (£50) was the most distinguished prize which the University could award. Peake sat for this in March 1888: there were eleven candidates, all senior to himself. He wrote to his brother; 'I am quite unprepared, and, as there is a very hot field, it is almost certain I shall get nothing ... I regard myself as quite outside the running.'[2] The following year, 1889, he sat again and was successful. Amongst the congratulations he received was a note from Dr Fairbairn:

---

[1] A.S.P. to George Peake, 9 November 1887.
[2] Ibid. 7 March 1888.

'It has been fairly earned and well-deserved. I was particularly pleased to hear from Sanday how good your papers had been.'[1]

In 1890, despite weighty competition, Peake gained the Ellerton Essay Prize for an essay on 'The Relation of Montanism to the Doctrine and Discipline of the Catholic Church'. Upon the fly-leaf of the surviving manuscript is his *nom de plume* τὸ πνεῦμα μὴ σβέννυτι προφητείας μὴ ἐξουθενεῖτε—'Quench not the Spirit; despise not prophesyings.' The Rev. J. Harryman Taylor, who was Peake's friend and contemporary, has an interesting reminiscence of the occasion:[2]

The time for sending in the essay drew near, and he had not written a line. Then one day he set to work. He wrote all that day and through the night, with very short intervals for refreshment, and all the day following. During the afternoon of the second day I called at his rooms. He seemed very tired and nodded to me, but it was evident that it was not a convenient time for a visitor, and I left at once. Sometime during the night the essay was finished.

Early in 1890 Peake sat for the Senior Greek Testament Prize, and although not successful, he was placed *proxime accessit*. He wrote to his brother:

... I saw Professor Sanday on Monday; he was sorry I hadn't got it, but said he had heard that several of my answers were better than anything Walmsley, who got it, had sent in; but his work was more complete: that is I had confined myself too much to answering a few questions fully.... He thought that *proxime* would mean a substantial present of books for me. I hope it will.

During these immediate years Peake also turned his thoughts towards the securing of a College Fellowship in the University, and early in 1889, at the suggestion of one of his tutors at St John's, he sat for a Theological Fellowship at Magdalen. There were fourteen entrants, and, being the youngest competitor he was not successful, though he was placed fifth in the list.[3] In October he sat for a Fellowship at New College. Halfway through the examination he wrote: 'I haven't particularly shone in it, and I am not expecting to secure it. There are nine men in'[4]—a verdict that proved to be right.

In October 1890 Peake sat for the Merton College Fellowship and was successful. The Fellowship carried with it dinner in Hall, a full suite of rooms and the sum of £200 for seven years. It was awarded upon a written examination of nine three-hour papers and lasted four-and-a-half days. The competition was unusually keen, several of the entrants being double-firsts.[5] This year it was a unique award in that Peake was the first Nonconformist layman to be elected to a Theological Fellowship at Oxford.

---

[1] Quoted in a letter of A.S.P. to George Peake, 27 March 1889.
[2] *H.R.* January 1930.
[3] A.S.P. to George Peake, 24 February 1889.
[4] A.S.P. to George Peake, 2 October 1889.
[5] A.S.P. to Samuel Peake, 2 November 1890.

H. J. A. Murray, President of the Oxford Union Society, wrote: 'My warmest congratulations on your splendid success at Merton. Isn't it a fact that you are making history'? Not only did he receive abundant congratulations on his success,[1] but the occasion was celebrated by Primitive Methodist friends at a 'complimentary luncheon' given on 21 November in Birmingham, when about a hundred laymen and ministers were present, amongst them the Rev. Samuel Peake and Mr George Peake, and in addition many ladies. In the course of his moving speech, in reply to a toast of congratulation, Peake declared:

... Though modest in most things I cannot claim modesty on the ground of ignorance of the subject of this toast. I know him well, better than any of you. I can generally manage to preach a bit if I have a good text. This time I have a very poor one—myself! Though very thankful to you, kind friends, I am still more thankful to the kind friends I have had in the past. First of all my parents. Of my sainted mother you have already heard something. Some of you knew her, and here I joy to confess that very much of my success in life is due to her influence and teaching in earlier years. I desire to state also my sense of deep indebtedness to my father, whose untiring sacrifice and deep devotion to my interests have made the joy of this day possible. My brother is now literally where he has always been really—side by side with me. To the other members of my family I feel a sense of indebtedness.

In regard to my election, I think it is a pure accident that I should be the first Nonconformist to win that honour. This election should not be regarded as the victory of a minor over a major sect. Denominational rivalry has had nothing to do with the matter. I have received the warmest congratulations from Churchmen, even High Churchmen, including authors of *Lux Mundi*. Hence my election cannot be regarded in the light of a sectarian triumph. It rather indicates the change which is working in the theological world.... The true boon of the election lies in the fact that it declares the decline of party controversy. I am at present editor and secretary of an Oxford movement founded by Professor Sanday, in which High Churchmen and all shades of Nonconformists meet together for the investigation of New Testament facts. We meet harmoniously and even affectionately. Sectarian prejudice finds no place amongst us.[2]

As this was not a teaching Fellowship Peake had no tutorial work. At this period the Senior Common Room at Merton had an illustrious membership including A. C. Bradley, L. T. Hobhouse, J. Burnet, H. H. Joachim, William Wallace and A. E. Taylor, and this provided the enjoyment of stimulating discussion.

Remembering the sectarian antipathies of the time it is not altogether surprising that a rumour spread abroad that the fact that Peake was the first Nonconformist in Oxford to hold the Fellowship had resulted in

---

[1] With typical caution in a letter of congratulation his father wrote: 'It will have some effect on your influence at Mansfield; but be careful how you use it. Ever remember that one of the greatest and best traits in a man is humility, and kind disposition that makes all men admire you' (8 October 1890.)

[2] *Primitive Methodist World.* 27 November 1890.

certain Anglican protest. The following is typical of surviving letters in which this is mentioned:

I see as usual the High Church party are showing their unholy feeling against you, because of your Nonconformist principles, but I trust they have only power to bark and not bite.[1]

Again:

I note that there is a possibility of your having a stormy time with the High Churchmen. The thing is disgusting. When will bigotry be buried? Fight on—great principles are at stake. It will all help to the advance of Nonconformity.[2]

The situation is dealt with, not without some humour, in a letter from an Oxford friend:[3]

... I was startled to read the other day that some High Churchmen were binding themselves by a solemn vow to have your blood. I am sorry to learn from a later correction that the report is untrue! High Churchmen on the warpath trying to scalp A. S. Peake would have produced some fun! But although you have escaped this peril, are you never visited at midnight by ghostly appearances of some dons of the old high-and-dry Tory school? In particular has there never entered your rooms a shade with decanal habiliments and a strong tongue, who has introduced himself to you as the late Dr Burgon? I am sure that his spirit cannot be enjoying the repose it deserves, if it is able to picture you holding 'camp-meetings' in the quad, shouting 'Praise the Lord' in the Chapel, and holding a love-feast in the Hall!

Although these rumours were false, they were sufficiently widespread for Peake himself to write a public disclaimer:

Mansfield College, Oxford. Oct. 25.
1890.

To the Editor of the *Primitive Methodist*
Sir,
Will you kindly contradict a quite unfounded rumour that the High Church undergraduates at Merton intend to protest against my election as a Nonconformist to a Theological Fellowship? I find that several have been led to attach importance to the statement of the *Birmingham Daily Post*, so, in justice to the Merton High Church undergraduates, I feel it my duty not simply to contradict the report, but to say that I have received already what courtesy the Church Society was able to offer me. I have never found the differences in theological opinion affect in the slightest degree my kindly relations with men of all shades of opinion, and many strong churchmen have been among my warmest friends.
I am, Yours etc. A. S. Peake.[4]

On 22 October Peake entered Merton and a few days later wrote to his brother:

[1] Joseph Lawley to A.S.P., 19 October 1890.
[2] J. J. Lawrence to A.S.P., 16 October 1890.
[3] H. W. Horwill to A.S.P., 1 November 1890.
[4] *Primitive Methodist*. October 1890. The same letter appeared in the *Primitive Methodist World* and the *Christian World*.

I went to Merton on Wednesday, and am settling down. The men are congenial and very good fellows and I am having a very decent time of it. I have had to furnish my rooms entirely.... I have given up my Mansfield rooms. The report about the High Church protest was ridiculous.[1]

So with Peake's entry into Merton and his recently formed association with Mansfield College a new stage in his life work had begun.[2]

IV

With the repeal of the Test Act in 1871 the universities became open to men of all Churches. As early as 1875 Dr D. W. Simon, Principal of the Spring Hill Congregational College, Birmingham, initiated discussion as to the advisability of securing for their students 'the advantages now open to Nonconformists in the older universities'. The difficulties were found to be insuperable, but Simon later returned to the charge, and to a private meeting put his ideas into definite shape. Dr R. W. Dale, who at first opposed the idea—'in the very nature of the case the national universities could never be used for the education of Nonconformist ministers'—changed his view, and, being the most powerful influence in English Congregationalism, this was an important step forward. In 1884 he formulated a scheme for the removal of the College to Oxford, which was later implemented, Dr A. M. Fairbairn to become Principal. Fairbairn moved to Oxford in the spring of 1886. The College was opened on 15 October, 1889.[3] Two tutors were appointed—Vernon Bartlet to teach Church History and W. B. Selbie to teach Hebrew and Old Testament. A letter from Peake to his brother, dated 4 July 1890, contains the following:

You will be glad to hear that Dr Fairbairn has offered me a lectureship at Mansfield in place of Selbie, who goes to High Gate Congregational Church. It will be temporary for probably a couple of years, but that is just what I want. One step enough for me. The salary is not very large but sufficient, £100 a year with rooms, fire and light. I shall go into residence next term. I have to lecture on Elementary Hebrew, Old Testament and Texts for the Doctrine of the Incarnation.

Peake only remained in his rooms at Mansfield for some three weeks before transferring to Merton. With the acceptance of this appointment the die

---

[1] A.S.P. to George Peake, 24 October 1890.

[2] In passing we may note at this point an illustration of Peake's wider ministry. One feature of Primitive Methodism was the formation of District Ministerial Associations. One such was the West Midland Association, of which Peake was made an honorary member, and for some years he regularly contributed papers to it.

[3] This development is set out fully in W. B. Selbie, *The Life of Andrew Martin Fairbairn* (1914) pp. 161-202. Cf. F. J. Powicke, *The Life of David Worthington Simon* (1912) pp. 109ff.

had been cast and the mould for his future career had been laid down—the teaching of the Bible and Christian Theology.

Later, G. Buchanan Gray was added to the staff—and for the rest of the years these three—Bartlet, Selbie, and Gray—remained Peake's lifelong friends.

With Dr Fairbairn Peake had the most satisfactory relation during his two years at Mansfield and he records this in terms of deep admiration.

As a colleague I found him all that I could wish. His advice was always gladly given, but he did not obtrude it. My sphere of work having been allotted to me, he never interfered with my method of doing it. Remembering who he was and what qualifications and claims he had to exercise control, I have always been grateful to him for his confidence.... No one spoke more kindly or more warmly appreciated the work that I tried to do.... While he kept in touch with my work I never remember his intervening, except I myself consulted him, to direct me how I was to do it.[1]

Of Peake's work during the two years at Mansfield only scanty record has survived, but there is sufficient to indicate the way in which events were moving. His work of teaching proceeded steadily and effectively; he began also the work of book reviewing and his early literary contributions. He wrote on 8 July 1890:

Bartlet introduced me to the editor of the *Christian World*. He had been at the Milton dinner, and it was Bartlet who suggested to him the reviewing business.

On 1 November 1890 he received an unexpected letter from Dr W. Robertson Nicoll, the Editor of the *British Weekly*

27 Paternoster Row, London

My dear Sir,

Professor Sanday kindly wrote to me about you. I venture to ask whether you wd contribute anything to *The Expositor* during next year. Also I shd like very much to make your personal acquaintance. Wd you not come and see me next time you are in London? My address is Bay Tree Lodge, Frognal, Hampstead, and we should be delighted if you would arrange to spend a night any time.

Your faithfully
W. R. Nicoll.

Peake was Nicoll's guest in London on Friday, 12 June. They rambled over Hampstead Heath and talked of Peake's future: in the evening in the library much of the conversation was about Robertson Smith. It was an important introduction to a friendship which lasted until Nicoll's death in 1923. Peake did not write the article for *The Expositor* immediately. Recognizing that *The Expositor* was the most important theological monthly in England, Sanday advised him to wait. To the *British Weekly* however he made early contribution much to Nicoll's satisfaction.

Early in 1891, at the request of the Rev. Colin C. McKechnie, Editor

---

[1] A.S.P.: art. 'Some Reminiscences of Dr Fairbairn', *Aldersgate Magazine*, 1912.

to the *Primitive Methodist Quarterly Review*, Peake contributed a paper on the Synoptic Problem, and as we shall see later this was the beginning of an increasingly important association with the periodical, for in 1892 he undertook the editorship of the literature section of the work.[1] A sentence in one of the editor's letters reveals the sensitiveness of the times to the new ideas of criticism and theories of revelation. He writes:

From the tone of your letters, as well as from what I have heard on reliable authority, I feel sure I can trust you to conduct the discussion of these important and delicate matters with wisdom and discretion, your youth notwithstanding.

In October 1891 Peake proceeded to the M.A. degree at Oxford.

Two further occasions belong to these years at Mansfield. In a letter to his brother there is an important entry:

... Mr Hartley and three of his family are coming up from Saturday till Monday, so Taylor informs me. They are on a driving tour.[2]

Taylor brought them round to Peake's rooms at Merton on the Saturday evening, and they had lunch with him on the Monday. For some time Peake had felt much dissatisfaction with regard to the ministerial training at the Primitive Methodist College in Manchester, and with some freedom spoke to his guests about the matter. Mr Hartley was deeply interested in Peake's view of ministerial training, and although he was unaware of any plan in Mr Hartley's mind, he soon discovered, in conversation with Taylor, that Mr Hartley was considering the question as to whether Peake could be induced to leave Oxford for Manchester. The outcome of this crucial conversation is well known, and it will be fully considered later in these pages.[3]

The second occasion was an even more personal one. In a letter to his brother[4] there is a somewhat naïve entry as follows:

I was at 63 Iffley Road yesterday, and had a pretty good time.... Miss S. (the elder) told me to come in to tea any afternoon; they will always be in by 4.30. They are coming to hear me preach next Sunday. I hope that will make a further impression.

A member of this household was Miss Harriet Mary Sillman, to whom eventually Peake made a proposal of marriage. Their engagement took place in the midsummer of 1890, an event which brought the following amusing effusion from his old friend Humphrey Nott, including an invitation to visit him in Herefordshire.

Dear Arthur,
    I write to congratulate you on being elected President of the Milton Society.

[1] C. C. McKechnie to A.S.P., 17 April 1891; 4 September 1891; 16 February 1892.
[2] A.S.P. to George Peake, 11 May 1891. The reference is to J. Harryman Taylor, who was in training for the Primitive Methodist ministry at Mansfield.
[3] A.S.P. *The Life of Sir William P. Hartley* (1926) pp. 133ff.
[4] A.S.P. to George Peake, 19 March 1890.

Is it a University or a St John's College Society? ... But all this pleasure I fear will fail to make up for the great unhappiness into which I hear you have lately fallen! If it is any consolation to you to know that your friends sympathise with you, you may accept my hearty condolence with you upon your engagement to Miss Sillman.

Just drop me about two particulars that I may better realise your distressing position, and thus be better able to sympathise more rationally with you. It may not be so very bad as I imagine—I trust not.

Can you manage to slip down here sometime for a few days and escape by stealth and without leaving address, from your fair enchanter? Should be pleased to see, harbour and protect if necessary, for I shall still remain your attached friend even in this time of distress!

Yours truly

H. F. Nott.[1]

The marriage took place on 29 June 1892 in the Parish Church at Cowley St John's. Of the significance of this important event it is fitting that Peake's eldest son, Leslie Sillman Peake, should speak:[2]

His marriage was important, apart from any domestic considerations because through it he came to understand more fully than he might otherwise have done, the ways and methods of the Church of England, and in later years this had its influence when he attended the Conferences at Lambeth on the question of Reunion. His marriage did not revive the youthful desire to take orders in the Church of England, but it did lead to a more personal interest in the denomination that claimed the allegiance of his wife, and mainly as a concession to her wishes he always conducted family prayers from the Church of England Prayer Book. She in turn frequently attended the Primitive Methodist Church along with her husband and children, though she always remained an Anglicna at heart.

In the nature of things it was inevitable that their home life together through the years was invaded by the monolithic demands of Peake's work, but with complete selflessness his wife supported and sustained him in his labours with perfect devotion. A close friend of the family over many years wrote to Mrs Peake at the time of Peake's final illness:

You have always seemed to me a model of unselfishness—the way you have cheerfully borne with his giving of his genius to the world—and all the time this had taken—instead of holding him back for your own pleasure and the children's. Many a wife would have been jealous even of his genius, but I am sure you have always been a very great help and a secret source of strength to him. And now you will be called upon to be his mainstay in life.[3]

In the summer of 1891 Peake spent two months in Heidelberg, during which time his mind was much exercised upon the question of the situa-

---

[1] H. F. Nott to A.S.P., 13 June 1890.
[2] L. S. Peake, *Memoir*, p. 97.
[3] Mrs Dorothy Holmes to Mrs Peake, 16 August 1929. Peake died three days after this letter was written.

tion in Manchester. Little has survived giving account of his stay there, but one interesting episode is worth recounting. He writes:[1]

> I have discovered a little Methodist meeting even here. Everything is in German, but I make a point of going and enjoying the service much better than anything else. I managed to get through a little conversation with the preacher the other Sunday. They have service in the afternoon followed by a class-meeting. They have a hymn-book of their own, but also a small hymn-book which they use a good deal, containing chiefly translations from Sankey. It was very interesting and cheering to get 'Rock of Ages' and 'Hallelujah! send the glory' in German. I have ordered both the hymn-books with the music.

Steadily, as we shall see in more detail, the issue regarding Manchester was being determined. Peake left Mansfield amidst mutual regrets. The following letter, dated 25 June 1892, indicates the esteem in which Peake's work was regarded, and the signatures include significant names:

> Some of the students at Mansfield College desire to make a present to you in view of your approaching marriage as a slight mark of their regard for you and their appreciation of your services as Tutor and Lecturer in the College. We cannot think of your departure from Oxford without feeling that it will result to us in the loss of a friend and of a valuable helper in our studies. We wish to thank you for your kindness and all the obligations that we owe to you, which are greater than we can express; and in your new life, your married life, and your work in the College of your own denomination we would wish you all joy and prosperity.
> We have been proud of having on the staff of our College one so distinguished as yourself in Oxford University. We trust that the connection you have had with Mansfield College may not be broken, although your tutorship ceases therein. And we feel assured that in your new sphere of instruction you will be the same faithful teacher and servant; you will imbue all with your own love of truth and knowledge, and ever promote the great work of theological study and the Kingdom of Christ in our land.
> We trust that you will find these books; Thayer's *N.T. Greek Lexicon* and Westcott's *Epistle of St John* of service to you.
> Signed on behalf of the subscribers,
>
> James Gordon Wall   A. Hallack
> A. E. Garvie   T. D. Rutherford
> W. E. Ireland   H. T. Spencer
> R. J. Rees

Peake left Oxford and Mansfield on 31 August, 1891.

V

We cannot leave the story of these years at Oxford without some reference

---

A.S.P. to George Peake, 20 August 1891.

to more external interests which claimed Peake's thought and attention, though some of these will be considered more fully later in these pages.

Even before going to Oxford he had already developed a deeply sensitive social consciousness and the impulses for social betterment which centred in a number of Oxford men—'The Oxford Socialists'—and which found expression in such projects as the Toynbee Hall experiment gave further stimulus to his interest. In the succeeding years there is little record of his direct activity in the movement, but Peake's concern for the welfare of the people remained constant and unabated throughout his whole life.

Politically Peake espoused the cause of Liberalism and had a strong allegiance to the policy of Irish Home Rule which Gladstone and the Liberal party led in 1886. This loyalty to the cause of Liberalism Peake maintained throughout his life with unflinching allegiance. Consequently he followed the movement of parliamentary elections with unabated interest.

Peake gave much time and thought to two further matters during these years. Very soon after his arrival at Oxford he entered into the work of Sunday School teaching and exercised a distinct influence towards reform in the work at the church in Pembroke Street. In addition he began the work of preaching in the Oxford Circuit, and likewise fulfilled a useful ministry. Of these things we shall write more fully in these pages later on. In both these matters he laid the foundation of his important influence in the years that lay ahead.

Despite the strain of academic studies there is some indication of a lighter side to his Oxford life, though doubtless his indulgence in recreation was all too scanty. There is a brief glimpse in a letter to his brother:[1]

... We are having hot weather, exceedingly scorching at times. On Tuesday we were down at Cufton Hampden,—a party of five—thirteen miles down river from Oxford. I bathed in the river once; it was pleasant, the water was warmer than the air. Just now I am lazy, and sleep most of the day and much tired out with the heat and languid atmosphere. My spirit fainteth! I am faint yet pursuing.

He also found a keen interest in chess and for a time played it by correspondence with his brother George.

It was natural that during these Oxford years friendships were forged between Peake and his contemporaries—and in time to come these still remained unbroken. Not a few names might be mentioned, but the following examples will serve to illustrate the influence which Peake unconsciously exerted in his contact with others.

D. Herridge, the son of a Primitive Methodist minister, who later held a mastership at New College, Eastbourne, wrote on the eve of Peake's departure for Manchester:

---

[1] A.S.P. to George Peake, 19 January 1887. At this time he had been working hard for the Casberd Scholarship and his Final Schools.

... I cannot say how much I am indebted to you for the *tone* you imparted to my life at Oxford. I may have an opportunity some day of publicly acknowledging that next to my own beloved father you have exercised more influence upon my life than anyone else. I feel proud to have shared your society and spent many hours with you. ... I feel more strong to endure and to battle than I should have done had I not had the joy of knowing you. *You* have supplied a want which no other earthly person has.[1]

Again:

... When I look back upon those happy times in old Oxford then the many occasions when we were together; the many walks, the many confidences come very vividly before me. ... You know what your influence on me was at Oxford; you know what a large part you played in my life while at the famous city—that influence has never left me, and I find myself under the spell again and again.[2]

William G. Torr, who joined St John's College shortly after Peake had taken his degree, was a fellow-member of the Bible-reading class in the College. A lifelong friendship sprang up between them. On the occasion of Peake's death in 1929—when Torr at an advanced age was compelled to spend much time in bed—he wrote the following to Mrs Peake:[3]

... Today he shares the joys of the Church Triumphant. His portrait is at the foot of my bed, where I spend a great many hours. I have sweet communion with my sainted chum. I have mentioned my dear old College friend in prayers every day for years, and I shall continue to do so, in spite of Protestant orthodoxy.

The Rev. E. R. Buckley, who went up to Oxford in 1886 was one of Peake's most intimate college friends and became the Rector of Colchester. In a communication sent to Peake's son he has afforded a further glimpse of these Oxford years.[4]

In a college which on the one hand was rather fast and on the other rather High Church, Peake was something of an unusual phenomenon. His dress was not fashionable though he was always neat. He always wore a short black coat and waistcoat, dark grey trousers, a turn-down collar and dark tie. To this he added a blue ribbon in his button-hole, for he was a staunch teetotaller, and Jaeger boots. His black bowler hat always looked a size or two too big, which made him appear rather top-heavy.

My first clear remembrance of him is that on a Sunday night after hall, about 7.30 p.m. towards the end of my first term, he came up to my rooms, where about a dozen freshmen, several of them rather of the rowdy kind, were assembled. I was a little anxious about how he would mix with them as I think he only knew one of them besides myself. I need have had no anxiety. He was

---

[1] D. Herridge to A.S.P., 17 June 1892.
[2] Ibid., 18 November 1894.
[3] W. G. Torr to Mrs Peake. 5 September 1929. After gaining the LL.D at Dublin University Torr became Principal of the New Way College, Brighton, S. Australia.
[4] L. S. Peake, *Memoir*, pp. 94–7.

the life and soul of the party. One of them—H. Y. Nutt—who had been a medical student and a trooper in the Cape Mounted Rifles before coming to College—began to tell very tall yarns, but every time Nutt told a yarn Peake capped it with a better, and so briskly did he keep the ball rolling that the party did not break up till five minutes to twelve, when Peake, who was living in lodgings and had to be out of College before twelve, left.

That evening illustrates his position in College very well, despite his drawbacks, for to be badly off, unfashionably dressed, a Nonconformist and a teetotaller were serious drawbacks in such a College as St John's in those days. His wit, his unfailing good temper, his courtesy and personal charm, made him one of the most popular men in College. The verdict of my dozen friends that Sunday night was unanimous. They all said: 'What a good chap he is: we didn't think he was a bit like that!'

Sometime in 1887 I joined the St Hilary Society (an inter-collegiate theological society of which Peake was a member), and from that time onwards saw him constantly, going for walks with him, going to his rooms and he coming to mine. His speeches at the St Hilary were always interesting and illuminating, and many a tussle did he have with High Church members of the Society. He was always good as chairman of the various College Societies. The quickness and aptness of his repartee were astonishing, and his most crushing retorts were always made in a gentle voice and with a winning smile. . . .

After taking his degree he remained in Oxford and made a living by coaching. When after taking my degree in 1889 I started to read Theology he insisted on coaching me for love for two years, though he must have had a hard struggle to live, for it was not till a year or more later that he finally got on his feet by winning in quick succession, the Denyer and Johnson Scholarship, the Ellerton Prize and a Fellowship at Merton.

He was no good at games. I don't think he ever rowed. I once played a game of lawn-tennis with him—only one set! I never repeated the experiment; perhaps he did not either!

He had a passion for 'Penny Dreadfuls'. At the time he was working very hard for the Denyer and Johnson scholarship, he read one every night. I remember going with him to a dirty little stationer in St Clement's to buy them. He would buy half-a-dozen at a time—usually Red Indian or pirate stories.

It was in my company, and I think at my instigation, that he paid his first visit to the theatre. J. L. Toole was touring in a play called *The Don*. Miss Eva Moore was playing the leading lady (Dora), and at the end of the play after Toole had come before the curtain and made a speech, there were loud calls for Dora! I can still vividly recall Peake standing beside me on a bench in the pit, rather flushed, very excited and shouting 'Dora' at the top of his voice. Many years after (about 1920) when I was passing through Manchester and spent an afternoon with him, I asked him whether he still went to the theatre. 'No,' he said, 'I have had to sacrifice it to Higher Criticism.' He explained that as some more conservative members of his Connexion looked rather askance at his championing Old Testament Criticism, he did not wish to give them a handle to say that Higher Criticism leads to play-going and such evil ways!

In these rather scattered reminiscences I have touched chiefly on the lighter side—the side of him I perhaps saw more of than his colleagues at Mansfield, such as Dr Bartlet and Dr Selbie. But I should like to mention a great debt I owe to Peake. I had been brought up in a narrow High Church school of thought. After I had been a year or two at Oxford my mind became very unsettled on religious matters, and it was Peake's sympathy and tact and wise counsel that kept me from drifting into agnosticism.

The significance of these nine years at Oxford cannot be better summed up than in the incisive words of Dr W. F. Lofthouse, written in 1958.[1]

The brief period spent at Oxford, though almost inarticulate compared with the immense product of the years that followed, needs the illumination of Manchester. But the thirty-seven years at Manchester, one may say with confidence, would have been impossible without it: and this we may surmise, for three reasons: because of what was given by the decade (it was hardly as much as that); because of what was withheld by it; and because of what, unconsciously it may be, it induced into his life.

Peake took from Oxford to Manchester a vast and rich store of knowledge, the technique of its propagation and advancement, and an intense understanding of culture in the fullest sense of the term, an endowment which became continually enlarged. But there were some things Oxford could not give him. It could not afford generous recognition of those whose religious experience fell into other moulds than the set form of worship associated with a tradition which, though ancient and somewhat outworn, could not be questioned. It had no sympathy with those who had and could have but 'the *foi du charbonnier* as Peake's friend A. E. Taylor used to call it'.[2] Yet this failure to give became for Peake a translation into a deeper loyalty and allegiance to those things that had been once delivered to him, and which he steadily determined to foster and proclaim. The result was that, despite the inner tumults of experience, Peake left Oxford a more determined Free Churchman than when he entered it. 'All the principles in whose presence the boy had been brought up called for their defence by the student and as a result he spent the remainder of his life in serving every one of them!'[3]

Throughout these years of academic study at Oxford Peake seems to have had a growing conviction that the new approach to an understanding of the nature of Scripture should be steadily disseminated to a wider constituency, and this to be done by those who were best able to spread it. This was the thing which unconsciously was induced into his life through his Oxford experience. This conviction lay behind all his work in future years. It was this conviction that he carried with him when he left Oxford—a precipitate of these years, the development of which he may have steadily become aware of. That which he had discovered for himself others must share. Again, in the final words of Dr Lofthouse:

Surely we may say that the seventh heaven of Paradise, the heaven of the great

---

[1] W. F. Lofthouse: 'Oxford Days' in *Essays in Commemoration*, p. 31.
[2] Ibid., p. 32.   [3] Ibid., p. 32.

doctors of theological learning is still entered by those who decided not to live but to know, and whose faces shine with a fresh light of joy whenever opportunity is given them to share with others what He whose Name is Truth has shared with them.[1]

[1] Ibid., p. 33.

CHAPTER THREE

HARTLEY COLLEGE, MANCHESTER

THE Primitive Methodist Church emerged as a distinct religious organization in 1811, and for the first half-century it was content to go forward without any special training for its ministry. For this there were valid reasons. Primitive Methodism was born out of a passion for evangelism, and its first fifty years belong to the creative stage of its history. The eagerness to seize new 'openings', and break up new ground often led to men being thrust into the work without any warning or intellectual preparation. Furthermore, financial considerations were also a serious issue, and the work was largely carried on by working-folk who possessed little education, and in some cases without a feeling that this was required for the task in hand.

It may be recalled, however, that Hugh Bourne, one of the founders of Primitive Methodism was a keen advocate of intellectual betterment, and also that some of those who belonged to the creative period in its history acquired, by the sheer weight of their own effort, a creditable degree of culture. Such names as John Petty, Colin McKechnie, James Macpherson, the two brothers William and Samuel Antliff, spring to mind. In 1850 came the establishment of the first Ministerial Association, issuing in 1854 in the founding of the *Christian Ambassador*, the precursor of the *Holborn Review*. Whilst these represented a vigorous attempt to discipline a movement towards a more effective ministry, this was no adequate substitute for a ministry thoroughly trained for the work.

It should also be remembered that in this matter of ministerial education there was some measure of suspicion. Much success and advancement had been achieved by those already in the work despite their lack of education; the younger minister might lose the passion for evangelism, under the influence of a training that was more intellectual in character.

The first impulse towards collegiate training came in 1865, when Elmfield College, York, which had been opened the year before as a secondary school for boys, was also utilized as a training school for the ministry, and some fifteen to twenty men were sent there for one year's study. The next advance came in 1868, when the Institute at Sunderland was opened; the residence was for one year only. The curriculum covered certain elements of ordinary education, with additional study in theology and the work of preaching. In 1875 the desire was expressed for an extension of the course of training to two years—though this did not find fulfilment until nearly seventeen years later, in 1891. Further, however, it was later decided that a second college, to supplement the work at Sunderland, should be established and that its location should be in Manchester. On June 24, 1878 the foundation stone was laid and the College in Manchester came into being, though because of financial reasons, the building was not completed until 1881, and the first company of students, ten in all, was admitted. The accommodation provided for thirty men. The two institutions continued to pursue their work side by side, but before long the Sunderland Institute was closed and the work transferred to Manchester. Its first Principal was the Rev. James Macpherson, who retired in 1887 after fulfilling fine pioneer service; he was succeeded by Dr Joseph Wood who, alert in mind, exerted much influence throughout the Church concerning the whole question of ministerial training, before he retired in 1893. Up to this point the Principal of the College had been responsible for the whole curriculum, and the course of training still was only one year in length.

Such, then, was the situation at Manchester at the time when Peake was a young graduate still in Oxford, and on the staff of Mansfield College.

I

As we have already noted, though in the academic groves of 'the city of dreaming spires', Peake was deeply concerned with the question of the training of the ministry as centred in the industrial city of the north; his dissatisfaction with the situation was deep.

Further, as we have also seen already, this concern had become focused more strongly in consequence of the visit of Mr W. P. Hartley to Oxford in May, 1891. Now the whole issue began to assume a more personal involvement as the result of the conversation in his rooms at Merton. Peake knew that, without any mention of his name, Mr Hartley had suggested a new policy to the College Committee, and indeed had offered to provide the salary of a tutor for five years. The outcome was that a proposal was made to Peake that he should consider the position in relation to himself.

In the light of these developments it was a natural thing that, as a member of the staff at Mansfield, he should consult Dr Fairbairn, as Principal of the College. Fairbairn greatly desired to retain Peake in Oxford, but he recognized that a call had come which was not to be resisted. He wrote:

Dear Mr Peake,

I have read your letter with deep sympathy and certainly appreciate your motive and all you would surrender. For many reasons I wish it were in my power to set before you a permanent career here worthy of your deserts. It would be a great personal pleasure to me to be able to help you in connexion with Mansfield, and the prospects of Theology in Oxford. But my own feeling must be made strictly subordinate to your sense of duty. And I feel what a great opportunity may come, nay, has come to you in your own Connexion. It seems to me as if you had been specially raised up and trained for the very work that is most in need of being done for it. And you are in many ways the only person that can do the work. You may lift up their ideas of the ministry, of the Church, may open their minds in no way cooling their piety, and may attain a position and influence any bishop might envy. It says much for your people that they have proved themselves able to appreciate this opportunity, and the promise such appreciation gives is one of the happiest elements in the situation. I hardly at this moment see how we can do without you; yet the less feel the possibilities of a career which such an appointment would open. Possibly your Connexion might come to see that your work could be done here; that for a few men you could do better in Oxford than in Manchester; but quite possibly you would need to do some service in the old Institute before any new enterprize could be proposed with any chance of success. What is before my mind is this: were they to appoint and maintain you here as resident tutor, sending only the picked men who could graduate, or had graduated, then these men could be taken in as Taylor[1] has been, to be educated in Mansfield while you would be at once their tutor and a member of our staff. I am sure our people would do all in their power to make some such arrangement possible.

But on these points we may have a talk soon. I shall, if you are able to be out, try and arrange tonight. . . .

                              Ever yours,
                              A. M. Fairbairn[2]

On June 4, Peake met a sub-committee of the College committee for preliminary discussion of matters involved, and he intimated his willingness to accept appointment should it ultimately be offered to him, and if so that he would be willing to come in July or August 1892. Some preliminary conversation took place as to the nature and extent of the work he would wish to undertake.[3] The proposal to recommend to the Conference that he should be appointed was unanimous.

On June 12, on his way to attend the Conference at Northampton—the first he had ever attended—Peake stayed overnight in the home of Dr W. Robertson Nicoll, in London. During a long walk over Hampstead Heath Peake explained that he might be leaving Oxford to serve his own Church in the College in Manchester. Nicoll was sympathetic with this,

---

[1] J. Harryman Taylor, who took his theological course at Mansfield and entered the Primitive Methodist ministry in 1892.

[2] A.M.F. to A.S.P., 3 June 1891. This letter is quoted in *The Life of Andrew Martin Fairbairn*, by W. B. Selbie, pp. 244-5. Peake's letter does not appear to be extant.

[3] Minutes of sub-committee, 4 June 1891.

but demurred at Fairbairn's suggestion of the possibility of students being sent to Mansfield, and that Peake should return to Oxford and be their tutor and as a member of the Mansfield staff. Nicoll's feeling was that every denomination has its own ethos, and that this would be endangered if the Primitive Methodist students were trained in a Congregational College. Peake did not wholly sympathize with Nicoll's view on this point, but when he entered upon the work at Manchester eventually he became convinced of his personal duty to remain there, rather than to try to realize the wish the Principal of Mansfield had so generously expressed.[1]

At the Conference, the President, Dr Ferguson and Mr Hartley introduced Peake to the assembly, and at a later point in the proceedings, when the College Report was under discussion, he urged the appointment of a new tutor to whom a free hand should be given, and said that he would finance the scheme for five years.[2] He then mentioned Peake's name in illustration of the kind of appointment he had in mind. On his return to Oxford Peake received notice of the definite proposal and that he should be asked to meet the College Committee for consideration of details. He received this by telegram from Mr Hartley on June 19.[3]

Two letters written to his father disclose Peake's mind and spirit in this time of crisis.

The first was written from Brobury Court near Hereford when, whilst preaching at Staunton-on-Wye, he was the guest of Mr James Farr.

You will have seen from my article in the *British Weekly* that I think something should be done in our connexion for the better education of the ministry. I am quite convinced that unless something is done in this direction the Connexion will fail to advance. Our people have failed to keep pace with the advance of the nation in education and general culture. My mind has been much exercised on the disgraceful state of the Connexion in this particular and in the means of remedying it. I think it is the main problem before me at present, as it supplies us with the starting point from which we must proceed to solve our other difficulties. Others are feeling this too, and a scheme is on foot for revolutionising the Theological Institute. The idea is that the students should remain for at least two years, if possible three, one of which is to count in the latter case, as a year of probation. Also that a graduate should be appointed as Tutor with a free hand in tuition without interference from the Principal. Mr Hartley has promised two hundred pounds a year for five years, if this scheme can be adopted. Of course this raised the question at once as to my own position and responsibility towards it. I feel that the Connexion should have the advantage of what prestige and position I may have, and also of my educational privileges. In fact I have been driven to the conclusion which as a matter of duty I feel

---

[1] A.S.P. art. 'Sir William Robertson Nicoll' in the *Holborn Review*. January 1926.

[2] Conference MS. Journal, 1891. Minute 465. 'That Mr Hartley's generous offer to provide the said Tutor be accepted; that the College Committee enter into negotiations with Arthur S. Peake, B.A. and with him exchange opinions as to subjects of tuition, entrance examinations, and with a view to his appointment at the Conference of 1892.'

[3] A. S. Peake: *Life of Sir W. P. Hartley*, p. 136.

bound to accept that if the Connexion wishes me to take the position, and will adopt a scheme which will guarantee a reasonable prospect of success in the work, I shall do so. Of course it will mean considerable sacrifice. I don't think any one but myself knows what it will mean to me to leave Oxford, but that counts with me as nothing if I can see my duty clear. And I think I have never seen it clearer than in this case. I have reason to believe that it will make a considerable difference to the position of the Institute, and the financial support given to it. I am told that it would restore confidence in the Connexion and give it a status it has not had before. My wish in the matter is to do what would be best for the Connexion, and the country at large, and I think that is the sphere in which I can do it. Dr Fairbairn with whom I have communicated is very much distressed at the idea of my going, and would like to offer me a position worthy of my merits. But he says his wishes must be strictly subordinate to my sense of duty, and he thinks my duty is to go. He says that it seems to him that I have been specially raised up and trained for the work and am in many ways the only one who can do it. I don't feel that I am doing anything specially noble in going, though some have told me so, because when a thing becomes a matter of duty it ceases to be a matter of choice. Of course, nothing is settled at present, but Mr Hartley has sent me a telegram saying: 'Conference decided that a Committee meet you personally to talk over College course, entrance examinations and your probable engagement.' I think you will see and sympathise with my position. If I go it will not be because I wish to go, but because it is my plain duty. It may still come to nothing, but for the sake of the Connexion I do hope the opportunity will not be neglected. If I were I should wish it to be in 1892, in a year's time.[1]

Some six weeks later, whilst he was on his summer vacation in Heidelberg in Germany, he referred more briefly to the matter again in a second letter to his father.

... With respect to Manchester I don't know that I have much to add. Of course the matter has been very long thought about, and for some time, before it seemed at all likely to come to anything. I had thought a great deal about the Institute. I don't feel that I have any right to consult my interests in the matter: it is simply a question of duty. The only question to be decided is whether it is my duty to go. It is clear that I have nothing much to gain by going, and that it will be a great trouble to me to leave Oxford. This being so all my prejudices were naturally against my going, and if I come to the conclusion that I should go it will be in spite of my feelings and wishes to the contrary. Just now the Connexion is in a very critical condition. It is neither one thing nor the other. It is passing through a period of transition. I think that the time has come for a step forward, and I feel that matters are just in that stage when I can materially help the Connexion. The training of the ministry is perhaps the most important work that can be done and very essential to our future prosperity. As matters are at present the training that is given is most inadequate. So much so that the Institute has never commanded the confidence of our people, for the truth is that it really does not deserve it. Several who know the opinion of the Connexion think that there can be no doubt if I went that confidence would be restored and

---

[1] A.S.P. to Samuel Peake, 24 June 1891.

the College properly supported. Besides Mr Hartley's offer is on condition of adequate provision being made for tuition by a graduate of a British University. I think I told you Dr Fairbairn's opinion. He is very much distressed as he has told me again and again at the thought of my going. When I said goodbye to him he told me that he didn't know what he should do if I left. But yet he feels that it is my duty to go, and he thinks that I have been specially raised up and trained for the very work that is most in need of being done for the Connexion. He feels that a great opportunity has come to me, and that I am in many ways the only person who can do the work. I am bound to attach a good deal of weight to his knowledge and experience in these matters. Of course I should have nothing on my hands except the tutorial work. The idea is that the Principal should keep to his department, and that I should have a free hand in mine. Much of the work would not require elaborate preparation, and I am inclined to think that I should be able to reserve a good deal of time for my own work. I am hoping too that if I go the work I do will have a beneficial influence on me in more ways than one. There is no idea of my doing anything except teaching.[1]

It will be observed that in this second letter there is a considerable reiteration of detail named in the first, together with a distinct attempt on the part of Peake to reassure his father as to the rightness of his decision. This seems to imply that there was some hesitation, if not opposition, on his father's part to the new venture. This was indeed the case, for his father had some reluctance and even uneasiness. This expressed itself in a letter to his son,[2] following the visit of Peake to the Northampton Conference.

I must congratulate you on the hearty manner you were received at the Conference. No doubt binding yourself down to the course you intended to adopt at Manchester would interfere somewhat with your freedom. But I think under the circumstances, it was the best thing to do, and the Conference appears very much pleased.

This hesitation within the family circle was shared by George Peake, whose concern for his brother was always so deep and genuine. He wrote from London:[3]

I don't feel quite satisfied that you are taking the best course in leaving your work in Oxford for our Manchester College, and I think the step is of such great importance that I trust you will give it most careful thought and consideration before finally accepting. It is not necessary to point out the sacrifice you are making, but it certainly does seem to me that your prospects of doing really good, useful and original work in Oxford have opened up so clearly that they should not be lightly thrown on one side. I believe you are acting from a high sense of duty, but I am doubtful if it is your duty, and this is where I think you are making a mistake.... Certainly Dr Fairbairn in his letter seemed to encourage you to go, but then I don't see how he could have counselled you in any other way, as in the letter which you wrote to him I am afraid you handi-

---

[1] A.S.P. to Samuel Peake, 5 August 1891.
[2] Samuel Peake to A.S.P., 17 June 1891.
[3] George Peake to A.S.P., 1 July 1891.

capped his reply. If it is the welfare of the P.M.C. you have at heart is it not possible you may do it as much or more good by remaining at Oxford? Does not the positive influence which you have attained give you a splendid and unique opportunity of gaining for our church a more recognised position among the Free Churches? Have not your own successes made for us one step in the right direction, the more so as the attention of the Connexion has been called to the question of culture and higher education as never before, and undoubtedly during the next few years many Primitives will pass through Oxford and Cambridge?

However much may be the good you would do in Manchester, the Connexion and yourself will, I still think, be the losers by your removal from Oxford. At Manchester you will doubtless do good and sound work, but your influence will be greatly restricted to the students you teach; but in Oxford you are a link between your own Church and the life and thought of a great University; your opportunities for doing good are infinitely superior, and you can lead with more advantage and influence to much greater purpose.

Despite the strength and cogency of these arguments Peake replied to his brother from Heidelberg, in even stronger terms than in the letter he wrote to his father.[1]

... As to Manchester, of course you are aware that as yet nothing has been definitely settled.... I think just now a crisis has come in the history of the denomination, and one which it is my duty to take advantage of, since our future to a considerable extent will depend on our action now. I think it is just as well that I should have the direction of the movement in my hands now, with a view to guiding it more efficiently still when we are prepared for the next step. I am not without hope that if I leave Oxford now I may return rejoicing bringing my sheaves with me. My chance of influencing the Connexion for good depends very largely on my present decision ... I feel that our people should have what I can give.

These letters have been quoted at length to show how profound and inevitable was Peake's sense of duty in this decision, a line of action that he was prepared to pursue, despite what must have been for him the most deeply felt opposition on the part of those nearest to him, the members of his own family.

It should also be remembered that elsewhere there was a measure of hesitation as to Peake's eventual appointment, and of this he was not unaware. He was only twenty-five years of age, comparatively little known in the denomination, and there were those who raised the question of his theological soundness. Further there had arisen some misconception as to Peake's precise intention, for the term 'classical tutor' had been used to distinguish his proposed work from that of the Principal in whose hands the teaching of theology had always been, though this misunderstanding was eventually resolved.[2] In May, 1892 Peake met the full

---

[1] A.S.P. to George Peake, July 1891.
[2] W. P. Hartley to A.S.P., 17 September 1891. 'I think you may rest contented that the use of the word "classical" was simply either ignorance or inadvertence.'

College Committee and placed his plans before it. A resolution was passed recommending the appointment to the Conference to be held at Norwich. Mr Hartley was present to advocate the proposal which he had been the first to suggest.

At the Conference in Norwich the following resolution was passed unanimously: 'That we appoint Arthur S. Peake, M.A. to the tutorship of the Theological Institute, Manchester'.[1] In advocacy of the cause of ministerial training, an enthusiastic public meeting was held in the Queen's Road Chapel, under the presidency of Mr Hartley, at which the Principal of the College, Dr J. Wood and Peake himself spoke. It was distinguished particularly by the presence of Dr Fairbairn, who at the opening of his address spoke the following words:[2]

I feel it a great pleasure for me to stand here alongside my friend and brother Mr Peake, and to wish him godspeed in the work he has undertaken. I know I speak the language of sober truth when I say he is acting in the highest sense of loyalty in resigning ambitions that in many respects are noble and true. Mr Peake occupies this distinguished position that he not only has taken the highest theological honours that the University of Oxford can give, has not only in free competition taken its most distinctive theological scholarship, but he has also the honour of being the first Nonconformist who was by open competition elected to a Theological Fellowship in an Oxford College. His life has not only been blameless, but it has been marked by an integrity and yet by a grace and gentleness strangely eminent amid difficulties that only those who know them can imagine. He has been able never to surrender a principle and never lose a friend. I know him not only as a friend, but as a tutor in the College where my life is lived, and all my interests lie, and I know no man could have been more faithful and more diligent, more accurate, more successful and inspiring a tutor. Personally to me his removal from Oxford is a great loss; to you it is a great gain. When he first came to me for advice upon this matter all that I could say to him was this: 'Your own people have the first claim; if you have the heart to serve them, serve them with your whole heart'. He comes to offer you these services. Will you not receive him as he comes, and when he comes, and takes up his work among you; will you not welcome the faithful son who has come away from the University with all its attractions, and with all its temptations with his heart true to his people, and with the feeling that his life-work is with his people? Will you not trust him, stand by him, and supply him with every opportunity his heart can ask for the service of the work he has undertaken? Success does not lie with him but with you!

Writing over thirty years later Peake recalled the impression which Fairbairn's speech had created:

Dr Fairbairn was rather uncertain as a speaker, but at his best he stirred and moved me as scarcely any speaker to whom I have listened. That night he 'got away', and his speech, which was greatly conceived and magnificently expressed, was inspired by a passionate conviction and transfigured by an emotional glow

---

[1] Conference Journal. 1892. Minute 90.
[2] *P.M.W.* 16 June 1892.

which places it in my memory among the finest it has been my lot to hear. It produced a profound and an enduring impression.[1]

The threshold having now been finally crossed, it must have been gratifying to Peake to receive the following letter from his father,[2] who as we have seen found himself reluctantly compelled to accept his son's decision:

... I am glad that the Conference gave Dr Fairbairn such a grand reception and hearty vote of thanks, and also that it bestowed its honours and praise on you in such a hearty and sincere manner. In no other Connexion could you have received such marked attention and gratitude.

It is worth while to record Peake's judgement upon this momentous decision written many years later[3]

Looking back to that action across the intervening three and thirty years I pay a sincere and prayerful tribute to the generous confidence it implied. But its intrinsic significance went much deeper than any personal element in the situation. It meant that, for the first time, the official training of the ministry in the Primitive Methodist Church was in contact with the modern spirit and outlook. That it fell to me to be the pioneer in this respect was more or less accidental; the essential thing was that, whether through one channel or another, the new light should be suffered to shine.

II

Peake came to Manchester in July 1892 to begin the new task. It was of the greatest importance that by official resolution he was allowed a completely free hand to frame the new curriculum for the College teaching. It was agreed that he should open up classes for Old and New Testament Theology, Old and New Testament Exegesis and a course of lectures on the History of Christian Doctrine. The study of the Greek New Testament was to be compulsory and Hebrew might be taken by the students in their second year. The teaching given by the Principal of the College was to remain as hitherto.

Although the Conference had been unanimous in the matter of Peake's appointment it was not wholly surprising that among the more uninformed elements in the denomination there should be some prejudice. This is exemplified in a confidential letter written by an enlightened layman some eighteen months after Peake's work had begun:

As an ardent Primitive and admirer of your great abilities, I venture to address you on a subject that you are as I know almost entirely ignorant of, and one which may seriously concern you. There is a strong feeling, how strong I had

---

[1] A. S. Peake: *The Life of Sir W. P. Hartley*, p. 140.
[2] Samuel Peake to A.S.P. 20 June 1892.
[3] A. S. Peake: *The Life of Sir W. P. Hartley*, p. 141.

no idea till recently, existing amongst certain of our ministerial and lay brethren regarding your Scripture expositions at the Institute. It is their intention to raise the question at next Conference, and as one who is in thorough sympathy with your teaching this must be my sole excuse for addressing you, so that when the time comes you may be in a position to defend your positions. There seems to be a crisis ahead of us, more especially when I consider the utter nonsensical language of some of the perturbed spirits, one going so far recently as to describe your teaching as 'German rationalism pure and unadulterated'. Your recent articles have interested me very much and I have been greatly benefitted and helped thereby. I do hope the superfluous energy of the dissatisfied may expend itself before Conference, but I am in a singular position for judging, as my business takes me to all parts of the country, and speaking candidly I do not think it will. I am anxious for the future of our Church, and believe it to largely depend on our coming ministers and hence on you. This must be my excuse for writing.[1]

In a letter a fortnight later—March 6—the same writer declared:

There is one point I am much concerned about and that is the annoyance that these people who are dissatisfied, may cause you. I know well what a sacrifice you have made by taking your present position, and, as one who appreciated that sacrifice, I hope you will in no way be dissuaded by any pressure from your present method of instruction.

Such criticism of Peake's work never assumed serious proportions and the answer is found in the fact that for thirty-seven years his appointment was confirmed *nemo contradicente*. The fact was that taken as a whole the Church growingly maintained a friendly attitude towards him, and through the years the unfailing interest of Sir William Hartley, who became the sponsor of many schemes for improvement of College life and work, was his constant friend and advocate. But above all it was Peake himself, by virtue of the quality of his own personality, and the manner of his advocacy of the new approach to the truth of the Scriptures, in addition to his sheer genius for friendship, which steadily overcame any hostility.

Soon after his arrival Peake turned his attention to the reconstruction of the College Library, the contents of which he found not only unsatisfactory but positively inadequate. In December 1893 he wrote a long letter to the *Primitive Methodist World*, appealing for contributions both in money and in kind and stating that Mr Hartley had generously stepped in to relieve the more pressing necessities. Peake set forth a long and detailed list of the most important requirements, though warning would-be donors against the sending of duplicates:

It is said that in an American village once, a sale of flat irons took place at the shop just before a wedding, and that the whole stock was transferred to the pair in the shape of wedding presents. We want to prevent a similar catastrophe, so ask our friends to write what books they would like to send to us!

[1] E. B. Robinson to A.S.P., 23 February 1894.

Peake's labours in this respect created the foundation of what through the years became an outstanding library.

It is fortunate that a manuscript account[1] of the very beginning of Peake's work at the College has survived, from the pen of one of the fourteen students who entered College in 1892, fourteen others being already in residence.

The twenty-eight of us sat at our desks—it seems a long way back on 'the pebbled shore of memory' to that day in August, 1892, when we all sat together and stood up as there walked into the old lecture room a slight figure with gown on. He went to his desk and gave his first lecture to us. He was almost young enough to be one of us, only a few years separated us; perhaps hardly any years from the oldest of us, but he had come with the breath of Oxford and we were proud of him, and he had come with the fragrance of sacrifice attached to his work and we reverenced him. He became our hero. . . .

He took seven subjects—we wondered how many more he could teach—and he taught Greek in addition, and took it without a book, and when one of us ventured to suggest that the book said so-and-so, he just answered: 'Then the book must be wrong'! He laid hold in his masterly way of the facts of Scripture, and opened them out to us in such a way as to give to us the feeling that there was nothing we ought to reverence more in spiritual things than true fact; that we ought to love facts first, and theories after, if any ever came at all. He taught us to so look for the facts that he turned us every one into questors. We sought for the facts of the Scriptures, and the facts of the spiritual life. Then he taught us the spiritual significance that lay in the facts and we began to see the meaning in things, and while our reverence for knowledge grew we were also growing in the thought that there must be something greater than gaining a mere knowledge of facts. We were out for a message and out for a gospel and we needed to see beyond the facts. He took hold of the 23rd Psalm for us and taught us what it meant, and did more, he never left us until we had seen the Shepherd. He took hold of the story of the Gospels and took them to pieces and we wondered if any Gospel was left. He took us a little further and still further and gradually opened out the meaning of what lay behind the analysis, until the face of Jesus Christ began to peep out, and that is where the new things came in which was equal to the old. No dry bones of criticism alone but a highway of critical enquiry till we found a spiritual vision. As he taught—at least I speak for myself—I came to see that I had mistaken the scaffolding for the building, the theories about Jesus for the Christ Himself, and the things under debate for creative personal experience. He gave us perhaps the first thing that is required for college—knowledge enough to know how little we knew.

How did he do it? We were new men; we had never heard of criticism before we went there: we were blinded at first . . . It was through the prayers on a Sunday night that we found that he was a man who kept the altar light burning and we were able to bring our lamps and light them at his altar.

[1] The writer was the Rev. Frank Holmes, who was minister at the Great Western Street Church, Manchester, at the time of Peake's death in 1929, and who ministered to him in the Royal Infirmary, Manchester, in his final illness. He wrote: 'He was a giant before men but he was a child before God. He desired prayer and the relation between tutor and pupil was reversed as the pupil prayed for his tutor. No honour came to me or ever could come to me equal to that one.'

In the early years the conduct of his classes was somewhat hampered by the fact that lectures had to be taken down by the students from Peake's dictation. This method had obvious disadvantages, not least in that it restricted to some degree the amount of material that could be given, though since he invariably suggested a course of reading upon the subject concerned, the students were directed to further fields. Later on lecture outlines, and in some subjects printed copies of a more or less full text, were supplied, and placed in the hands of the students before they met in the lecture hall, thus allowing time for discussion. The situation has been described by one of the early students:[1]

In my time Dr Peake dictated his lectures word for word amid a silence only broken by the chiming of the quarters from the clock-tower, or by an occasional question from the floor of the hall. The lecturer's voice would flow in calm measured fashion, unhurried, unhasty, never metallic or wooden, but vibrant with the feeling suitable to the theme. Now and again would come a pause, pens would drop, and some remark or the telling of a humorous incident would light up the serious topic in hand. Any attempt at ill-timed interruption would be quietly but effectively scotched, but any pertinent query would receive fitting answer, illuminating and satisfying.

Peake adopted the extempore method in the delivery of his lectures making only occasional reference to notes which contained heads of topics to be treated for occasional reference or quotation necessary to illustrate a point or clinch an argument. Some of these small cards and sheets of paper are still extant.

The student carefully listening to the lecture gained the impression that he was witnessing a mind at work. Not only was information imparted but he saw in Peake 'a living example in method'. 'He gave the impression that he was balancing the evidence afresh in his own mind testing it anew, and finding the conclusion which it permitted.' His thought was expressed 'in tense and nervous English' together with a certain hesitation in delivery as he felt for the precise and suitable word, 'revealing an exceptionally acute and living mind'.[2]

In addition to his defined curriculum Peake also taught English, though often unconsciously on his part, by counsel and correction. Many men listening to his voice carefully enunciating sentences entirely lucid and with warmth of colour learnt the better how to speak in their native tongue—and on those occasions outside the syllabus of college teaching when he would lecture on Robert Browning or George Meredith there came the opening of a new door for many whose knowledge of English Literature was scanty.

His more informal talks on the formation of a minister's library were highly valued. The addresses which he was accustomed to give at the

---

[1] W. E. Farndale: 'Impressions of an Early Student' in *Essays in Commemoration*.
[2] J. T. Brewis. *P.M.L.* 5 December 1912.

beginning of each college year were solemn occasions, containing wise counsel as to the use of time and opportunity which residence in college afforded, and an appeal for the acceptance of a high and lofty conception of the ministerial vocation, were regarded as being the utterance of one whose own life exemplified the things of which he spoke.

Thus steadily through the years, one by one, his influence over the students under his care became immeasurable.

It is not surprising that in 1903 on the tenth anniversary of his appointment, the students past and present decided to make a presentation to him. The gesture was entirely spontaneous and nearly two hundred and fifty students subscribed. The presentation took the form of a beautiful oak library cabinet. At the gathering Sir William Hartley presided, and an address was given by Dr Fairbairn who voiced the congratulations of Mansfield, as did Dr J. Hope Moulton for Didsbury and Professor Robert Mackintosh for Lancashire College. In his simple but frank address Peake combated a rumour current in some quarters respecting his teaching and urged that his one aim had always been to hold his students to the centre of the Christian faith:

So far from drifting into Unitarianism, my whole tendency is the other way. A belief in God is a difficult thing in face of all the pain in the world, but in Christ I get my guarantee in God. I believe in Christ, therefore I take courage and believe in God.

The following extract from a letter accompanying the presentation reveals the esteem in which Peake was held:

... We trust Mr Peake because of his ability, scholarship and experience, but especially because of his evident love of truth, and his sustained devotion to the Church of Jesus Christ.

We love him for the fine qualities of character which, by the grace of God, he has revealed in his various dealings with us. The personal influence exerted by Mr Peake is enormous. It is a distinctly welcome assurance that side by side with great mental power and learning, Mr Peake daily exhibits those traits of Christian character which raise our conception of human nature. To know him is to have an education in courtesy and modesty, in gentleness and goodness. The steadiness of his faith and the consistency of his life have stamped upon many minds a sense of the reality and power of God in the soul. The value of his guidance and counsel and help always cheerfully given in the College and afterwards is incalculable.

That this esteem was held by others as well as by his students is illustrated by a letter written by one of his colleagues, the Rev. A. L. Humphries, M.A., who had become a member of the staff in 1902, and who was unable to attend the occasion of the students' presentation.

My dear Peake,
    ... The value and content of your services to the College it would be difficult to exaggerate. As a training institute for our ministry it occupies in every way a

much higher position than that which belonged to it when you joined the staff eleven years ago. To that heightened estimation in which the Institute is held no one has contributed more than you. By your wide and accurate scholarship, your modesty of bearing, and manly, unaffected goodness you have left an abiding mark upon all who have sat under your tuition. We watch with pride your growing reputation both within and without our Church. To those who have come near to you, as some of us have done, there is nothing in you that we note with greater pleasure than your profound loyalty to evangelical truth and to the essential principles of Methodism. More than many think who judge you simply by your views on Biblical Criticism, you stand in the old paths and speak on the great verities of the Gospel with no uncertain sound. To me, my work at the College, whilst congenial in any case, affords greater pleasure because of my association with you, and most happily do I join in the congratulations and commendation which will be offered to you tonight.

Ever sincerely,
A. L. Humphries

As we shall discover, this esteem in which Peake was universally held deepened with the passing of the years.

III

At the Conference of 1891 in Northampton, again on the initiative of Mr Hartley, an important decision had been taken in regard to ministerial training, by which the normal period of student residence was increased from one year to two. At once this raised the question of some extension of the College buildings, which at that time could only accommodate twenty-eight men.

To a large number of ministers and laymen Mr Hartley sent a letter[1] explaining a scheme for extension, and declaring that of the sum of £5,000 required he offered to provide one third. Of the ensuing development we must now give some account.

In 1892 at the Conference in Norwich the important Jubilee Thanksgiving Fund was inaugurated, with the object of raising £50,000, and it was decided that from this Fund £12,000 should be set aside for the building extension and for a necessary investment for future demands. By the time of the Conference in Edinburgh in 1895, land had been secured and plans prepared and an estimate of cost obtained. The extension of the buildings was delayed, however, because some had yet to be convinced of its necessity. When the project was actually in hand, Mr Hartley assumed the entire financial responsibility. The building was planned on an ampler scale. The total cost was £12,500, and the share for the College from the Jubilee Fund was handed over to it intact. The foundation stone was laid on 12 May 1896 and the extension was

---

[1] A.S.P., *Life of Sir W. P. Hartley*, pp. 138-40.

completed; its formal dedication was the outstanding event of the Conference in Manchester in 1897.[1]

An important change associated with the new development was the decision to extend the course of training to three years, with the result that Conference gave to the College the full complement of sixty students for whom there was now accommodation. The demands for the stationing of ministers in the circuits, however, was so great that only a small number of students had the opportunity of staying for a third year.

Under the circumstances Mr Hartley, who was anxious that the three years should become the normal course for every man, offered at the Newcastle Conference of 1903 to provide a further extension, including the erection of a College chapel. With the acquisition of additional land the site now covered more than five and a half acres. The building thus planned on the assumption of a three years' course was now able to accommodate 105 students, thus permitting over thirty men to enter the ministry annually. The cost of the new extension was over £20,000 and the building was opened on 18 June 1906 when again the Conference was in Manchester. The dedicatory sermon was preached in the new Chapel by Dr Fairbairn, and in the evening a large meeting was held in the Free Trade Hall in the city, with Mr Hartley in the chair. The meeting was remarkable for the tremendous tribute paid to Mr Hartley as the far-seeing layman who had made so outstanding a gift, and also for that paid to Peake the scholar, whose valuable work had made the gift so necessary and so desirable.

It was in full recognition of Mr Hartley's munificence that at this Conference of 1906 a resolution was passed to the effect that henceforth the College should bear the name 'Hartley College'.

It is obvious that these rapid developments during these years should involve new arrangements in the inner life of the College. As we have seen for a year after his coming to the College Peake included New Testament Greek in the subjects he taught. In the following year, however, the Rev. Daniel Neilson, M.A., B.D., who was a minister in a Manchester Circuit, was engaged as an assistant tutor in the subject. In the same year, Dr John Watson became the Principal, and whilst he retained the subjects taught by his predecessor, Dr Wood, he added Logic and Psychology to his course, and also introduced German as an optional subject. The appointment of Principal was always for a term of five years, and when Dr Watson retired it was decided that his connexion with the College should continue, and so by the appointment of the Conference of 1898 he was placed in a Manchester circuit, and thus remained as an assistant tutor. By the appointment of the new Principal, the Rev. George Parkin in 1898, further advance was made, for in addition to the teaching of Pastoral Theology and Homiletics as normally, he

---

[1] The munificence of Mr Hartley was recognized by the Conference by the presentation of his portrait in oils; this now hangs in the College Library.

commenced classes in Hebrew, as an integral part of the College curriculum. In addition, and at Peake's special request, he lectured on New Testament Exegesis. These changes were largely due to Peake's foresight in the matter of curriculum development, and from this pattern the situation remained unchanged for several years. In 1901 the serious illness of Dr Watson necessitated his retirement, and there now came the appointment of a full-time tutor, free from all circuit responsibilities, in place of the two assistant tutors. In 1902 the Rev. A. L. Humphries, M.A. was appointed. In 1903 on the initiative of Mr Hartley, who was concerned that the students should be more thoroughly grounded in the study of English Language and Literature, the Rev. W. Lansdell Wardle, M.A., B.D. was added to the staff, and to him the work of the classes in Hebrew was assigned.

No further change occurred until 1908 when Mr Atkinson Lee, M.A., a layman and lecturer in the University College of Aberystwyth, became a member of the staff. The purpose of this appointment was to strengthen the curriculum on the philosophical side, particularly in view of the needs of the third year students. Mr Lee took over the teaching of Logic and Psychology and ultimately developed his own work in Metaphysics to include courses on the Philosophy of Religion. It was at the suggestion of Peake that the curriculum was extended into this field.

The staff now consisted of the Principal and four tutors and, apart from the normal change of Principal each fifth year, there was no change until Peake's death in 1929.

The purpose of this rather detailed account of these years 1893-1908 in the life of the College has been to indicate the changes which were for the most part at the suggestion and initiative of Peake himself, as the architect of the system of teaching and the arrangements for implementing it, a fact which reveals the greatness of his administrative ability and foresight. Further behind these changes lay the fact that inevitably Peake's own greatness as scholar and teacher was increasing the demands made upon him, the most important of which was the call of the newly-formed University of Manchester, which had been created from Owens College, in 1904. There was an increasing association of the College with the opportunities which it provided for some of the students. To this new development we shall turn later on. There were also literary demands for Peake's contribution in the field of scholarship, and these were becoming more and more insistent.

In 1913, the year before the twenty-first anniversary of Peake's appointment to the College, it was the students who were foremost in the desire to celebrate this important occasion of his 'coming-of-age' in the life of the College. As ten years earlier, a further letter signed by all the men conveying their appreciation was sent to him; a revolving summer-house expressed in a more tangible way their real affection for him. The family had moved from Manchester to Freshfield, near Southport, on account of the health of the children, and it was there that the summer-house was duly established. In this in the following years Peake did a great deal of his work. One of the students, speaking as one who was present in the common-room when the presentation was made, afterwards declared that those assembled felt that 'there was a human majesty about him which commanded reverence'.

But there was also an official movement on foot for due recognition of the 'coming-of-age'. The ceremony took place on June 11, 1914. A subscription portrait in oils, the work of Mr A. T. Nowell, of Kensington, was presented to him by the Trustees of the College.[1] Further in the already fine College Chapel three richly stained glass windows, designed by Mr Anning Bell, A.R.A., were installed by Sir William Hartley, a gift in honour of his friend, of whom, as he proceeded to unveil the windows, he declared: 'I look with unalloyed satisfaction to the day when Dr Peake and I met twenty-three years ago at Merton College, Oxford, and that I am still alive to work with him to advance the education of students intended for the Primitive Methodist ministry'.

The design of the windows, which had been suggested to the artist by Peake himself, represented the focal points in his teaching of the Bible. Remembering that the windows are no longer in existence,[2] a brief description may be allowed.

The large central window above the communion table was a representation of Christ at Calvary. With the Cross in the background there was the calm figure of Jesus in the centre; Roman soldiers on the right hand held back the rabble while on the left were the sorrowing women. At the base on the left was a picture of Bethlehem, on the right, one of Jerusalem. The inscription ran: 'Unto Him that loveth us and loosed us from our sins'. The window in the north transept of the chapel represented Elijah, the great prophet of the Old Testament at the sacrifice upon Mount Carmel. The prayer of the prophet was inscribed below: 'Hear me, O Lord, hear me, that this people may know that thou art the Lord God'. The window in the south transept depicted Paul, the great apostle to the Gentiles, preaching at Athens. On either side were the listening Athenians and beneath were the words: 'Whom, therefore, ye ignorantly worship, Him declare I unto you.'

Later in the afternoon on the day of celebration it was announced that Sir William Hartley wished to celebrate the occasion not only by the gift of the windows, but in addition by the founding of a number of scholarships for the benefit of needy students, particularly those for whom the expenses of their college course were found to be onerous. This gave profound satisfaction to Peake, glad to know that they had not been overlooked.

[1] This portrait hangs in the College Library and is reproduced as the frontispiece of the present volume.
[2] The windows were entirely destroyed in a German air raid in December 1940.

In the dining hall, before adjourning to the College grounds in which a garden party was held, and knowing that the portrait would find its place in the Library, a gift of silver rosebowl, fruit dishes and flower vases was presented to Mrs Peake and her husband as a tangible reminder of the great occasion.

It was typical of Peake's concern for others than himself that, after the great day was over, he found time to write letters of appreciation to those who, behind the scenes, had done much to secure its success: his letter to the College cook is an example:

Dear Cook,
Now the celebrations of Tuesday are over my thoughts turn in gratitude to those who did so much to secure for us so happy a gathering. And I feel very much was due to you and all your ungrudging labour. Please accept this expression of personal thanks. You will know that this was one of the great days of my life, and I am glad that the happiness with which I look back on it is not marred by any feeling that things had not gone smoothly. Will you kindly convey the same warm thanks to those who have worked with you, especially to Violet? I am grateful to them all. They did us credit in the eyes of our guests.
Yours sincerely,
Arthur S. Peake

It was a deep disappointment to Peake that Miss Elsie Cann, who had been his private secretary for ten years, was unable to be present owing to serious illness. In a letter he wrote to her he pays tribute to the devoted service that she had rendered to him in his work—another illustration of his quality of sympathetic understanding:

June 5, 1914
Dear Miss Cann,
I hope you won't worry any more about the 11th, should the doctor refuse to let you come. You know how keen a disappointment it will be to have you, of all people, missing: but I would far sooner this than that you should undertake a strain too severe for you to bear. And I know well what a disappointment it will be to you.

One of the pleasures of anticipation that I had in mind was in thinking that, when my work was receiving such recognition, you would be there to receive your share in the recognition, for you deserve to have no little credit for what I have done. Your loyal, unselfish labour, your unfailing considerateness, the strenuous industry, the temper and spirit in which all has been done during the long happy years of unbroken harmony and fellowship in a common task that we have spent together, are beyond all my thanks and praise. And I should like you to have felt, as I was speaking, that I was not monopolising all the gratitude and congratulations, but giving you in my heart some portion of the tributes I was being paid. I feel that it is not right when people calmly annex to themselves the sole credit, when others should receive their part in it. And when I think of what your part has been, it is not just of the mechanical work that forms so much of it, but of the keen and eager interest you have taken in it, and the sympathy you have always shown me. I know that if you cannot be with us, you will be with us in spirit. But I should like you to know this one theme of my thought as I look back over the years at Hartley College, in which you have filled so large a place.

I trust and pray earnestly that all may go well with you, and that you will soon be fully restored. Never mind about the work: do your best to get well.
With kindest regards and best wishes for all
Yours faithfully,
Arthur S. Peake

IV

The years that followed this great occasion were not marked by any outstanding event. The normal course work in the College proceeded steadily until the time of the outbreak of war, when the work had to be adjusted, and eventually for a period, entirely suspended, as in June, 1917 the College buildings were taken over by the military authorities for conversion into a Red Cross hospital. After peace was declared the work was resumed, seventeen students who had been demobilized being placed in the old wing of the College in March 1919. Not till the following year—in August—did the College building revert entirely to its ordinary use.

As we have already noticed, during these years Peake's work at the College was at times challenged to some degree by outside criticism on account of its modern approach to theological and biblical matters. But as time progressed the opposition faded away. On one occasion at a College function Peake himself summarized the change:

Synchronising with my coming to your College strong hostility to the training of ministers evidenced itself. But it has now disappeared. It was beaten down not by any frontal attack. We won the confidence of the Church simply by attending to our own work steadily and conscientiously. And no more responsible labour producing such far-reaching issues exists today than the glorious work of education of young men for the Christian Church.

From time to time, however, another type of criticism raised its head, perhaps inevitably, remembering the great variety of outlook and temperament among the students themselves. That students should become critical of College structures and administration is by no means unknown in educational institutions—and theological colleges are no exception—and so it was that here and there in the College there were, at times, those who questioned the soundness of the curriculum and the administrative arrangement. A College Common Room can sometimes feel quite convinced of its own omniscience in regard to what is the most suitable training for the ministry. However, during these years, such elements of restlessness were invariably overcome in particular by the gracious and tactful attitude of Peake himself as the senior member of the College staff. Confidence being restored, work together was resumed at the highest level.

In 1918, however, a more serious occasion of criticism arose not from within the College, but in open correspondence within the pages of the denominational paper. It was perhaps inevitable that, arising out of the situation of ferment everywhere developing out of the stress of war conditions, when most ideas and institutions were being challenged to inquiry and reform, the structure of the College administration and curriculum should come under fire. There were those who strongly dissented from the arrangement whereby the Principal of the College was appointed for a five-year term of office, the one thus appointed being a senior minister whose duties would be administrative, and whose teaching would consist only of Pastoral Theology and Homiletics. Would it not be a sounder policy to place the principalship in the hands of a member of the tutorial staff? Certainly the limitation to five years was open to question. But an even more serious criticism related to the nature of the curriculum and it was suggested that a committee of enquiry should consider the whole question.

At times the correspondence became sharp in tone and words were not always wisely chosen, but the motives behind it were honest and sincere. By it, however, Peake, with his native sensitiveness, was deeply wounded in spirit. In particular it was the criticism of the College tuition that naturally hurt him and brought deep distress. This was not surprising for, after all, largely through his own foresight and labour, the curriculum had been steadily built up, and it seemed therefore like a personal challenge to his ability and position. Eventually, however, this public outburst died away and by expression from many quarters, both official and unofficial, Peake became reassured of the repose of the Church's confidence in him and his work.

In 1919 after the re-opening of the College for normal working, an important development took place by the amalgamation of Hartley College and the United Methodist College staffs and students, though the latter remained in their respective buildings, the United Methodists being in Victoria Park. This co-operation enabled new subjects to be added to the curriculum, and more personal oversight of students was made possible. The following year proved that the venture had been amply justified, and the co-operation became a congenial and settled policy.

In the early summer of 1920 Peake and his family returned to Manchester, having dwelt for some eight years at Freshfield, near Southport. The sojourn there had proved greatly beneficial in terms of health, but for Peake himself it imposed weighty burdens as it involved almost daily journeys into Manchester and then the return home, though during term time he stayed overnight at the College when necessary, to ease the burden of travel, particularly in the later periods.

The years following the return to Manchester were marked by constantly increasing demands, over and above the work at the College and at the University. It was not only the pressures of a great number of lectures, but the preparation which lay behind them which began to take toll of Peake's strength. He wrote in 1922:

The real strain is not in the lecture room, but in the study involved in keeping in touch with the development of criticism, history and theology in both Old and New Testaments. It is practically the whole field of Biblical scholarship that I have to cultivate, though I cannot with the utmost effort do it to my satisfaction. As you will know, most scholars limit themselves either to the Old Testament or the New.[1]

Nevertheless the work continued for the remaining years until his death in 1929, which marked a milestone in the history of the College. Its significance cannot be better expressed than in the following words:

His passing marks the end of an era in the history of Primitive Methodism—an era created by himself. No one has been able to affect our Church for its permanent good as he has done, and no loss has even been so keenly felt as his departure.[2]

V

For the moment we must retrace our steps to recall the additional service which in the earlier years of the work at the College Peake undertook.

Soon after he commenced his duties at Hartley College it became clear that it would be impossible for him to ignore approaches for service beyond his own denominational commitment however great might be his unquestioned loyalty to his own people.

It was in 1892 that an approach was made to him from the Lancashire Independent College, which was not far distant from Hartley College. A vacancy had occurred through the death of Dr Alexander Thomson, who had been responsible for the teaching of the Hebrew Old Testament, and was at the same time minister of the Rusholme Road Congregational Church in Manchester. During his illness early in 1895 much of the work was placed in the hands of the Rev. T. Lewis, a college tutor, who, in contrast to Dr Thomson was in sympathy with the new approach to the Bible. This gave the opportunity for an expansion of Old Testament teaching in the College. Eventually a removal to the staff of the Congregational College at Brecon opened the door for the committee to invite Peake to assist in the work, and in the session 1895-6 he began to lecture on Old Testament Introduction and Theology, later taking over the work on Old Testament Texts. Dr Robert Mackintosh, who was a

---

[1] A.S.P. to the Rev. William Eccles, 3 October 1922.
[2] The Rev. George Bennett (quoted L. S. Peake: *Memoir*, p. 127).

member of the Staff at Lancashire College, has recorded his impression of Peake's association with the College:[1]

We always felt him to be an exceptional man—a layman who was more than welcome in every meeting of ministers, and a staunch Methodist, who knew and certainly did not dislike Congregational ways. For years we enjoyed his presence in the Education Committee, and also in the General Committee of the College. He was an invaluable adviser as well as a delightful friend. And when Dr Adeney became Principal of Lancashire College and instituted a system of staff-meetings—there were four of us including Dr Peake in those days—Dr Peake willingly attended these smaller gatherings also. Had he been a Congregationalist outright he could have done no more for us. All the supporters of Lancashire College—those who had hesitated about the new policy as well as those who welcomed it from the first—fully appreciated the advantage to the name and fame of our College, due to our having captured a share in the services of Dr Peake.

The Rev. George Shillito, a Congregational minister who was a student in Peake's classes at the College in the early years has supplied this additional interesting note:[2]

The classes were uneventful because they were so efficient. Work went on steadily from week to week without sensation of any kind. His teaching was so thorough that few questions were needed; when they were asked the answers were frank and comprehensive. In his classes we seemed always within the atmosphere of scholarship and intellectual sincerity. The only time I ever saw him at a loss in an emergency was when a student from North Lancashire demanded truculently: 'D'you believe i' the flud?'. At that period Peake was not intimate with the Burnley accent!

Peake's influence was like that of a river gently overflowing its banks, and quietly fertilizing all the adjacent land; then subsiding without surge or tumult, leaving a surprising increment of prosperity behind it. He seemed to take possession of one, and remained in possession without a symptom of domination.

In the winter session of 1904 Peake received an invitation from Principal Thomas Sherwood,[3] of the Victoria Park United Methodist College, to lecture to his students. Peake mentions this invitation in a letter to his father:[4]

You will be surprised to know that the United Methodist Free Church College asked me to lecture there once a week. I could not have found time to go over to that side of Manchester on purpose, but as I have to be at the University for two hours on Wednesday afternoon and it is near, I go there at 12, and stay to dinner, then go to the University. As I have not any new lectures to prepare for them it adds not very much to my work, and it is a little contribution towards Methodist Union.

[1] L. S. Peake, *Memoir*, pp. 133-4.
[2] Ibid., p. 135.
[3] Thomas Sherwood to A.S.P., 31 October 1904.
[4] A.S.P. to Samuel Peake, 10 November 1904.

Peake's classes at the College covered Old and New Testament Introduction.

In 1912, following the death of Professor Hogg, Peake had to undertake additional work at the University, and it became necessary for him to relinquish his work in these more limited spheres at Lancashire and Victoria Park Colleges. This was of course a great loss to both Colleges, but opportunity was provided for the students from Lancashire College to attend Peake's lectures at the University; and, as we have seen, the amalgamation of Hartley and Victoria Park Colleges in 1919 brought both staffs and students into a common fellowship and a renewed opportunity of participation in Peake's teaching ministry.

CHAPTER FOUR

THE UNIVERSITY OF MANCHESTER

DURING the twenty-five years (1880–1904) of the life of the Federal Victoria University two unsuccessful attempts were made to found a Faculty of Theology. Both these attempts had their origin in Owens College, Manchester. Partly owing to the opposition from the constituent colleges of Leeds and Liverpool, and from certain old-fashioned Liberals who believed that it was a dangerous step to introduce theological study into the newer Universities because it would result in their being put under ecclesiastical domination, the issue of which might be bitter disputes, and because of serious practical difficulties in providing the required instruction, the proposal fell through. When the break up of the Federal University took place in 1903, however, the door opened for the establishment of a Faculty of Theology in the newly-founded University of Manchester.

Local conditions were in many ways favourable to this new proposal. There were eight theological Colleges in Manchester.[1] Dr Moorhouse, Bishop of Manchester, approved the proposal from the beginning, and his successor Bishop Knox warmly supported it. The heads of the Free Church Colleges were, perhaps, the most effective advocates of the policy.

In the autumn of 1903 the Senate drew up a report recommending the establishment of a Theological Faculty under certain conditions, and defined the subjects of study and examination. One condition was that provision should be made for instruction in Comparative Religion—the study of other religions as well as Christianity and Judaism—and this subject should be compulsory.

A major problem was financial. However, Mrs Rylands, who already had been a benefactor of Owens College, was approached and she agreed to give £400 annually for five years, and shortly afterwards Professor Rhys Davies was induced to accept appointment as the Professor of

---

[1] These were: Egerton Hall (Anglican); Lancashire Independent (Congregationalist); Baptist College; Didsbury (Wesleyan); Hartley (Primitive Methodist); Victoria Park (United Methodist); Fairfield (Moravian); Somerville (Unitarian).

Comparative Religion. Afterwards from one of her bequests a permanent endowment was provided, and in her memory the Rylands Professorship of Biblical Criticism and Exegesis was given permanent establishment. To this professorship Arthur Samuel Peake was appointed.

This was a unique appointment for it was the first time that a non-Anglican had been chosen as a Professor of Divinity in an English University. The committee on whose recommendation this appointment was made included the important figures of Dr Alexander McLaren, Dr Caleb Scott, Principal of Lancashire Independent College, the Bishop and the Dean of Manchester, and Sir Alfred Hopkinson.

This new Faculty of Theology was outstanding in two aspects: it was the first British University to establish such a Faculty on entirely undenominational lines[1] and further it was the first of the modern universities to teach as well as hold examinations in Theology.[2]

In the process of formation a wise and important step was taken in seeking the advice of some outstanding theologians outside Manchester. Special visits were made to Professor Sanday of Oxford and to Dr A. M. Fairbairn of Mansfield College, and when these distinguished critics gave their support of the policy it was felt that the scheme rested on sound foundations. In these advisory discussions Fairbairn was specially anxious that the particular stress of each denominational college should be preserved,[3] and we find him writing to Peake with some measure of concern:[4]

I am sorry that we shall not have the pleasure of seeing you in Oxford this summer.... I wanted to consult you touching various things, especially the mission on which I was in Manchester. It struck me that our people did not at all understand the question at issue, and it might have been well if we had met for a brief talk, say in the Rylands Library. I sent a protest to Hopkinson the day after the Committee as I cannot in conscience accept the conclusions reached in the form in which they were stated and argued. My feeling is that the scheme as it has been drafted and put into force will involve the ruin of all the higher teaching in our Colleges, transferring the centre of gravity as regards theological teaching from them to Owens College. It was that for which I was fighting, and which lay at the back of my mind, and made me fear that whilst the Churchmen clearly saw what were the principles in debate our friends did not ... I do feel that our Colleges, Lancashire, yours, Didsbury, the Baptists' and so forth have the whole question in the hollow of your hands; and that if

---

[1] Complete freedom in teaching was safeguarded by the requirement which is fundamental in the constitution of the University, as laid down by John Owens: 'Nothing will be introduced in the matter or mode of education in reference to any religious or theological subjects which shall be reasonably offensive to the conscience of any student.'

[2] At this time the University of London was only an examining body in Theology and gave no teaching in the subject.

[3] As early as 1879, when proposals were afoot for founding the Victoria University in the North of England, Fairbairn had raised the question of the establishment of a theological faculty and had called a conference at Bradford of those representing the Nonconformists to consider it. W. B. Selbie, *Life of Andrew Martin Fairbairn*, pp. 215-6.

[4] A. M. Fairbairn to A.S.P., 16 May 1904.

you like you can settle it in a way to enhance your own work, but if it be allowed that Owens College or the University provide the major part of the teaching then the days of your pre-eminence will be numbered. Please think over this matter and let me know your mind, and if your own idea is that any good can come out of my attempting to visit Manchester towards the end of June I shall try to do so.

Peake was appointed Dean of the new Faculty, and this seems to have given great assurance to Fairbairn, for shortly after writing the above letter he wrote again[1] (presumably after Peake had given him elucidation of the situation in regard to the problem concerned):

... You have great opportunities and great influence, and I am sure they did very wisely in appointing you Dean. In the circumstances of course I won't go to Manchester, or even propose it. What concerned me altogether was the chance that the institution of a degree in Theology be offered to the Colleges. It is a great means for bringing them into immediate relation with the University, and I am sure the Churches would rise at once to the position of equipping them so as to bring them to the dignity of academic institutions. I am glad to find you so hopeful, and with you as Dean I cannot but feel that all will yet be well.

As an autonomous and inter-denominational Faculty of Theology the system thus created at Manchester fulfilled all requirements, and Professor T. F. Tout, who along with Peake had so important a place in the establishment of it, wrote significantly and with confidence of its promise for the future:

Though our experiment is still young, we believe that events have already justified our boldness, and that the Faculty established on this dual basis will continue the old system of separate theological colleges for each denomination with the advantage of a wider and freer academic school. While we wish our teaching in all subjects to be equally free we cannot, as practical men, blind our eyes to the fact that a large proportion of our students in the Faculty of Theology will be those who are preparing for the Christian ministry of the various denominations. We must respect their wants if we wish them to take part in the working out of our ideals.[2]

I

The early years of the new Faculty—as well, indeed, as the later ones—reveal how crucial was the work of Peake himself. Of course he was responsible for framing the curriculum, but his ability as an administrator soon became evident. His loyalty to the established principles upon which the Faculty rested, his foresight and tactfulness in dealing with

[1] A. M. Fairbairn to A.S.P., 27 May 1904.
[2] *Inaugural Lectures delivered by Members of the Faculty of Theology* (1905) p. 20.

differences of opinion within the Advisory Board, gave the key to the solution of the many issues and problems that were involved. As first Dean of the Faculty—a position which he held for five strenuous years—he proved his profound understanding of the situation. Again and again it was Peake's sagacious counsel that prevailed, not least, for example, in the interpretation and application of the stipulated requirement that Comparative Religion must be basic in the syllabus of teaching. Obviously the maintenance of a delicate balance was involved. One of Peake's most valuable achievements was the steady attempt to secure a closely knit unity between the University and the Colleges. As he wrote to the Vice-Chancellor nearly twenty years afterwards in 1923:

Our policy I think is to encourage the centripetal tendency and I have worked steadily though unobtrusively in that direction. It is much better than setting up little classes at three or four of the Colleges. We could not of course prevent the Colleges from offering classes, but I gather from what has been said at Faculty meetings that their preference is for university courses.

A considerable part of Peake's success arose out of his close association with the affiliated colleges, not only in the particular work which he undertook at Lancashire Independent College, the United Methodist College, and at Hartley College, but in his ready participation in the various occasions in the other institutions, frequently being their guest at times of important celebrations. All such participations revealed his fundamental interest in their work in connexion with their wider interests.

For a good number of years the work of the Faculty was hampered by the lack of adequate accommodation and administratively this was a pressing concern on Peake's mind. With the passing of the years Peake's responsibilities increased and on the death of Professor Hogg, who taught Semitic Languages and Literature, the additional work fell upon Peake's shoulders, and this, as we have seen, necessitated the relinquishing of his duties at both Lancashire College and at the United Methodist College. He had previously had to decline the invitation of the University to give courses of extra-mural lectures under the auspices of the Board for Extra-Mural Studies.

For twenty-five years, until his death in 1929, Peake represented the Faculty and its interests in the Senate of the University, and his successors inherited the sterling work which he did in securing its recognition in the formative years.

As Rylands Professor of Biblical Criticism and Exegesis, Peake's work was comprehensive in its extent and superb in its quality. Dr T. W. Manson, who held the chair from 1936 to 1958 has summarized his significant contribution in words that form an eloquent tribute to Peake's work:[1]

---

[1] *Essays in Commemoration*, pp. 34–5.

He set a standard which neither of his successors[1] has attempted to emulate; and it seems likely enough that no future holder of the chair will be more adventurous than they. For he understood Biblical Criticism and Exegesis quite simply as covering everything from Genesis to Revelation, and proved his competence in this very wide field both by the spoken word and by published work. He also made it plain that in this branch of study there was one aim only, the discovery of the truth, and one method only, the most careful sifting and weighing of all relevant evidence. By the quality of his work he showed that theological scholarship was intellectually respectable, that theology was not a soft option, and that as a scholarly discipline and a field for research it made as rigorous a demand and offered as good opportunities for original and creative work as any other branch of scholarship. He showed this not only in his own lectures, articles and books but also in the high standards which, under his leadership, the newly constituted Faculty set for its students. From the outset it was made plain to them that nothing less than their best would be offered to them and expected from them. So the Faculty made its way in the life of the University, not by making extravagant claims and promises, but by going about its business in an honest, diligent and workmanlike manner. And there was none more capable than Peake of showing just what had to be done and how to do it.... There can be no finer testimony to the quality of his building than the simple fact that the history of the Faculty is the history of fifty years of friendly and wholehearted co-operation between the University and the Colleges.[2]

We may fittingly add the sentence from the lecture delivered by Professor F. C. Burkitt in celebration of the twenty-fifth anniversary of the founding of the Faculty, when he declared that in the main its success was due to Peake's 'eirenic and enlightened guidance':

... I suppose every man and woman in this assembly feels the loss of Arthur Samuel Peake. And yet perhaps there may be many who hardly realise the debt which we all owe to him. For the twenty-five years about which I have to speak to you he has been the guiding and persuasive voice and a constant personal example, saying in an era of transition and changing values, 'This is the way, walk ye in it!'[3]

When, in 1925, the Council of the University invited Peake to become Pro-Vice-Chancellor, it was no mere compliment for the long service he had rendered, but a realization that his wide knowledge of University affairs, together with his consummate wisdom and tactfulness would make him an ideal figure for such a post of public responsibility. As is made abundantly clear by the deeply moving resolution passed after his death in 1929, no member of the Senate was held in higher respect, and amongst his colleagues he won universal esteem, and even affection.

---

[1] i.e., C. H. Dodd (1930–1935). T. W. Manson (1936–1958).
[2] Dr Manson also points out that at a later time, when the University was faced with the task of erecting a School of Education in which University and Training Colleges should work together, the conviction of its possibility and how it should be done came from a consideration of what already had been accomplished in the field of Theology.
[3] F. C. Burkitt, 'Twenty-five Years of Theological Study'. *H.R.* January 1930.

II

It was natural that a strong connexion between the University and Hartley College should develop. As early as 1907, Mr Hartley wrote to Peake urging that such students as were competent should enter the University and take their degree. The system at the University was the completion of an Arts degree taken in three years, followed by the B.D. which was a further two-years course. For the Hartley College student the five-year course, followed by the normal period of probation required by the regulation of the Primitive Methodist Conference, involved a weighty burden both on the student and financially on his friends. There were three types of student to be considered; those who on entering College had graduated, and could therefore proceed to the course of B.D., which could be completed in two or three years; those who having already matriculated could take the five-year course for the B.A. and B.D. degrees; those who, having ability for it, could begin the ordinary College course and perhaps at the end of two years, having gained matriculation, could take the Arts course in three years. A modification of the probation period by one year, was eventually approved in the first two cases.

In the light of the financial position thus involved for both the students themselves and the College Committee, Mr Hartley agreed to take the whole cost of financing the project by the payment of fees for university students, a provision that was continued until his death. This was an important contribution to ministerial training and gave a maximum opportunity for increasing contact between the College and the University. In all this scheme Mr Hartley was guided entirely by Peake, even in regard to advice concerning individual students' courses, as the following letter indicates:[1]

I note that one of the students wishes to take a class in Hellenistic Greek in addition to his Arts work, and from what you say I think he should do it. . . . I leave it entirely to your judgment. You can just act as you think is the best, and I shall be agreeable whatever it may be. I leave the whole matter in your hands both present and future to act as you think is best, giving me the minimum of work and correspondence.

A further illustration of Peake's concern for the welfare of the students is found in his keen interest in the Primitive Methodist University Students' Union, of which he was President, and for it he sacrificed much time and energy, being always the most punctual and regular attender, sharing in their summer rambles and other activities. One of the students, Miss Dorothy Bell, who was Vice-President of the Union, has recorded a pleasing glimpse of the friendly interest he took in the work of the Union:

[1] A.S.P., *Life of Sir William P. Hartley*, p. 148.

We loved him for his laughter-making. Some of us kept special 'scrap-books' of his sayings and anecdotes; he could always remember the right story. In the train, on one of the return journeys from one of our rambles, he recited to us curious epitaphs, and on a page from his diary he wrote down for me his favourites.

When he was forced, through an attack of influenza to be absent for the first time from a meeting, as a surprise for the programme he sent along some 'limericks' of his own composition.[1]

And there is another reason why we so loved him. He took such an interest in us. If he saw us in the street or on the tram he would go out of his way to speak to us, remembering whether we were arts or science, whether we were present at the last P.M.U.U.—and making us feel important.

It was undoubtedly this genius for friendship that won for Peake the admiration of all who came into contact with him.

III

One occasion of outstanding pleasure for Peake was in 1908, when as Dean of the Faculty of Theology he presented to Lord Morley, the first Chancellor of the University, his former colleague at Mansfield, Dr A. M. Fairbairn, to receive the first honorary degree of Doctor of Divinity bestowed by the University. Peake not only acclaimed Fairbairn's greatness, but acknowledged the part Fairbairn had played in the creation of the new order, and his words also reveal the felicitous style of utterance in which Peake was so great a master. So significant was the occasion that we venture to set down his oration:

It is with singular pleasure that I present, for the first Degree of Doctor of Divinity conferred in this University, my former teacher and colleague, Dr Fairbairn. His services to theological science time would fail barely to enumerate. With a profound belief in the trustworthiness of reason, and the rationality of history, it has been the main passion of his life to understand and interpret religion. Intimately acquainted with the comparative study of the various forms it has assumed, he has risen from the mass of intricate detail to large and luminous generalisations in the philosophy of religion. An alien in no part of the dominion ruled by the queen of sciences, he has been especially distinguished as an exponent of historical and constructive theology. Himself a preacher whose sermons have been characterised by solidity and depth of thought and by a massive and inspiring eloquence, he has laboured to create a learned ministry, with an adequate technical equipment, based on a broad and generous culture. Of this, Mansfield College will be his enduring monument.

---

[1] Among the limericks thus composed was the following:
A conceited Professor called Peake
Did twelve months' work in a week:
When they said, 'You will rue it
If you will overdo it',
He replied: 'Don't you know that I'm PEAKE?'

He did much to frame the scheme of theological studies in the University of Wales, and we gratefully remember the help he gave us in our own similar enterprise. He will pass into his retirement followed by the gratitude of many who owe much to his writings, and with the warm and deep affection of those who date a new epoch in their lives from the time when they sat in his classroom and came under his influence. It will be their desire that, as the evening closes after its strenuous day, he may find it a season of tranquillity, brightened by many memories, and by the assurance of the place he holds in the hearts of all his pupils.

Remembering as he did the earlier as well as the later years, this must have been for Peake a crowning moment in his experience.

IV

It is fitting at this point that we should recall the academic honours that were bestowed upon Peake himself.

On the first Degree Day following the inauguration of the Faculty of Theology at Manchester, the honorary degree of Bachelor of Divinity was given by the University to Peake himself. There were some who thought that a more fitting recognition would have been a doctorate. It was Dr J. Hope Moulton who wrote the following,[1] expressive of his own feelings on the matter:

My dear Peake,
 ... Somebody told me that the University was going to give you a B.D.—according to a veracious newspaper! What on earth does it mean? Does it veil some more sensible proposal? I greatly hope that the first D.D. will be the Dean, if honorary degrees are allowed—there would be universal agreement as to the fitness of that. But B.D.!! βαβαίαξ.

The simple explanation was that it was the highest recognition within the Faculty of Theology that the University could allow, as by regulation honorary doctorates could not be given to members of the University staff.

In April 1907 the University of Aberdeen conferred on Peake the degree of Doctor of Divinity, *honoris causa*—an occasion which brought him many felicitations. The event was more significant in that Peake was the first Nonconformist layman to be given this distinction by a Scottish University. His friend and colleague Dr Robert Mackintosh of Lancashire Independent College wrote: 'Well done Aberdeen! I told Scotch friends years ago you ought to be a D.D. They mumbled something about confining the degree to reverend gents!' Dr Fairbairn was particularly gratified: 'I am glad that the degree is to be a D.D. It is much better to take it where there has been no ordination than to take another.'

[1] J. H. Moulton to A.S.P., 5 April 1905.

Similarly Dr Moulton: 'I am delighted to hear of the honour Aberdeen is conferring on itself. I like the combination "Esq. D.D." ' Thus addressing a postcard to Peake he added: 'I use with pleasure the piquant combination of your address—I very nearly said 'peakuliar pleasure' and 'peakant combination'. A rather amusing letter came from George Peake:

Dear Arthur,
    We were very pleased to hear of the honour which you have had offered to you by Aberdeen University. But we shall, I think, rather regret the loss of 'Professor Peake'. Maggie told Irene, and asked her how she would like her uncle being 'Doctor'. She said, 'I don't mind—he will be the same to me.'

The pleasure of the important occasion of the conferment was greatly heightened because Sir William Hartley travelled to Aberdeen and was received as a guest of the University.

Although as far back as 1871 a government bill was introduced which abolished all ecclesiastical and theological tests for professors, tutors, fellows, and scholars in the older universities, clerical fellowships were still retained, and members of the Theological Faculty were still obliged to be clergymen of the Church of England. No Nonconformist could obtain a theological degree.

From several quarters, including prominent Anglican scholars, the question of freedom in theological teaching at Oxford was raised, and also by Peake himself in 1913, emphasizing the openness of the opportunities provided by the University of Manchester. This prompted the following letter of support from his friend Professor C. H. Herford of Manchester:

I must write a line to thank you for your splendid letter to the M[anchester] G[uardian]—a capital service to the cause of freedom in theological teaching. The bigotry you oppose is now one of the greatest obstacles to the extension of the view that, apart altogether from the results of theology as dogma, religion as a fact of human nature and of human society, is of supreme interest and importance.[1]

Despite attempts to alter the position, it was not until 1920 that the way was opened for the admission of other than members of the Church of England. In that year a number of eminent Nonconformist scholars were given the degree of D.D. *honoris causa*, and Peake was included in this number.[2] All were ordained ministers (with the exception of Baron von Hügel and Peake himself). Thus he became the first Nonconformist layman to attain this distinction. One who witnessed the

---

[1] C. H. Herford to A.S.P., 6 May 1913.
[2] In addition to Peake the following were those presented for the D.D. degree: The Very Rev. James Cooper, Professor of Church History in the University of Glasgow; the Rev. John Skinner, Principal of Westminster College, Cambridge; the Very Rev. Sir George Adam Smith, Vice-Chancellor of Aberdeen University; H. St. John Thackeray, Cambridge; Baron von Hügel.

conferment was C. J. Cadoux, who some years afterwards wrote to Peake[1]

... I have not had the pleasure of meeting you, but I have long been indebted to you for your works in biblical study, and I shall always remember witnessing the degree ceremony in the Sheldonian at Oxford, when you and five others received the Oxford D.D. It was a great occasion in Free Church history!

On the occasion of the conferment Sir William Hartley was again present, much to Peake's gratification. Naturally congratulations in abundance were sent to Peake, and his feelings regarding the occasion were expressed in his reply to a resolution of the Hull Conference in 1920.

... I should at any time have received this honour from my own University with much gratification; but to have been chosen as one of those whom the University has selected to mark the removal of the restriction in the granting of Divinity degrees is, alike in the occasion itself and the eminence of the scholars with whom I share this distinction, a particular pleasure. Nor can I think of any academic honour that would be more precious to me than this.

Shortly before the occasion of presentation Peake received the following letter from Baron von Hügel, a letter which he counted as the most valuable compliment ever paid to him.

13 Vicarage Gate,
Kensington W.
Dear Professor Peake,   12 June, 1920
   It was a very genuine pleasure to find you amongst those who on the 24th inst. are to receive the honorary D.D. at Oxford. When I first heard of the University thinking of myself in the matter, I told my wife and daughter that the honour would be big or little, in proportion to the significance or otherwise of my fellow Doctors; and that I should feel it a very real honour if they had also proffered this degree to Professor Peake! Indeed, you were the only name for Great Britain that occurred to me, though now I see that Sir George Adam Smith also especially deserves the honour, and indeed that my good friend, John Skinner also will form a very worthy recipient. Professor Cooper I must admit I know nothing of; and Mr Thackeray I am vague about. But it is pleasant indeed to have two friends—yourself and Dr Skinner—amongst one's fellow recipients, and to know well about a third, Sir George Adam Smith.
   Looking thus forward to meeting you at Oxford soon, with congratulations,
   Yours sincerely,
   F. von Hügel[2]

V

Because of Peake's prominent position in Manchester it was inevitable

---

[1] C. J. Cadoux to A.S.P., 10 April 1926.
[2] In the diary of von Hügel there is the following reference: 'We were three clerics—all Scotch Presbyterians: and three laymen—a Primitive Methodist (Peake): an Anglican layman (Thackeray), a Catholic (self).' M. de la Bedoyere, *The Life of Baron von Hügel* (1952), p. 318.

that he became widely involved in duties beyond the demands of the University itself. He undertook important work for other universities as external examiner for higher degrees. Because of his deep concern for the diffusion of biblical knowledge he eventually undertook courses of lectures outside Manchester in such places as Bolton, Oldham, and other Lancashire towns. He had long regarded the value of Summer Schools for the extension of Bible teaching,[1] and as far back as 1899 he had given a series of lectures at the school at Woodbrooke, in Birmingham, established by Dr Rendel Harris.[2] He lectured at similar gatherings in Oxford and Cambridge and Edinburgh. In 1907 he gave a course of lectures under the Board of Theological Studies in association with the University of Liverpool, and later on addressed members of the University on 'The Historical Basis of Christianity'. Similarly he delivered a series of lectures at the University College of Aberystwyth. In 1910 he was made an honorary President of the Theological Society of the United Free Church College, Glasgow, and his lecture on the occasion evoked warm appreciation from Dr James Orr: 'Your lecture gave great delight and has raised your high reputation more highly in our College.'[3] A similar honour was bestowed upon him by the Theological Society in the University of Edinburgh in 1914.

In Manchester itself Peake became deeply involved in various external associations. For many years he was the President of the Manchester branch of the Classical Association;[4] he was Vice-President of the Egyptian and Oriental Society, established in 1911 by his colleague Professor Hogg; he was an active member of the Hellenistic Seminar founded by Professor J. H. Moulton; and similarly an active member of the Dante Society. Two particular interests were the Society of Friends, to which he delivered courses of lectures, and the Jewish Community in Manchester, where his discourses on the Old Testament were greatly esteemed.

All these numerous commitments made immense and additional demands upon one whose physical resources were all too slender. It was eventually on this ground that, much to his regret, Peake had to decline

---

[1] Peake was probably influenced by the experiment of a Summer School promulgated successfully by Fairbairn in 1892, as a pioneer of the movement.

[2] Peake wrote to his father (26 August 1904): 'I had a good time at the Friends' Settlement at Woodbrooke.... I was at the second Summer School in 1899, and have been at every one they have held since (except one) to which they invited me. The Warden said before my first lecture that he thought I had done more for the Society of Friends than anyone else, who was not himself a Friend. The school this year was intended to help them (more particularly men) to meet the difficulties raised in their classes by recent attacks on Christianity.'

[3] J. Orr to A.S.P., October 1910. Cf. J. Fitzpatrick to A.S.P., 25 October 1910: 'It is not too much to say that you have done much to give a finer conception of the Bible; you have made Christianity a larger and more precious religion: above all you have given that inspiration which makes preaching an increasing delight, while at the same time it is a heavy burden.'

[4] In 'The Year's Work in Classical Studies', edited for the Journals Board of the Classical Association, Peake wrote an annual review of New Testament literature for seven years: 1907–11; 1913–14.

the pressing and repeated invitation sent to him in 1924 and 1926 to deliver the Cole Lectures at Vanderbilt University, Nashville, U.S.A.

It was natural that the growing success of the Faculty of Theology at Manchester should attract the attention of other universities where the establishment of Faculties of Theology were being considered as desirable. It is not surprising, therefore, that approach should be made to Peake to whom Manchester owed so much. These approaches involved him in considerable labour and correspondence.

In 1915 the Editorial Board of *The Welsh Outlook* decided to open a discussion on the desirability of making a theological faculty in the University of Wales—'a teaching faculty on the lines of the University of Manchester . . . the success of the Manchester experiment has encouraged us to move in this direction'. In Wales the seminary system had long prevailed. The Editor wrote to Peake:[1]

One of our chief troubles in Wales is our sectarianism, and the different denominations need to be convinced that your system does not tend to weaken the student's denominational loyalty. A few words from you on the point as well as on the advantages of making the theological department of the Welsh University a teaching faculty would carry much weight. . . . As a kind of *preparatio evangelica* it would help very much if you would be good enough to give us a brief description of the Manchester system and its advantages.

To *The Welsh Outlook* Peake wrote an article giving a detailed account of the working of the Manchester Faculty, and this exercised a definite influence upon the Welsh development. In July 1917 Peake was elected a member of the Theological Board of the University of Wales.

In 1925 a similar desire was expressed for the establishment of a Faculty of Theology in the University of Birmingham, and Dr W. F. Lofthouse was deputed to approach Peake for advice:[2]

We naturally thought of Manchester, and although the circumstances at Manchester are very different, we felt we could not move forward in any direction, with much confidence without having some knowledge of details with regard to Manchester and its Faculty. I was deputed to see you if possible on the subject. . . . I am sure you will be interested in the suggestion, but you will agree with me that the utmost circumspection will be needed and that a failure would be disastrous.

Even abroad the value of the Manchester experiment was recognized. It was in 1920 that Dr D. L. Ritchie, Principal of the Congregational College of Canada, wrote to Peake setting forth the position in regard to the relation of the various Colleges in Montreal to McGill University.[3]

---

[1] Richard Jones to A.S.P., 11 March 1915.

[2] W. F. Lofthouse to A.S.P., 10 May 1925. In June 1926, after a stay in Peake's home, Dr W. F. Howard wrote to Mrs Peake: 'Dr Peake has greatly helped me by giving me this glimpse into methods and aims, for we are carrying on a campaign for getting a Faculty of Theology started at Birmingham University.'

[3] D. L. Ritchie to A.S.P., 10 December 1920.

Here, as you may know, we have a United Theological Faculty (Anglican, Congregational, Presbyterian, Methodist) working together in one Divinity Hall. The Colleges themselves are affiliated to McGill University; the United Faculty is not, and with the centenary of the University falling October, 1921 new proposals are in view. To help us we are gathering information from other Colleges and Universities that work together, and it has been left to me to enquire as to methods of British working. I know generally the arrangements at Manchester, but want particular evidence of the relations that exist between Victoria University and the Theological Colleges. Can you kindly help me?

Here we have a further illustration of the constant demands being made upon Peake and the measure of his importance in the theological world in the first quarter of this century.

There remain to be considered two important spheres in which Peake took a vital part, and which, though external to the University, were indirectly related to it.

The first is connected with Peake's work for the Society of Old Testament Study, which had been formed early in the summer of 1916. At a Conference of Old Testament scholars in Oxford, it was arranged for a meeting to be held in King's College, London, in January 1917, where the Society was to be formally constituted. Peake's name was included in the list of original members. The advent of the war prevented further meetings until 1919, when, in July, a meeting, scantily attended, was held in Manchester. At this meeting Peake read a paper on 'Hebrew Prophecy in Recent Discussion'. Of this small number Peake not only pressed for the continuation of the Society, despite the immediate discouragement, but in the years ahead none did greater service than Peake, who rarely failed to attend the gatherings. A member of the consultative committee of the Society, his first outstanding contribution was his editorship of a book of essays, *The People and the Book* (1925), as an attempt to expound the general position of Old Testament studies. Peake became President of the Society in 1924, and at the occasion of his inaugural address more than fifty members were present. A further particularly important contribution was Peake's preparation of *A Scripture Bibliography*, with annotations on the books listed, and concerning which the secretary of the Society, Dr Theodore H. Robinson, wrote:[1] 'Probably no other man living had the combination of knowledge and sound judgement which enabled him to do the work so successfully.' A very considerable correspondence between these two scholars has survived, and it reveals the extent to which Peake was involved in the whole business and activity of the Society.

The last paper which Peake prepared for the Society was on 'The Servant of Yahweh' for the January meeting in 1927 but because of illness he was unable to attend and the paper was read for him. A recovery

---

[1] In a letter to L. S. Peake, quoted in *Memoir*, p. 153.

of health allowed him to be present in the following July at the international gathering held in Oxford.

After Peake's death in 1929, Mr (later Dr) C. R. North sent to Mrs Peake the text of a resolution passed at the Society meeting, and spoke of the manner in which Peake had 'added lustre to the Society'.

... He was one of the small band to which it owes its birth, and had served as President and in many other capacities, with unstinting devotion. We remember especially the great help he gave to the Society in connection with its literary projects and the sagacity of his counsel in its business affairs. We lose in him not only one of its most diligent and distinguished members, but one whose willingness to help us as individuals and whose genial comradeship endeared him to us all.

A further comment—from the pen of Dr T. H. Robinson—may be recorded: 'To describe his connection with the Society would almost be to write its history.'[1]

The second institution with which Peake was intimately connected was the John Rylands Library in Manchester, which, in 1899, had been built and endowed by Mrs Rylands in memory of her husband.[2] In the preliminary arrangements for the creation of the Library, Peake was in constant consultation with Mrs Rylands at her home at Longford Hall, Stretford, regarding rules and regulations which she had carefully thought out for its management. The first meeting of the Council of Governors was held at the Library on 18 December 1899, and the original agenda has survived, bearing in Peake's own handwriting his notes of the important decisions. In the list of proposed contents he underlines one phrase: 'Theology to be the strong point of the Library'. This emphasis is borne out by a conversation Peake had with Mrs Rylands following the inaugural dinner at which all the governors were present. Peake wrote:[3]

Later in the evening I had an opportunity of a conversation with Mrs Rylands in which I said that the fear had been expressed that the Library would be a museum of rarities,[4] and how glad I was that she had made it so rich in modern works valuable to students. She replied that her desire was that a student in any of the subjects covered by the Library should be able to find at his disposal all the latest and best literature, without waiting, for him to use. One of my first tasks was to discover how far the best recent literature on the Bible was already provided. I found a large number of gaps, especially in the foreign literature, and

---

[1] T. H. Robinson in *H.R.* 1929.
[2] The Library building was opened on 6 October 1899, and at the ceremony Dr Fairbairn, an old friend of the Rylands family, gave 'a striking and masterly address'. W. B. Selbie, *Life of Andrew Martin Fairbairn*, p. 380.
[3] *H.R.* January 1925.
[4] Mrs Ryland had purchased the unique Althorp Library at a cost of nearly £250,000 and later she purchased the rare MSS belonging to the Earl of Crawford and Balcarres for a sum little short of the same amount.

made a detailed report about them. Mrs Rylands, hearing of it, ordered the whole of them to be procured without delay. She was especially anxious that theology should be kept well to the front and once sent me an urgent message to that effect. Another thing which I recall with gratitude touched the purchase of German books. I generally prepared on my own account a list for each meeting of the book-committee containing suggestions of recent theological literature. The criticism was more than once made that we were buying too many German books. During that time Mrs Rylands asked me to see her on a matter about which she desired to consult me. When we had talked this over she asked me how we were getting on with our work, and I told her about my difficulty. She said she would back me wholeheartedly, because we could not have the best literature unless the German books were purchased. Fortunately as time went on, the member of the Committee who had felt specially doubtful came round to my view.

Peake was also responsible for securing a copy of the rare facsimile of the *Codex Vaticanus*, and when the Crawford MSS. were purchased he was consulted about the cataloguing, and when at his suggestion that Mrs Rylands should invite Mr Hogg to settle in Manchester to deal with them, he carried through all the negotiations.

Dr William Temple, then Archbishop of York, recalled that in his days as Bishop of Manchester, he was a member of the Book Committee of the Library. At each monthly meeting the Librarian produced a long list of new and important publications. As chairman Peake would ask if any member had other volumes to suggest. Very rarely was ever even a solitary suggestion forthcoming, the Librarian having anticipated all. Then Peake would produce a list of six or seven books which were not found in the Librarian's list—sometimes concerning subjects which were not in his own particular field of biblical and theological studies.[1]

In 1914 the Library at Louvain suffered ruthless destruction by the Germans, and the John Rylands library gave splendid service in assisting its reconstruction. Through this project, initiated by Dr Guppy, the Librarian, about fifty thousand volumes were gathered at the Library from many contributors, and in this work he was greatly helped by Peake and his colleagues. Peake himself donated a large number of volumes from his own library. Of this splendid enterprise, Professor A. Van Hoonacker wrote: 'Our debt of gratitude towards the John Rylands Library is very great indeed and can never be forgotten.'

In addition to all his valuable advice and administrative service mention must be made of Peake's writings for the *Bulletin of the John Rylands Library*, and as a regular contributor to the series of lectures arranged by

---

[1] L. S. Peake: *Memoir*, p. 7. This was borne out by Professor C. H. Herford, who was Peake's colleague on the Committee for fifteen years. He wrote of 'the long list of books belonging to all branches of religious science, comparative, domestic, anthropological, theological, anti-theological, philosophical, all of which we were staggered to find that Peake had seen, most often read, while of all he had a considered judgement'. Letter to the *Manchester Guardian*, 22 August 1922.

the Library. Some of Peake's most erudite and important monographs were given in this way, and to some of them we shall give attention later on.

The close friendship which sprung up between Dr Guppy and Peake is illustrated by a letter which the former wrote to him:

I should like to take this opportunity of thanking you for the generous help and encouragement which you constantly afford to me in the work of the Library. Service in the Library under such conditions is very pleasant, and I cannot help feeling that I do not as often as I should express to you the grateful appreciation which, though not expressed, is none the less sincere.[1]

VI

The weight of ever-growing responsibility during the Manchester years for one whose physical resources were slender and always taxed to the utmost, might well have caused Peake to consider relinquishing some of his labours. His ever-strong sense of duty, however, never allowed him to consider any relaxation of the strain with which his work was carried on. The suggestion that he might consider a removal to a less exacting post of duty was rigidly set aside. The following illustrates his firm and inflexible sense of duty to his work in Manchester.

In 1919 he received a private note from Dr W. B. Selbie, Principal of Mansfield College, Oxford, who was faced with the problem of finding a successor to a member of the College staff, Dr James Moffatt, who was about to remove to Scotland. The suggestion had been made to Dr Selbie that perhaps Peake might be willing to consider a return to Oxford. To him Selbie wrote privately:[2]

... Briefly it is to the effect that you ought to have less work to do than you have in Manchester, and that there is a possibility that you might consider returning to Oxford again. As you know the work here is by no means heavy. If such a thing is out of the question as I half suspect it is, you will not hesitate to tell me so, but if there is the least chance of your being willing to entertain the idea, I should very much like to know of it before we go any further. No one knows that I am writing to you, and no one will know unless the matter is to go further.

That Dr Selbie's doubt about Peake's return to Oxford was well-founded the following letter, written by Peake in reply, leaves no question.[3]

Gairloch, Freshfield
Liverpool. June 5,
1916

My dear Selbie,

Moffatt was staying with me a little while ago and we travelled to Cambridge

---

[1] H. Guppy to A.S.P., 4 November 1913.
[2] W. B. Selbie to A.S.P., 4 June 1915.
[3] A.S.P. to W. B. Selbie, 6 June 1915.

together, and I gathered from what he said that he would feel it his duty to accept the call of his own church if the Assembly appointed him to the Chair. I am very sorry that you are losing him, and I am sure from what he said that he will be very sorry to go.

I very much appreciate your letter, and it is quite true that I am overburdened at Manchester and it is all the heavier that I have to do the work from Freshfield. And it would be delightful to be back again at Mansfield with you and the others as colleagues. The work would be most attractive, and the conditions under which it would be done, and it would be specially stimulating to have a picked body of men like Mansfield students to teach.

But it is quite out of the question for me to come. Were it simply my connexion with the University I should carefully and seriously balance the claims. I might feel that my duty would be best done by remaining in Manchester, but I am by no means sure this would be so. What is really decisive is my relation to Hartley College. While my own Church desires me to remain, and I have strength enough to do the work, I am bound by duty, honour, affection and gratitude to remain. I don't think I have any illusion about my work. I am constantly dissatisfied with it. At the same time I don't see any one yet on the horizon who would fill my place if I left. And apart from this our people have got used to me, they have become fond of me, and even those who have been suspicious have come to trust me. The consequence is that I am in a very favourable position for carrying further the work which needs to be done, and which I have been doing for the last 23 years. Materially also the position is very favourable. Sir William Hartley has twice enlarged the College, and largely on my account. He must have spent not much short of £40,000 on the College since I came; it may be more than that.... Of course, this is not the paramount consideration; but the clear duty to my denomination. At the same time it would weigh heavily, as would the very handsome treatment our people have given me, notably in the celebration of my majority.

Of course this is a confidential letter, and we are very old friends, so I can speak more fully than I could otherwise without feeling that you will think I am unduly puffed up. I need hardly say that I do not share the estimate that our people express about me, for I know of short-comings that they are in no position to recognise, and am often depressed about my work than otherwise. But their estimate whether right or wrong is in itself a very important fact and they have left me no room to doubt that they would be dismayed were I to leave the College. And so I am afraid I must stay and indeed it would be a very great wrench to leave, although I often wish either that my work was much lighter, or that I had more strength to carry it.

With kindest regards and many thanks,
Yours ever,
Arthur S. Peake

So it was in Manchester that Peake remained until his life-work came to its close.

CHAPTER FIVE

THE INTERPRETER OF THE BIBLE

WHEN we turn to a survey of Peake as a writer we are immediately faced with a colossal task, for from his pen came some twenty books of solid scholarship, a large number of important monographs, a colossal quantity of articles and book reviews, all written in that lucid style which was one of his great characteristics. The fact is that he was a ceaseless writer whose pen was never idle, and always before him there lay a formidable quantity of subjects awaiting exposition and treatment out of the richness of his fertile mind, always guided by inflexible principles from which he would never deviate. From his vast range of reading and acquaintance with everything that had already been written on the subject in hand, he possessed an amazing skill in marshalling material and evaluating it, allowing it to pass through the crucible of his own mind, stating with scrupulous fairness opposite points of view, and finally precipitating with extraordinary insight the deposit of truth, which he declared with clarity and conviction.

There were for him certain principles that were basic, and these had been secured through the long and arduous years of training at Oxford; from this starting point he went forward to fearless enquiry, and therefore in everything he produced he revealed the greatness of a master mind.

The greatness of that mastery becomes more significant when it is remembered that in nearly every case his works were dictated as his mind moved steadily through the subject concerned—the consequence of possessing a power of memory which could draw fresh from the vast storehouse of his mind the things required, producing in clear and logical sequence the stages of his argument. It was this power of disciplined control which characterized his lectures, to the amazement of those who listened to him. In this particular he was a confessed contrast to the practice of another eminent scholar, Dr J. H. Moulton, who was one of Peake's closest friends, and who wrote:

I have been trying to think what I would do with a secretary if I had one. . . . I have always envied you from afar your genius for talking your books and reviews. With me it is a cunning spirit residing in my pen that makes my sentences for me and my speaking style differs altogether—a clear case for χωρίζοντης if any should lay hold of a verbatim report and a written paper.[1]

Peake's mastery of the English language was superb, and at times there was a certain poetic quality in his writing. It is this quality of exactness and lucidity that lends a certain fascination to all he wrote.

Despite the vastness of his literary work we must make some attempt to evaluate his achievement.

Throughout his writings, almost without exception, Peake was, directly or indirectly, the interpreter of Scripture. The recognition of this will form the structure of our survey of his voluminous work. His task of biblical interpretation falls into two categories—the interpretation of the Bible in terms of an understanding of the Bible *as a whole*; the interpretation of the *text* in terms of truth by way of exact exegesis, and therefore as a commentator of Scripture. The right understanding of the very nature of Scripture was a *sine qua non* for the interpretation of any part of it by way of commentary or detailed study. Peake was convinced that much of the difficulty and confusion with reference to an understanding of the Bible is due to the prevalence of incorrect conceptions of what the Bible really is. The life-work he set for himself was to make known far and wide a sound understanding of the *nature* and the *content* of Scripture.

One thing becomes indubitably clear in making a survey of Peake's writings, namely that in biblical interpretation he possessed equal mastery alike in the field of the Old Testament and in the New. This it was that made him almost unique as a biblical scholar in his generation. Few if any other scholars have attempted the task.

I

We turn first to the writings *on the nature of Scripture*.

Peake's first book, published in 1897, was *A Guide to Biblical Study*[2] and it contained a significant Introduction written by his former teacher, Dr Fairbairn. In estimating the importance of the book it should be borne in mind that it was written at the end of the nineteenth century, and though some of its assertions may no longer be tenable, it was at that time entirely representative of the stage of biblical scholarship which had then been reached. Moreover it was the kind of book that needed to be written. Peake clearly defines his purpose in the opening pages:

---

[1] J. H. Moulton to A.S.P., 26 December 1911.
[2] The book bore the dedication: 'To my Father with grateful affection'. On receiving the volume his Father wrote to him 8 October 1897: 'Your surprise has just come to hand, for which I am very grateful, When I opened it and saw that you had so kindly and affectionately dedicated it to me, tears came into my eyes, and I said: "Heaven bless him!".'

This book is intended for those who wish to make a systematic study of the Bible, and its purpose is to indicate the methods that should be employed and the problems to which attention should be directed. As it is not designed for scholars, it is untechnical in character; and although it contemplates a long course of study, it will, I hope, meet the needs of beginners.

The book attempted to exhibit in a general way what was the outcome of the extraordinary critical activity in the field of biblical knowledge—as a starting point for those who were not specialists, but interested students of the Bible, desiring to begin a special study of it in relation to the then new methods of critical enquiry. It was an attempt to provide the means with which the student, carefully reading the Bible, might intelligently and personally work out his own conclusions. Peake realized that such folk possessing that desire were a growing number, and for these he must seek to open the doorway to truth.

In this, his first book, we perceive at once the true critic's faculty for weighing up both sides of a question—for example, his discussion of the authenticity of the Pastoral Epistles, and his statement of the Synoptic Problem—but equally clearly he expresses his own conviction and preserves an independence of judgement. The book is particularly valuable in the way in which it discloses, in both Old and New Testaments alike, the great facts of the religious life, and, in common with all Peake's work, it brings out strongly the foundation truth to which the biblical records bear witness.

The chapter on 'Books' also reveals for the first time in Peake's writing his remarkable skill in the preparation of bibliographical material, a work in which in many fields he was afterwards to prove himself expert.[1]

One feature of the book is that the student is taught to see what is known and established and to distinguish it from what is still *sub judice*, and it is therefore wise in its warnings. 'The Bible is to be studied just like any other book. We can come to it with no prepossessions but simply with an open mind' (p. 8). 'It is unhistorical exegesis which reads the New Testament into the Old. . . . No quarter must be given to allegorical interpretation, which leaves the Bible at the mercy of every fad and caprice of the exegete' (p. 115). 'It is a golden rule in the study of the prophets to start from the principle that the prophet's main interest is with his own time, and only when this rule is observed do the prophets become intelligible. . . . It is only the incurable conceit of human nature to imagine that the prophets had a peculiar interest in the closing years of the nineteenth century or the fortunes of the British Empire' (p. 116).

The following extract not only reveals Peake's profound insight into the experience of Paul, which was the foundation of all his later writing on the subject, but is also a felicitous example of the poetic quality of much of his writing:

---

[1] At Peake's request, Dr G. Buchanan Gray added a bibliography of literature on the Hebrew and Greek text, and also a chapter on language for more advanced students.

In this experience he knew himself to be one with Christ. And as one with Him he was lifted to a new point of view, to new sympathy with the universal grace of God. From the barren island of sectarian prejudice, on which he had so long been stranded, he had been plucked by a miracle of mercy and swept into the strong current of God's eternal purpose and eternal love, which bore along the whole universe to the summing up of all things in Christ.[1]

In reviewing the book it was the recognition of Peake's insight which prompted Dr Marcus Dods to write:[2]

The familiarity which he shows with the subject, revealed in the well-digested statements he makes, and the lucidity and consistency with which he constructs the theology of Paul and exhibits it as an organic whole, must win the admiration of every reader, and prompt the wish that the same hand would elaborate that chapter into a volume.

Despite Peake's life-long intention that he should write this whole volume—which undoubtedly would have proved to be his *magnum opus*—it was never written, though what might have been was foreshadowed in his monograph *The Quintessence of Paulinism* (1917).

A Guide to Biblical Study was 'a handbook in a very true sense: a light to show the way to be taken; a key to open doors into treasure houses; a quickener to patient and prolonged reading'.[3] We have given rather considerable treatment to this book because, as Peake's first book, it is a valuable pointer to all his subsequent writing. Moreover it was a much needed book. Perhaps the most shrewd comment upon it is the following extract from a review:

The line of study suggested by it cannot well be neglected if the Church of England is to maintain herself at least upon a level with Nonconformist bodies in theological learning.[4]

In his later years Peake declared his intention to re-write *A Guide to Biblical Study* in a revised and expanded form, but this was never done. Nevertheless much if not all of what such a revised volume would have contained found expression in what proved to be one of his most important writings, and which he wrote in 1913; *The Bible: Its Origin, Its Significance and Its Abiding Worth*. To this we now turn at some length.

In a very real sense this book may be regarded as perhaps the most important work because it revealed with the utmost clarity the foundations upon which all his other work was built—namely an understanding of the true interpretation of the biblical records as the classic documents of the Christian faith. He was intensely aware of the immediate situation in religious thought about the Bible, and declares in the opening sentence of the book, 'This volume has been written in the hope that it may prove

[1] Op. cit., p. 197.
[2] The *British Weekly*, 28 October 1897.
[3] *P.M.Q.R.*, January 1898.
[4] *The Times*, 21 October 1897.

helpful in the present perplexity.' That this proved to be the case is shown by the fact that in the year of its publication a second edition was called for, and by 1921 it had run into no less than seven editions. Shortly after its publication a notable Scottish scholar wrote:[1]

I have read your volume and am greatly impressed by its timeliness. I can't imagine any treatment of the subject better fitted to meet the vague feeling, so widely current, that the Bible has been quite discarded by modern investigation. You have shown exceptional skill in approaching the subject from so many important avenues. The work is indeed a handbook of the most valuable type of apologetic.

Similarly Peake's former teacher, Dr S. R. Driver of Oxford,[2] wrote in warm commendation:

Your book has duly reached me, and I have read several chapters in it—especially those on criticism and inspiration—with great interest and approval. I think them *admirable*. You have taken just the right points and put what you had to say in a lucid and convincing way. Critics have been suffering lately a great deal from misconception and misrepresentation: and your chapters ought to do a great deal to place criticism in its true light. . . . I congratulate you very warmly.

Professor Gilbert Murray welcomed it as meeting his own personal need:[3]

Many thanks for *The Bible*. I wish I had more time to study theology of your sort carefully—I do not much care about other sorts! I feel my knowledge at present so dreadfully precarious and superficial.

On receiving the volume the famous anthropologist J. G. Frazer wrote:[4]

. . . Though I have not time at present to read it, I have read enough to see that it is marked by that combination of learning, candour, good sense and good temper which your friends expect from you, and which is sadly wanting in some of those who write on these controversial topics.

Although it is impossible in the space at our disposal, to give an adequate account of the volume—which runs into over five hundred pages—a statement of its chapters will give an indication of its wide range and the clear sequence of its treatment. The early chapters deal with the current position of the Bible in existing thought; the method and temper of the apologist; the new light thrown upon the Bible by the discovery of new manuscripts and the original languages in which it was written together with the building up of the Bible into the canon of

---

[1] H. A. A. Kennedy (of New College, Edinburgh), to A.S.P., 4 November 1913.
[2] S. R. Driver to A.S.P., November 1913.
[3] Gilbert Murray to A.S.P., 2 November 1913.
[4] J. G. Frazer to A.S.P., 2 November 1913.

Scripture, with the problems involved in the process. Seven important chapters, fundamental to the whole enquiry, are concerned with the legitimacy of criticism in its various aspects, showing the movement through which biblical criticism has passed and further declaring its most probable and most assured results. All this is preliminary to the core of the book which is concerned with the evolution of the Scriptures as a written record of the self-disclosure of God in history and in experience. Following this, the remaining chapters on the relation of this line of interpretation to biblical theology, the authority of the Bible, the nature and mechanism of inspiration lead to a final chapter on the permanent value of Scripture as taken in its entirety. A significant chapter deals with the misuse of the Bible.

In 1922, under the title *The Nature of Scripture*, Peake gathered together a collection of papers and addresses which, although miscellaneous as to date and occasion, were characterized by unity of theme and purpose. The earlier essays are concerned with the critical method as applied to the Scriptures, and also with its results; the later, for the most part, deal with the values that remain in the literature of the Bible when sober criticism has done its work and its results have been frankly accepted. The book was written primarily for the non-specialist reader, for those who hesitate between the traditional and critical views of Scripture, and in particular for those who fear that the acceptance of the modern critical outlook will weaken the influence of the Bible and result in disastrous consequences for faith and life. Peake realized that there were many for whom his earlier book of five hundred pages might be too formidable. The issue of these collected papers was timely indeed. In the Preface Peake writes:

The recent course of discussion[1] has suggested that the publication of this volume might serve a useful purpose. The advocates of traditional theories on the Bible have been stirred to new efforts. It must be said with regret that these have in some instances been marred by a painful absence of Christian temper and the courtesies of controversy, and by a lack of that scrupulous fairness and accuracy of statement which is the first essential in debate.

Peake regarded his book as 'the fulfilment of a mission' in the interests of what he believed to be the truth about the Scriptures. As with the earlier book this volume was an immediate success, a second edition being called for before the end of 1922. Undoubtedly it had a steadying effect as a useful piece of work in the field of Christian apologetics.

It is fitting at this point to estimate the precise significance of these

---

[1] In part the reason for this resurgence of the traditional view was the challenge arising from the issue of *Peake's Commentary* in 1919. In 1922 the outstanding advocate of the traditional view, Dr W. H. Fitchett, had published his book *Where the Higher Criticism Fails*. In the same year a massive correspondence appeared in the *British Weekly*, to which Peake found himself compelled to reply. The activities of The Bible League also had become vigorous and severe.

three volumes concerned with biblical interpretation, written as they were within the period of thirty years from 1892 to 1922.

The traditional theories which suggested that the Scriptures contained everywhere the immediate word of God to the soul resulted in an atomistic view, for in the use of the Bible it had to be admitted that not all parts of Scripture yielded the same spiritual blessing, and so in practice large portions remained unused. Further, the theory of verbal inspiration left many of the problems, both textual and ethical and theological unanswered, despite traditionalist attempts to overcome these difficulties. The allegorical and typological use of Scripture,[1] particularly with reference to the Old Testament, often led to misuse, not seldom in extravagant form. The inerrancy of the Scriptures was assumed and categorically insisted on.

The challenge to the inadequacy of this traditionalist view was not by any means new. The year 1860 saw in England the publication of a volume of essays by seven members of the Church of England, under the title *Essays and Reviews*, which created a storm of protest because of its declaration of this new approach to the Bible. Particularly important was the essay by Benjamin Jowett of Oxford, 'On the Interpretation of Scripture'. In the last quarter of the nineteenth century English scholars recognized that the only adequate approach to a sound biblical interpretation was by the use of the historical principle and the new movement had definitely established itself before the century had closed.[2] Actually the years of greatest crisis were over before Peake's influence was widely felt, and he himself seems to have given the chief credit for effecting so peaceful a transition to S. R. Driver, the Oxford scholar.[3] This was unquestionably the position held by an increasing number of English biblical scholars before the turn of the century, but there remained a gulf between its acceptance by the leaders and the following of the mass of lay folk and the less 'advanced' ministers. Only in the final decade of the nineteenth century had the value of the critical view filtered down to any marked degree among the laity in the churches.[4]

Peake wrote his first book *A Guide to Biblical Study* in 1897 and in so doing he stepped straight into the arena as a valiant defender of the new viewpoint, determined to spread the truth as widely as possible. He took

[1] Cf. T. W. Manson, *Bulletin of John Rylands Library*, xxxiv, p. 312: 'When we get into the field of allegorical interpretation and typology, it often seems as if the only limits to what can be done are set by the resources and fertility of invention of the expositor.'

[2] There is an admirable summary of the development in W. B. Glover, *Evangelical Nonconformists and Higher Criticism in the Nineteenth Century* (1954).

[3] L. S. Peake, *Memoir*, pp. 74–5.

[4] The Rev. Charles A. Berry, an outstanding figure amongst the younger Congregationalists, declared in an interview in 1896: 'While it is too early to say how far the results of the Higher Criticism have affected our congregations, I can discern a real difference in their attitude.... The school of Higher Criticism has voiced the general sentiment of our average intelligent layman, and has relieved them of the sense they once had of disloyalty to the Bible. It has given our people a more rational and satisfying belief in the great truths of Scripture.' J. S. Drummond, *Charles A. Berry* (1899) p. 247.

up the challenge and continued it in the books that followed—*The Bible: Its Origin, Its Significance and Its Abiding Worth* (1913), and *The Nature of Scripture* (1922). With deep insight he had discerned the need of the situation and counted it his mission for the rest of his life to endeavour to meet it. Here we have the secret that lay behind his unflinching conviction that the fruits of his scholarship must be made available for ordinary intelligent folk who were seeking after the truth of the Bible. Peake's position is summed up in a comment which he made years later after reading a book written by an Old Testament scholar who was one of his closest friends.[1]

One of the things that specially attracts me in your work is that you do not limit yourself to the learned side of it, but realize the duty of a Biblical scholar to help ordinary people. This side of our work appeals to me greatly, and although I feel distressed by the distraction from other work of the more academic type which it involves, I think scholars do owe a duty to the Church and to the people. This seems to me all the more important just now because, although we are not submerged, as I fear America seems likely to be by the tide of obscurantism, we are suffering and are likely to suffer more from its arrogant temper, its use of the money power and its not too honourable methods.

A survey of these three volumes at once makes clear Peake's standpoint as an interpreter of Scripture. As a biblical critic he stood upon the foundation of the historical principle in relation to interpretation and pursued by the method of scientific enquiry. Therefore any historical study of the Bible inevitably involved critical study. More than once Peake declared that he had no interest in criticism for its own sake, but affirmed again and again that the ultimate purpose was the discovery of truth concerning the content of the Bible and its permanent message. There must be a careful examination and sifting of evidence, both internal and external, whatever might prove to be the result of such examination. The aim of criticism was to restore the true text of Scripture; to determine problems of date and authorship; to estimate the qualities of the writers and the historical worth of the documents themselves; to seek to arrange the material in chronological order and to determine the relations between the various parts. As the mark of integrity in all scientific study is that a former view comes to be abandoned in the light of new evidence, there should be no surprise if a revision of the findings should be then found necessary. The method of approach should be wholly inductive and the starting point should be a resolve to examine the Bible itself without preconceived ideas, the one desire being to discover the truth. Peake's attitude may be summed up in the words of Benjamin Whichcote, the Cambridge Platonist:

God expects that the reader of Scripture should be of an ingenuous spirit and use candour.... for the Scripture is to be read as a man would read a letter

[1] A.S.P. to J.E. McFadyen, January 1923.

from a friend, in which he doth only look after what was in his friend's mind and meaning, not what he can put upon the words.[1]

Thus Peake regarded criticism as the instrument for opening up the truth of Scripture by discovery of its original meaning.

An important result of this historical approach to the Bible is that it is seen *as a whole*, and its permanent value is discovered in much that in itself could hardly be accounted to be of direct moral and spiritual significance. There is a great deal in the Bible which, separated from the whole, has little value, yet for an appreciation of the Bible taken in its entirety it may be indispensable. It is only on this basis that the permanent value of the Old Testament can be vindicated; in addition the problems raised by sub-Christian morality of the Old Testament can alone be resolved. Unless there is a final break with the atomistic view of the Bible, its full significance, as containing the classic documents of the Christian faith can never be discovered.

Moreover, a further outcome of the historical approach to the Bible is an enlargement of the idea of inspiration. The earlier view of the Bible at its best regarded the Holy Spirit as simply enlightening the minds of those who were its writers, but by this new viewpoint that action of the Spirit is seen to be both wider and deeper. Not only individuals but the whole nation of Israel is seen to be the object of Divine inspiration. The sense of the unity of the Bible begins to emerge, and is seen to indicate a process of development in which the significance of the human factor in Scripture can be discerned. Underlying all is the idea of God as revealing himself in history and experience.

Thus the Bible is seen to be not primarily a handbook of history or of ethics, but a record of God's gradual self-disclosure 'through the Spirit's leavening of a material too often uncongenial'. In fragmentary portions only was it possible for God to speak His word to the people whom He had chosen: and it was only in the fullness of time that the Word came to be declared with finality in an incarnation—in one who was a Son. Thus came 'the self-translation of the language of God into the speech of time'. In the Jesus of history the self-revelation of God attained its climax, and as the Old Testament contained the story of the earlier stage of this process, so in the New Testament there is the record of God's last and greatest declaration: 'No man hath seen God at any time; the only-begotten Son hath made the declaration' (John 1:18).

This is the truth that lies behind the current phrase 'progressive revelation'.[2] The Bible is the record of this progressive revelation of the character and purpose of God in the history and experience of man.

[1] B. Whichcote (1609-1683). *Sermons* II. p. 245. Cf. B. Jowett in *Essays and Reviews* (1860), p. 377: 'Interpret the Scriptures like any other book.... The first step is to know the meaning, and this can only be done in the same careful and impartial way that we ascertain the meaning of Sophocles and Plato.'

[2] The term is not new; it was used by Benjamin Jowett in 'On the Interpretation of Scripture' in *Essays and Reviews* (1860) p. 348

'Progress is there and in the progress revelation.' As it is the same light which manifests itself in the dawn and yet comes to its full revelation in the noonday glory, so in the Christ of the New Testament there is the climax of the whole complex process of revelation to which the Bible bears unmistakable witness.

It will be observed that Peake lays equal stress upon *both* history and experience as significant in the process of revelation. This was in contrast to some nineteenth-century writers who, whilst recognizing the importance of the historical nature of revelation, were inclined to lay the greater emphasis on the subjective element of personal experience in the matter of the revelation of Christ to men. The insufficiency of this position Peake clearly discerned, as the following letter shows.[1]

People say they are so sure of the truth of Christianity from their own consciousness that if the whole of the New Testament were lost their faith would still remain unaffected. I very strongly believe this to be not simply a mistake but a very dangerous form of teaching. Dr Dale and Hugh Price Hughes are the leading representatives of this false theory. On the contrary I say that Christianity is a *historical* religion, resting upon certain facts, and unless these facts are true the experience of which they speak is a delusion.

We have delineated the line of argument to which these volumes bear witness in vast detail throughout, and in the following passage Peake himself summarizes his own conclusions:

The Bible is the record of revelation. It is not the revelation itself. That was given through history and experience, in life and personality. But a record of it was needed that it might be preserved for posterity, and this we have in the Bible.... It was necessary for the meaning of history to be made clear, and the need was met by gifted men who were sensitive to the spiritual forces at work beneath the surface and the far-reaching plan which controlled the movement of events. We have then the double process of revelation and interpretation, and the record of this is contained in Scripture. It lies in the nature of the case that the supreme value and authority attaches to the final stage in the process; but the whole movement has permanent significance, and the New Testament did not make the Old Testament obsolete.... Fragmentary and incomplete, marred by imperfection and impoverished by the limitation of the medium, yet the process of revelation in Israel is organically one with the revelation of God's only-begotten Son, and he who would understand the climax aright must retrace with patient care the long and steep ascent by which it was finally reached.[2]

So we see that it was to the advocacy of this approach to an understanding of the Bible that Peake committed his life-work, to extend that advocacy so that it might reach the minds of all those who were seeking after the truth of the Scriptures. It was this fact that constitutes his uniqueness as an interpreter of the sacred writings. To an unnumbered

---

[1] A.S.P. to Samuel Peake, 9 December 1892.
[2] *The Nature of Scripture*, pp. 234f.

host not only through his writings but by general conversation and correspondence, at great cost to himself in both time and energy, he unfolded the truths of the Bible as he saw it. From his earliest days, a lover of the writings of John Bunyan, it is probably true to say that no figure in those immortal pages would have afforded him more satisfaction than to be known as Interpreter—'the man that stands at the gate, at the head of this way, that if I called here, would show me excellent things—such as would be a help to me in my journey'. Peake's vast and varied correspondence shows how many folk were willing to echo the experience of Christian who had dwelt in 'the House of the Interpreter':

> *Here I have seen things rare and profitable*
> *Things to make me stable*
> *In what I have begun to take in hand.*

Of the importance of the interpreter's vocation Peake had no doubt:

It would be out of place for me to insist that a book so largely created by experience needs experience in its interpreter, but at least I may emphasise this, that for a full understanding of it, the interpreter needs a sympathetic insight into religion. He should bring with him to his task a loving and reverential regard for every form in which the religious instinct has expressed itself. Nothing should lie beyond the range of his sympathy from the wild curses of corybantic emotion to the deep, calm brooding of the contemplative mystic. He should seek by an effort of imagination to sink himself in those types of experience which are most alien to him, as well as those which are most congenial, and in that way fit himself to be an interpreter of the greatest religious literature the world has known.[1]

Such requirement Peake certainly fulfilled.

Yet Peake's task as an interpreter could not be an easy one. It was inevitable that there were those who, deeply anxious that their faith should not be disturbed, were resistant to new ideas. There were even those who, with bitterness and acrimony, challenged Peake without mercy. There is a significant passage from the pen of Benjamin Jowett, which, though written as far back as 1860, is not without meaning for Peake's time and task.

The path of the critical interpreter of Scripture is almost a thorny one in England. It is not worth while for any one to enter upon it who is not supported by a sense that he has a Christian and moral object. For an interpreter of Scripture in modern times may feel that it is a matter of duty not to conceal the things he knows. He does not hide the discrepancies of Scripture.... He is not afraid that inquiries which have for their object the truth, can ever be displeasing to the God of truth; or that the Word of God is in any sense a word to be hurt by investigations into its human origins and conception.[2]

---

[1] 'The Present Movement of Biblical Science' by A.S.P., in *Inaugural Lectures delivered by Members of the Faculty of Theology* (1905), pp. 62–3.
[2] *Essays and Reviews* (1860), p. 376.

Such was Peake's own experience in his own loyalty to truth, and it was on account of this that, though unwillingly, not seldom was he forced into the arena of controversy. In printed journals and newspapers as well as by private letters to numerous correspondents, he defended the cause for which he stood, and did so often at great length at the cost of time and patience. As an apologist Peake was always obedient to his own dictum: 'We must know the worst; we must show that we know the worst; we must be prepared ourselves to state the worst that can be alleged against us.'[1] Perhaps the greatest thing about this ministry as an apologist was Peake's temper and spirit. He is always courteous, allowing all that he feels possible for good to his opponent, yet firm in the statement of his own case. Although Peake himself is the defendant in the case, the impression given is, nevertheless, that of a judge carefully and detachedly presenting a case for judgement, impartially stating both sides and then finally revealing his own conviction in clear and unmistakable terms, leaving the matter in the hands of the reader to accept.

As we have already observed, the task of interpretation is a difficult one. Yet the cumulative effect of an examination of Peake's writings is the impression that it is one of the highest tasks upon which the mind of man can be engaged—to bring forth and make known to others the unfolding of the glory of God's character and purpose as revealed in the history and experience of mankind. To this end, as we have seen, the interpreter himself needs nothing short of 'fashioning in himself the mind of Christ', and Peake himself had attained to this high level of experience; this had become the dynamic of all his work. He had fully understood the profound meaning of the words of John Robinson, the Pilgrim Father, 'The Lord has more truth and light yet to break forth out of his holy word,' and the richness of the experience of discovery Peake would have others come to know and share, a richness nowhere more fully declared than in this golden passage from his own pen:

We turn to the Bible to gain an ever renewed sense of its uniqueness of its inexpressible value. It is a light whose radiance illumines our way, while its glow cheers our hearts.... It is the river that makes glad and sweet the city of God, a river with clear shallows and unfathomed depths, reflecting now the bright untroubled sky and now the dark and lurid thunder-cloud, bathing our tired spirits in its warmth and softness, or bracing them by the vigour of its cold, moving here in a great stillness, and there in a rushing flood, cleansing us from our defilement, reviving us as we drink its life-giving waters, bearing us on its broad bosom through an enchanted land.[2]

---

[1] *The Bible: Its Origin...*, p. 27.
[2] *The Nature of Scripture*, p. 248.

II

We now turn to a survey of Peake's work in the field of Old Testament criticism and interpretation.

No volume by way of a critical introduction to the Old Testament came from his pen, and though eminently equipped for such a task, the probable reason for the absence of such a work was the fine quality of the book written by his former teacher Dr S. R. Driver, whose *Introduction to the Literature of the Old Testament*, published in 1891, Peake, in 1914, still regarded as 'our standard work', 'a place which it has through its nine editions continued to hold'. Further, as we have already seen, it was Peake's intention to re-write his book *A Guide to Biblical Study* (1897) and if he had done so the purpose of an Old Testament Introduction would have been served.

Nevertheless by article and monograph Peake expressed his views on the background of the Old Testament, particularly in his stress upon the soundness of the Grafian theory as to the composition and date of the Pentateuch. As early as 1892 he wrote an important article on 'The Textual Criticism of the Old and New Testament', dealing with prolegomena in defence of the critical position. 'The objective historical method is the note of the new textual criticism, as dogmatic caprice was a mark of the old.'[1] In 1907 a long article on 'The Problem of the Old Testament' came as a defence against the traditional position asserting 'the confidence with which critics affirm the validity of their main conclusions'.[2] In 1903 Peake delivered an important lecture in the John Rylands Library series on 'The Movement of Old Testament Scholarship in the Nineteenth Century', and in the following years from time to time, he produced summaries of recent literature on the Old Testament. A most important account appeared in 1928 under the title 'Recent Developments in Old Testament Criticism', being a John Rylands Library Lecture and containing a detailed survey of twentieth-century discussion. In its concluding paragraph there is the following statement:[3]

The net result of the recent critical movement, it seems to me, is that we are left in the main very much where we were a quarter of a century ago. Reactionary and radical conclusions have still their representatives, new theories make their appearances from time to time. They probably contain their elements of truth and necessitate minor readjustments. I believe that critics will tend steadily to retreat from the extravagance of criticism represented by such writers as Duhm, Marti and Hölscher. But I am disinclined to anticipate that we shall see any great movement in the direction of reclaiming Deuteronomy for the pre-prophetic period, to say nothing of Priestly Document. The relative dating of the codes advocated by the Grafians will, I am convinced, remain

---

[1] *P.M.Q.R.*, 1892. p. 116.
[2] *Contemporary Review*, April 1907.
[3] *John Rylands Library Bulletin*, 1928. pp. 29–30.

and the absolute dating will also, I think, not be seriously altered. And in the other departments of Old Testament Criticism I anticipate a similar maintenance of what I may call a central position. . . .

Old Testament criticism for its own sake would have its intellectual interest as the unravelling of a tangled skein; but if that were all it would assuredly not repay the colossal labour which has been lavished upon it. It is because it is the indispensable preliminary to the reconstruction of the history, which in its turn can alone enable us to follow the movement of revelation from its lowly origins to its supernatural heights, that the literary criticism of the Hebrew Scriptures is completely justified by its works.

It should also be noted that Peake contributed four important articles on Old Testament Introduction to *Peake's Commentary on the Bible* (1920): 'The Development of Old Testament Literature'; 'The Chronology of the Old Testament'; 'The Poetical and Wisdom Literature'; 'The Prophetic Literature'.

We now turn to the second category of Peake's Old Testament writing —his commentaries on Old Testament books. It was in this field that he did his most important and lasting work. Five Old Testament commentaries came from his pen, two of which—*Job* and *Jeremiah*—were in 'The Century Bible' series and are still regarded as important.

In 1905 Peake published the commentary of *Job*, a natural sequence following his book on *The Problem of Suffering in the Old Testament* written a year earlier. Twenty years before this, A. B. Davidson had written his commentary,[1] and in the interval new problems had arisen. New commentaries, mainly in German, had been produced, but were not available to English readers. To Peake this seemed to justify a statement of the position as it stood in 1905, but he also felt that he had his own contribution to make. So he came to produce a commentary which for the reader who has no theological training is still the best available, and it can hold its own alongside the more technical works being read by the more advanced student.[2] With his intimate knowledge of the vast literature on the subject, as in all his work, he makes use of the suggestions of his predecessors, so that all that was of value in the earlier works finds its place, yet always with due acknowledgement and at the same time with his own evaluation of the issues involved. Thus this volume comes to possess a unity and a standpoint all its own, and marked by extreme clarity of expression.[3] Whilst the Commentary itself takes full note of all

---

[1] A. B. Davidson (vol. i. 1862—all that was published) and in addition in the *Cambridge Bible* (1884). The latter was issued in a revised edition by H. C. O. Lanchester in 1951.

[2] 'If we had to select one book instead of ten our choice would inevitably fall on this, for it is an admirable introduction for the lay reader, and a work which is indispensable for the trained student.' *The Expositor*.

[3] J. H. Moulton to A.S.P., 20 February 1905. '. . . I must no longer keep waiting my words of heartiest thanks for the little book. The Introduction is simply splendid. The man must have no music in his soul who isn't moved to eloquence on such a theme; and when one of your calibre gets on it the result is something to remember. . . . That you have produced *the* edition

the results of recent research and presents careful investigation of all the critical problems involved, perhaps the most fascinating part of the book is to be found in the brilliant Introduction, in which Peake is seen at his best.[1] His deep appreciation of the richness of Hebrew poetry is illustrated by the following excerpt:

Man's brief life is like the flower opening in beauty and suddenly cut down, the swiftness with which it passes is illustrated by the weaver's shuttle, the courier, the speed of the light skiffs on the river, or of the eagle as it swoops on its prey. The completeness of his disappearance from the earth when he passes into Sheol is compared with the vanishing of the cloud.... Natural phenomena are described by graphic images. Clouds formed the garment and swaddling band for the infant sea, new-born from the bowels of the chaotic deep.... The dawn is a woman creeping over the crest of the hill, and the rays of light are her eyelashes. Darkness is a coverlet in which the wicked are shrouded from sight, suddenly the light comes and twitches the covering away, so that the wicked are shaken out of it, and stand revealed in the glow of day. And under the light the world lies all clear like clay freshly stamped by the seal, or like a body clothed with its close-fitting robe. The caracole of the horse is compared to the leaping of the locust....

And with what power and beauty are the marvels of the universe set forth! The laying of its foundations amid the songs of the morning stars, and the joyous shouts of the sons of God; the birth of the sea, and the staying of its tumultuous heavenward leap; the punctual dayspring flooding the world with light; the springs that feed the sea from the nether deep; the gates of Sheol; the dwelling of light and darkness; the stores of hail and snow made ready for God's battles; the sluice cut through the firmament by which the torrential rain descends; the frost that turns the streams to stone; the rain that falls on the waste afar from man; the nightly constellations, obedient to God's behest; the lightning with its purposeful movement—all pass before the mind as God unrolls the panorama of the universe.

To the writing of the commentary Peake brought a rare combination of qualities—ripe scholarship, spiritual insight penetrating far beyond the husk of mere grammar, and a faculty of expression charming in its ease and lucidity.[2]

---

of *Job* for some time to come cannot be questioned.... A year which has brought me two such books as the Hartley Lecture and the *Job* is indeed *annus mirabilis*.'

A further letter came from Professor C. H. Herford, Professor of English Literature in Manchester University, dated 7 November, 1910. 'The Edition of *Job* appears to me in one sense, even more direct, as an edition of a great literary classic; in which capacity it seems to me, measured by all the standards that can be qualified to apply, altogether admirable. I may say that I lately found it of practical service in dealing with a London "extension" dissertation on "The Book of Job" compared with "Prometheus Bound".'

[1] 'Peake always regarded this book as the best of his earlier works and some are of the opinion that it was never surpassed by anything he did later.' L.S.P., *Memoir*, p. 229.

[2]. Two interesting letters make reference to Peake's book. Professor Gilbert Murray wrote, 2 July, 1905: 'I should like very much indeed to have your Commentary on Job, especially as a present from you. I have just seen it in the libraries, but I have never worked at Job. Curiously enough, George Adam Smith once suggested I should try to translate it. I wonder if I could. Probably my Hebrew is not equal to the task.'

The second commentary, also in 'The Century Bible' series, is on *The Book of Jeremiah* and *Lamentations*, in two volumes in 1910 and 1912. Peake recognized that the Book of Jeremiah had suffered from 'an ungrateful neglect', for whilst in Germany some of the greatest Old Testament scholars had done important work, the last significant commentary in English was that of T. K. Cheyne, written some twenty-five years earlier. In the Preface Peake declares that it was Wellhausen's article 'Israel' in the ninth edition of the *Encyclopaedia Britannica* which first opened his eyes in his undergraduate days to the significance of Jeremiah. Later the impression was deepened by 'the truly wonderful pages' given to him in the same author's *Israelitisch und Jüdische Geschichte* (1894). He acknowledges his deep indebtedness to the work of Graf, Giesebrecht, Duhm and above all to Cornhill, 'with whose standpoint he is glad to find himself largely in sympathy'.[1] In the writing of his commentary he admits to his 'hero-worship' of Jeremiah, 'to which I am happy to plead guilty'! As a critic his attitude is conservative, though no problem of the book is left unconsidered. 'The author gives the impression that he is determined to allow nothing to be taken from Jeremiah to which the prophet has any reasonable claim.'[2] The book contains an excellent Introduction, covering seventy pages, and it consists of a discussion of Jeremiah's life and times, the prophet's teaching and appraisement of the literary value of the book. In particular Peake emphasizes the fact that many arbitrary decisions arrived at on the basis of metrical hypotheses are not well-founded, and avoids the delusion that everything in the way of manipulation of the text, seeking to improve the order or increase the literary beauty of a passage is *ipso facto* justified. The discussion concerning the problem of the relationship of the Greek and Hebrew texts is particularly valuable. The commentary itself is marked by the lucid exegesis that characterises Peake's work. 'The editor's comments really interpret' is the comment of a distinguished Jewish scholar.[3]

As in the case of his commentary on *Job*, Peake recognizes the richness of the poetic quality of *Jeremiah*, but it was the greatness of Jeremiah's character that most appealed to him. In his view no prophet more nearly approached Jesus in his abandonment of himself to his mission, and in

---

Theodore Watts-Dunton wrote to the late Mr Sydney Walton: 'I return you, with many and best thanks, the copy of the 'Century Bible' edition of 'The Book of Job' which you sent me. I have been studying it a good deal and have a copy for myself. It is a thing to possess and you have done me a real service by directing my attention to it'.

[1] A review by Dr Max Lohr of Konisberg, in *Theologische Literaturzeitung* (18 February 1911).

[2] W. L. Wardle in *P.M.L.* 8 December 1910, speaks of Peake's 'astonishingly accurate judgment of the exposition of these German scholars'.

[3] Dr Israel Abrahams in reviewing the book in the *Jewish Chronicle*. The same writer also remarks: 'Professor Peake rightly refuses to follow Duhm in making rhythm the *test* of the authenticity of passages in the book. Jeremiah used a particular rhythm, but not everything in Jeremiah which does not display that rhythm should be regarded as spurious.'

his conception of personal religion, and in turn it is significant that he prefixes a quotation from F. W. H. Myers' 'St Paul' to his book.[1] The following excerpt from Peake's Introduction may be allowed:

There is no one in the Old Testament who speaks to our imagination and our sympathy as this lonely and tragic figure. He was not without great merit as a poet; he portrays Nature and human emotions with the hand of a master, and strikes the deep chords within us as few have done. But it is the man himself who most appeals to us. We hear him crying to God to let his cup pass from him, and yet we see him forced to drain it to the dregs. We can tell one by one the bitter ingredients mingled in his draught; the dark sins of his people that had grown inveterate, the lighthearted folly with which it went dancing on the road to its inevitable destruction, the scorn and hatred heaped upon him for treason to the country he loved beyond his life, the irritation at his rebukes, the incredibility of his warnings. We watch him as he staggers and totters under the weight of the cross to which God had doomed him, a life-long agony for the sins and sorrows of his people, for God's pain and his own. It is God alone who can relieve him. But it was God who appointed his task and would not relent. And thus we find in his book a new thing. Unlike other prophets he has written down for us his emotions, his heart-broken appeals to God. Thus he becomes the prophet of personal religion because he has learnt the deepest meaning of religion in his own personal fellowship with God. So he rose to his conception of the New Covenant and anticipated in that great prophecy the central truth of Christianity.[2]

In the spring of 1929, when on a tour of Palestine and Egypt, Peake, with one member of the party, rode out upon a donkey—the only available means of transport—to visit Anathoth, on pilgrimage. He said, with some amusement, that if in the world beyond he should meet Jeremiah, he would like to be able to tell him that he had visited his birthplace!

Included in these volumes is the commentary on *The Book of Lamentations*. Peake sets aside the traditional view and discerns four different writers: the poems cannot be dated within very close limits, though probably chapters two and four are the oldest, written by one who had witnessed the tragedy of the exile, and not later than 580 B.C.: chapter five, and possibly chapter one, probably towards the close of the exile; chapter three would seem to have been written later. Peake is aware however that arguments for a pre-exile date are not without force. The same careful critical approach lies beneath this commentary as in the case of those previously considered.

The three remaining Old Testament commentaries written by Peake are to be found in *Peake's Commentary on the Bible (1920)*, and by the

---

[1] 'It would not be too much to say that what Paul was to Peake in the New Testament Jeremiah was to him in the Old Testament.' L. S. Peake in *Memoir*, p. 253.

[2] Op cit., p. 30. Of the Commentary J. H. Moulton wrote: 'It will fill an aching void for a long time to come: no one will try to supersede it, and any attempt would be likely to fail.' J. H. M. to A. S. P., 30 October 1910.

nature of the case are different in form and length following the general structure of the whole work; the method of treatment being the use of the paragraph rather than the verse-unit, each section being expounded as a whole, though with separate notes where necessary. Each book in the Commentary begins with an Introduction in which the general background is set out. The three Old Testament books with which Peake dealt are *Genesis, Isaiah 1-39*, and *Jonah*. It is not necessary to touch on these in any detail, but sufficient to say that, throughout, the clear and accurate scholarship which marks the larger work is evident, and each commentary is a marvel of exegetical compression.

A further aspect of Peake's work on the Old Testament is to be found in the numerous studies that came from his pen.

In 1908 Peake published *The Religion of Israel*. This small book of less than two hundred pages was in the series of 'Century Bible Handbooks', the purpose of which was to provide instruction for the general reader as a preliminary to tackling larger works, and was intended for use alongside the commentaries in 'The Century Bible'. It is often more difficult to write a short book than to write a long one, and this small work is a marvel of compression and lucidity. In twelve chapters Peake sketches the growth of Israel's faith from 'the rise of the religion' to 'the waning of prophecy', and its transformation to apocalypse in the Book of Daniel. A thirteenth chapter deals with 'the sages and the psalmists'; finally he adds 'a brief account of the leading doctrines of Judaism'. Written from the critical standpoint it takes for granted a moderate acquaintance with this position, but it is written without technical reference. Owing to the imposed limitations, complicated problems are sometimes summed up and solved within a line or two, sometimes even in less. This limitation of space was also responsible for the omission of any sketch of Semitic religion and for more than the slightest account of the religious institutions of Israel. For the non-theological reader this book provided an introduction to the subject, as Wellhausen had done for scholars twenty years earlier.[1]

The book was greatly esteemed by Dr J. H. Moulton who wrote:

By dint of keeping your little book in my pocket for train journeys and other similar opportunities, I am able to thank you heartily for it, and assure you that I have lost no time in reading it. Certainly the time I have spent in reading it has been spent to pleasure and profit alike. It is as good as anything you have done—as clear as it could be and extraordinarily interesting.[2]

Professor Herford described it as 'a wonderful example of compressed

---

[1] J. Wellhausen, *Prolegomena sur Geschichte Israels*. (1883) Eng. trans. 1885.
[2] J. H. Moulton to A. S. P., 11 September 1908. Cf. Prof. A. Bertholet, Professor of Theology at Basle: 'I have read it from first to the last pages with unintermitting pleasure and very great agreement.' 25 October 1908.

and concentrated learning in a narrative which is always luminous and sometimes eloquent'.[1]

It was Peake's intention to write a two-volume work on the same subject, and he makes frequent mention of it in his letters. That would undoubtedly have proved to be a great work, but unfortunately he was never able, under the countless pressures on his time and strength, to fulfil it.

In 1904 Peake wrote what proved to be one of the most widely read of all his books, *The Problem of Suffering in the Old Testament*,[2] which was an expansion of the Hartley Lecture, delivered in Carr's Lane Church, Birmingham,[3] and was dedicated to his friend and teacher, Dr Fairbairn, who, on receiving a copy of the book, wrote, 'This last memorial of your affection I shall earnestly treasure!'[4]

The book sprang very much out of Peake's own experience. In the Preface he wrote:

I am only one of many for whom the problem of pain constitutes the most powerful objection to a theism adequate to our deepest needs.... Yet I shall be more than content if by my witness-bearing I help some souls, to whom the world's misery is a nightmare, to escape beyond it into untroubled peace.

Thus Peake's purpose was a distinctively practical one: 'What does the Old Testament contribute to the solving of the problem of suffering?'

The approach adopted is the historical one. Peake begins by pointing out that in the earliest times the problem did not exist. The sufferings of the people were simply traced to the wrath of God on account of national disobedience, the woes of Israel being the fruit of her own ill-doing and were, therefore, to be regarded as righteous retribution. This consciousness of national sinfulness was so intense in the prophets that Amos, Isaiah and Jeremiah felt no surprise at the suffering that was the portion of Israel. Yet as time passed conditions changed. The national conscience was aroused by the discovery of the law and the promulgation of Josiah's reforms. The discipline of the exile turned the hearts as never before towards their God, and it became a severe trial of their faith, when, as loyal subjects of Yahweh, they seemed apparently forsaken by him and given over to their enemies. This was the perplexity in the mind of

---

[1] C. H. Herford to A.S.P., 7 November 1910.
[2] The book was reprinted by Epworth Press in 1947.
[3] It is worth while to record the impression of one who, on that occasion heard the lecture. 'Professor Peake, without any embellishment of oratory, held the audience for an hour and a half by sheer force of intellect and luminous statement, covering in that time a wide field and marshalling a vast array of facts in a way only possible to one who is thoroughly conversant with the subject. It was a spiritual stimulus that will abide for many a day.' *The Primitive Methodist*, 7 July 1904.
[4] A. M. Fairbairn to A.S.P., 15 June 1904. Some two years before Peake had discussed the subject with Fairbairn, who thoroughly approved of it, and at the close of a long letter (26 May, 1902) wrote: 'If you can give the idea such an expansion as I hint at, you could, I think, make the lecture a notable contribution to Christian thought and biblical theology.'

Habbakuk and the lament of heart-broken psalmists. It was Ezekiel who endeavoured to justify the ways of God to men. The dawn began to break, however, in the utterances of the Servant of Yahweh[1] in the Second Isaiah, to whom it was given to see in part at least the meaning of the mystery. Here is the first conception that suffering may be vicarious, and hence redemptive and regenerative in its influence. The poem of Job carries this line of thought still further, with the difference that here we are concerned with the individual rather than the nation—not with God's discipline of his people, but with the government of the universe. There comes the vision of God, which in satisfaction and acceptance of the divine will, there is release to rest and peace.[2] In the final chapter entitled 'Solution or Escape?' Peake declares that, while the Old Testament goes far in interpretation of the problem, yet it is not a solution: all speculative attempts at an answer break down,[3] but there is a way of escape, and this way of escape is indicated in the striking motto by Raymond Brucker which Peake placed upon the title-page:

Dieu, c'est le mot de l'énigme du monde:
Jésus Christ, c'est le mot de l'énigme de Dieu.

The key to the mystery lies in the Cross of Christ—the assurance of God's unfailing love, and in which the heart may find its ultimate peace.

We have set forth this fairly full analysis of this book because it reveals not only Peake's application of the historical principle of biblical interpretation, and his power to grasp the sweep of thought, but a profound insight into human need. In this book he speaks from the depths of his own experience.

It is not surprising that this great book received widespread commendation—in the words of one reviewer,[4] 'an instinctive and often very beautiful study of the perplexed minds which were seeking an explanation of sorrow they could not understand'. Perhaps the highest commendation is to be found in a review by Professor Bertholet, once a pupil of Duhm, and at the time Professor of Theology in the University of Basle, an acute critic who was one of the most accomplished of the younger continental scholars:

[1] An interesting change in Peake's interpretation of 'The Servant of Yaweh' is recorded. He had always resisted Duhn's plea for identification with an individual, and had insisted that the Servant should be identified with Israel, giving his adherence to the theory of the Servant as the *ideal* Israel, as expounded e.g. by Professor Skinner. Under the influence of Giesebrecht, however, he came to feel that the true identification was with the *historical* Israel, and this is the view Peake takes in this book, a view from which he never departed. It may be noted in connection with the Servant Songs, Peake gives in these pages his own luminous translation of the poems.

[2] 'To trust God, when we have every reason for distrusting him, is the supreme victory of religion. This is the victory which Job achieved' op. cit., p. 88.

[3] 'The most valuable thing the Old Testament has to offer us is not a speculative solution. It is the inner certainty of God, which springs out of fellowship with Him, and, defying all the crushing proofs that the world is unrighteous, holds its faith in Him fast' op. cit. p. 127.

[4] *The Guardian*, 5 October 1904.

To have set out frankly, and with so much clearness, the simple relative value of the attempt of the Old Testament to solve the question under consideration is above all, in a book intended for the laity, a most notable service, which I wish to call attention to with all possible emphasis.[1]

Some reviewers, however, levelled criticism against the book; in some cases because they felt that discussion of the purity of the text, questions of date and authorship, had been intruded into the book (though in fact these matters were almost entirely in footnotes and appendices); in other cases, because Peake had asserted the crucial importance of a trinitarian doctrine[2] as presenting the final 'escape' from the problem. But Peake's position is made entirely clear in a passage which may be regarded as a personal confession of his faith in the fact of Jesus Christ:

It is not given to me to stand where many stand, to surrender a belief in his Divinity, and yet to hold fast a faith in God's goodness. The longer I ponder the world's pain in itself, the more it seems to deny a moral government of the world, and the more I feel drawn to the conviction that on this, the greatest of all questions, *Ecclesiastes* has said the last word. And if I do not yield to this temptation it is because I ponder it also in the light of the Cross, on which the Son of God manifested the eternal love.[3]

In 1926 Peake delivered three important lectures at King's College, London, which were published in 1931 after his death. The subject of these lectures was *The Servant of Yahweh*, and with great skill he summarizes the theories which scholars have put forward as interpretations of the Servant, dealing first with those which hold the individual hypothesis, and then passing on to a consideration of the collective interpretation, finally declaring his own position to be that of the Servant as the empirical Israel—not a righteous kernel, not an ideal Israel, but Israel from the ideal point of view. In the concluding portion of the lectures Peake considers the secondary application of the Servant-poems which has been current in the Christian Church. He writes:

That the poet had the application to Jesus in mind seems to me excluded by the language of the poems, however striking the coincidence may be. But I fully believe that these passages meant much for Jesus himself.... If we could identify Israel with Jesus then the Christian application would be justified not exegetically but in principle. The Christian belief is that Jesus was the supreme revelation of God, and the sufferer for the world's sin. From that point of view the application would be justified. We could think of Him as the true Servant of Yahweh, and in him the essential significance of Israel, as the poet defines it, was concentrated.

In these lectures there is basic material which would have been used in

---

[1] Review translated from the German in the *Deutsch Literaturzeitung*, 11 March 1905.
[2] The *Yorkshire Daily Observer*, 28 July 1904. 'Jesus can become all that he is to the author without the metaphysical doctrine insisted upon.'
[3] Op. cit., p. 130.

the long-awaited commentary on Isaiah 40–66, in the *International Critical Commentary*, of which Peake's death deprived us.

From his early days Peake had a strong and sensitive concern for social issues, and this undoubtedly lay behind his readiness to accept the invitation to deliver the John Clifford Lecture in 1923. This he did at Stockport, on 17 September, under the auspices of the Brotherhood Movement,[1] an organization which strongly held his interest and sympathy and which he believed to be a strong moral and religious force in the life of the nation. The book bore the title *Brotherhood in the Old Testament* and contained a collection and classification of material, which resulted in a comprehensive picture of Hebrew society in its various aspects. Soundly based on Peake's critical position, he yet believed that 'those who prefer a more traditional attitude will find the value of the book but little impaired for their purpose'.

The book is frank in its discussion as it indicates without reserve the limitations of the Hebrew outlook on social issues, as well as showing the higher development of Hebrew legislation and custom. The main expressions of corporate life in the Old Testament are discussed in chapters on the family, slavery in Israel, friendship, the poor and defenceless, the administration of justice; sins against the brotherhood; war and peace; the unity of Israel and its relation to other people.

The book was timely for it expressed in its distinctive teaching those principles which sociologists at that time were also seeking to expound— the obligation of every man to every other man in the structure of the social order.

Two monographs on the Old Testament, both delivered as John Rylands Library lectures, must be noticed, being, as they are, extreme examples of Peake's accurate scholarship. In 1923 he published *The Roots of Hebrew Prophecy and Jewish Apocalyptic*.[2] After a careful survey of the evidence Peake asserts that 'it must still be regarded as very questionable whether there was in early Israel any developed eschatology at all.'[3] Passing on to the origin of Jewish Apocalyptic, he suggests that the general distinction may be best realized by placing *Amos* as a typical prophetic book alongside *Daniel*. The destruction of Jerusalem brought a transformation within the whole character of prophecy. The stroke of judgement had fallen and henceforth the prophet must provide for the future. The actual transformation is found in the message of Ezekiel. The anticipations of the prophets are conditioned by contemporary political conditions: deliverance can only come by Divine intervention.

---

[1] At one of their National Conferences Peake had read a paper on 'Spiritual Ideals of the Brotherhood Movement'.
[2] *John Rylands Library Bulletin*, January, 1922: reprinted, with slight additions in *H.R.* 1924.
[3] Op. cit., p. 15.

A natural systematization followed, a coherent scheme of future history, believing that the programme of history was laid down by God, to be interpreted in terms of varied symbolism. If to ourselves apocalyptic is likely to seem a decadent form of prophecy, it should be remembered that apocalypticism appealed to men of their own age, and represents an important element in the development in the history of Judaism and calls for a tribute to the amazing courage of the author's faith.

With a hostile world all about them, a world polytheistic and idolatrous, with the civil forces, military, political, social and intellectual massed against them, with sinister supernatural powers, as they believed, marshalling their forces against them, their faith rose to unprecedented heights. . . . Even when strength and endurance seemed to be strained to the uttermost, they nerved themselves still to bear their tortures, confident that the end was very near, and that soon in one radiant moment the kingdoms of this world would become the Kingdom of their God and his Messiah.[1]

The publication of this monograph was timely, as was the case with so much of Peake's writing. He possessed a remarkable insight into the relation between the message of the Bible and the thought and movements of his own age. The war had brought a strong resurgence of millenial ideas and his writing embodied an attempt to reassert a true philosophy of history.

All who are familiar with the history of modern interpretation of prophecy on apocalyptic lines are well aware that nothing is more common than to find the interpreter quite in good faith fixing the critical events in his own immediate future. It is a human frailty to believe that the times in which we live are specially important in the world's history. And if we are preoccupied with millenial speculation we easily find reason for believing that the end is very near. It is this conviction which, whether consciously or unconsciously largely guides the quest for identification of events in history, with prediction in prophecy and apocalyptic.[2]

The second monograph, *Elijah and Jezebel: The Conflict with the Tyrian Baal*[3] deals with a difficult subject. Most of the discussion of the problem raised was in German literature, and therefore inaccessible to English readers. Two points in Peake's argument were of particular interest: his contention for the high probability that there was a great set-back of the Tyrian cult in the reign of Ahab; his treatment of the ever fascinating 'gentle whisper' which Elijah heard from Yahweh in the theophany at Horeb. He leaves the reader in no doubt as to the greatness of Elijah as the prophet of Israel. We may quote the final paragraph:

The work which Elijah did was of incalculable value for the religion of Israel. It was the lofty privilege of that people to be the trustee of monotheism. Even

[1] Op. cit., pp. 23f.
[2] *John Rylands Library Bulletin*, p. 21 January 1923.
[3] Ibid., July 1927

if at that time monotheism was not the prophet's explicit and formulated creed, yet the monolatry which he undoubtedly championed took him a long way on the road.... He did not indeed stand alone, but he towered above all his fellow-workers in the vindication of Yahweh's right to the sole allegiance of his people. And his monolatry was an ethical monolatry.... Not without reason did later generations find in him the fittest comparison to couple with the great founder of the religion.

III

We now turn to Peake's work in the field of New Testament study. In 1919 he published his *Critical Introduction to the New Testament*, which was intended to serve those who were without leisure to study a lengthier volume, and also for some who would find a useful preparation for the study of more detailed works. Peake had provided a general approach to the subject in the second half of his essay on 'the Present Movement of Biblical Science' in *Inaugural Lectures by Members of the Faculty of Theology*, Manchester 1905. Written by scientific method, Peake declares with candour that his sole desire is to be 'loyal to the facts' and that he is 'conscious of no wish to be in the critical fashion or out of it'. As in all his writing, the book shows evidence of the author's mastery of all recent literature on the subject, especially the work of German scholars, but these are handled impartially and without dogmatic prejudice, yet his own judgements are clearly indicated.

The book is a complete summary of the results reached by modern critical examination at the time of writing. It had a wide influence, was many times reprinted, and in 1910 was published in America.[1]

Principal W. B. Selbie, of Mansfield College, Oxford, wrote to Peake:

I congratulate you on it most heartily. It seems to me just the kind of book that is needed, and Souter is going to use it here freely. How you manage to pour out things as you do passes my comprehension![2]

Professor George Milligan of Glasgow, wrote:

I was deep this morning in your *Introduction*. You have certainly the faculty of, if I may be allowed to say so, making abstract discussion clear.[3]

An interesting note on the book came from John R. Mott, the great ecumenical traveller, from Heidelberg, written to Dr D. S. Cairns, who, writing to Peake opened his own letter after sealing it, to insert the following:[4]

---

[1] Peake also wrote a useful Introduction to *The Pauline Epistles* in *Peake's Commentary* (1920).
[2] W. B. Selbie to A.S.P., 4 November 1909.
[3] G. Milligan to A.S.P., August 1910.
[4] D. S. Cairns to A.S.P., 25 July 1912.

I have been through Peake's book once and am going on the second round. He is so fair and so broad that he has quite captivated me and I want all my friends to read his *Introduction*.

As in the case of the Old Testament, so Peake's work in the New Testament field may be grouped into two categories—his work as a commentator on separate books, and his studies in New Testament themes. We turn now to the first of these groups.

Four commentaries on New Testament books came from his pen, two of them in the earlier years. His first commentary was on Colossians published in 1902 in *The Expositor's Greek Testament*, of which Dr W. Robertson Nicoll was the editor. As early as 1894 Nicoll had written to Peake:[1]

> ... I am getting up a Greek New Testament, the size of Alford's. Would you care to undertake one of the Pauline Epistles? Romans is allotted and also Philippians, but at the moment I think no other. Write to say what you think about this. You would have about two years to do it. Please keep this plan strictly private.

Peake's work on Colossians was completed by September 1898, but on account of the lateness of the other contributors in sending in their work for the volume, it did not appear until 1902, much to Peake's disappointment. Peake secured one great advantage for this commentary—namely permission to choose his Greek text,[2] whereas in the first two volumes of the commentary the Textus Receptus had been printed. It was owing to Peake's persistence that this choice of text was allowed for all subsequent contributors.

Peake admits that his chief concern was to expound the thought of the Epistle, the philological side having been represented by the English commentaries, specially in that of Lightfoot. A lengthy and very valuable section of the Introduction discusses the question of angelology, and, in regard to the false teaching to which the Epistle was directed, Peake rejects both Gnosticism and Essenism as its source; he holds that its origin lies in Judaism. 'We are certain of the Jewish nature of the teaching and if it can be explained from Judaism alone, we have no warrant for calling in other sources.' Written from Rome c. A.D. 59 the Epistle is accepted 'with confidence as the work of Paul'.

Reviewing the work Professor A. S. Geden declared: 'Of the work of Professor Peake on the Colossians there is nothing but good to be written.'

Peake's earliest commentary was *The Epistle to the Hebrews* (in the 'Century Bible' series) which he wrote in 1902. Again it is an example of his remarkable powers of compression, for all the admittedly difficult

---

[1] W. R. Nicoll to A.S.P., 30 May 1894.
[2] Ibid., 17 August (?): 'Please make your own text. I have come to the conclusion that upon the whole this will be the best way.'

issues associated with the book are dealt with, both in the Introduction and in the commentary itself. The central message of the Epistle could hardly be more forcibly expressed than in the following:

Christianity is that heavenly original of which Judaism is the flickering and insubstantial shadow. Its revealer is no perishable angel, who lives only that he may serve, or ceases to live that as impersonal force he may serve the better. He is the Eternal Son, Creator of the Universe and Lord of the world to come. Radiance of the Divine Glory and expression of the Divine Essence, he was the perfect revelation of God. Of heavenly origin he could lead his followers into God's heavenly rest.... Thus Christianity proved itself to be the perfect religion, in that it perfectly satisfied the religious instinct for fellowship with God.[1]

Dr Marcus Dods wrote in 1910:

Peake has a rare gift of compact lucidity. No better book could be conceived or is needed for English readers. Nothing better has been written on the Epistle than his chapter on its teaching.[2]

Two declarations in the Introduction to the book were important for the time when the commentary was written. The first was Peake's insistence that the Epistle could not be Pauline—for the traditional position on Pauline authorship was still widespread.

Nothing is so certain with respect to the authorship as the negative conclusion that it was not written by Paul. This is proved by a number of independent lines of argument, any one of which would suffice to make his authorship improbable, while some are quite inconsistent with it.[3]

Apart even from matters of language, style and structure, one line of argument may be regarded as conclusive, as illustrating the difference between the Epistle and the Pauline writings:

The differences as to the appropriation of salvation are even more radical. With Paul everything is included in union with the crucified and risen Lord, and participation in his experience. This is the very heart of the Pauline theology, but not a trace of it is to be found in *Hebrews*. Christ is our brother, who owns the ties of kinship, our Captain, our Forerunner, who dedicates the way to the holiest by his blood, by which we may follow him.... Never do we read that he is joined to the Lord in one Spirit, or hear any echo of Paul's immortal words: 'I have been crucified with Christ, and it is no longer I that live but Christ that liveth in me.'[4]

Further, seeking on the positive side for some declaration as to authorship, Peake sets aside the claims mentioned in tradition—Barnabas, Luke, Clement of Rome, Silas, Apollos and Peter—in each case giving careful consideration to each of these. He finds himself attracted to a theory then

---

[1] Op cit., p. 19.
[2] M. Dods, 'The Epistle to the Hebrews' in *E.G.T.* vol. iv. p. 244.
[3] Op cit., p. 28.
[4] Op cit., p. 32.

recently put forth by Harnack,[1] suggesting that the letter may have been written by Priscilla and Aquila, the former being the actual writer.

Peake's book was widely appreciated not only in this country, but in the United States. His old friend, Thomas Dyke, by this time a minister in Montana, sent to him the following notice:

> Professor Peake presents this topic in a manner at once scholarly and popular. We have never seen a volume on this anonymous epistle which was so full of helpful and suggestive material. Such a volume ought to be heartily welcome.[2]

The Rev. Samuel Pearson, of Broughton Park Congregational Church, and Chairman of the Lancashire College Committee, wrote:[3]

> I want to thank you very much for *Hebrews*. It is the only book I have brought away for this fortnight's rest, and well has it repaid me.... It has already given me an insight into the meaning of the Epistle which I never had before, and I think I could not better express my gratitude than by stating that fact. Its lucidity, comprehensiveness, compactness and fulness are very striking—and are all that I should have expected from work of yours.

A similar comment came from his former teacher, Dr Fairbairn:[4]

> Let me thank you for your book on *Hebrews*.... It is excellent, lucid, cautious, well constructed and well balanced. There are some points on which we should possibly differ, but the book as a whole could not be better.

In 1910 Peake published his *Heroes and Martyrs of Faith*,[5] a series of studies on the figures named in the famous eleventh chapter of the Epistle to the Hebrews, 'the bede-roll of great exemplars'.[6] The work possesses a devotional emphasis and is in no way concerned with critical or historical problems. The exegetical basis of the exposition of this chapter is to be found in the commentary. The book shows 'remarkable combination of entire simplicity with remarkable freshness'.[7]

---

[1] Op. cit., p. 37. Harnack in *ZNTW* (1900). Cf. Peake in *Critical Introduction to the New Testament* (1909 and later ed.). M. Dods, *E.G.T.* vol. iv. pp. 228–9.

[2] *The Pilgrim Teacher* (Congregationalist), Boston. 1902. Cf. B. W. Bacon to A.S.P., 3 June 1902 from New Haven, Conn.: 'your excellent commentary of *Hebrews!*'

[3] S. Pearson to A.S.P., 14 June 1902.

[4] A. M. Fairbairn to A.S.P., 5 March 1902.

[5] The chapters of the book were originally written as a series of articles in *P.M.L.* during 1908–9.

[6] *Manchester Guardian*, 25 April 1910.

[7] The following letter is worthy of quotation not only for its reference to the book, but for its own sake. J. H. Moulton to A.S.P., 7 March 1910:

> I expect we shall meet tonight but I must drop you a line of very hearty thanks for your delightful book. I have truly lost no time in reading it, for a timely week-end and a train journey—I have just been beyond your Mecca, Mow Cop—enabled me to finish it just as we neared London Road this morning. It is wholly worthy of you and it is quite needless to say more. Have you observed how your printer has committed a double blasphemy, by putting a *H* on p. 77 and a *h* on p. 79. It reminds me of the first edition of our new hymn-book, in which we were even turned into Mithraists by being made to sing:
>
> Jesus shall reign where'er the sun
> Doth *His* successive journeys run!

In 1920 Peake wrote the commentary on 1 *Corinthians* in *Peake's Commentary on the Bible*—again another example of his exceptional skill in compressing so much into so small a compass, no problem of the Epistle being left unconsidered.

In 1916 Peake gave a second Hartley Lecture, *The Revelation of John*. He was called upon at a few month's notice to take the place of another, and out of his immense store of learning he produced a masterly survey of the complicated theories, together with criticism and evaluation, which had been advanced on the questions of history, interpretation, and theology of this most difficult New Testament book—and in the second half of the work he gave an exposition of each section of the Apocalypse. A closing chapter dealt with its permanent value. The reader is able to follow the main movement in the drama without being lost in a maze of intricate problems which might arise in the discussion of minute details.

The writing of the book also was timely, following shortly after the close of the World War, because there were many who turned to its mysterious contents, regarding it as authoritative for a scheme of history and setting forth the future scheme, if only its symbolism could be elucidated. Peake decisively rejected both the 'futurist' and the 'continuous-historical' lines of approach, and if he appears to give an undue space to these speculations, the reason for so doing is clear. 'The great vogue given to continuous-historical interpretation by the European War makes it a matter of duty to explain why this whole system is to be repudiated both in principle and in detail and in all its forms.'[1] Peake affirms that the only theory which will afford solution is the praeterist; the Apocalypse is concerned with the contemporary situation and its immediate outcome.

Of this book Dr H. T. Andrews wrote in review:

Dr Peake's book will be for many years the standard work of its kind on the Apocalypse—and it is to be hoped that his frank statement of the modern position will clear away the mist of doubt and superstition that clings to the Apocalypse. He has embodied all that is best in the writing of his predecessors, and added to their discussion many new suggestions of considerable interest and importance.[2]

There is no clearer example of Peake's insistence that in all matters of

---

[1] Op. cit., p. viii.

[2] *H.R.* January, 1920. J. Estlin Carpenter wrote to Peake (21 March 1920): 'I admire the ease with which you carry so much learning and still more the simplicity and directness with which each position is faced and handled. You state alternatives with so much clearness and your judgments are expressed with such moderation that none of those whose views you criticise can take exception to a word.'

Also Professor R. S. Conway wrote (26 February, 1920): 'To my thanks let me add my warmest congratulations on the completion of such a substantial addition to knowledge; on the uniform and irresistible gentleness of its style—a real πειθοῦς ἱερόν—above all on the resolute courage with which you follow the Λόγος—for that is how to write it, not λόγος merely, and lead us all, humbly but most gratefully, after you.'

biblical interpretation the scientific, historical approach and method cannot be dispensed with if truth is to be discovered. Yet, as so often in his expositions, by his spiritual insight he lifts the reader to an understanding of the eternal quality of the Scriptures. Thus he writes in the concluding chapter:

What is of value to us is the author's undaunted conviction that the evils from which our world suffers are doomed to pass away, and that here on earth the kingdom of God is to be established.... Age after age men and women, passing through great tribulation or desolate from some sore bereavement, have found it as they have read of the countless hosts who passed from rivers of blood to fountains of living water, from the ruthless cruelty of men to the healing pity of God. And they think with longing and with hope of that blessed future in which the heart will never be hungry nor the spirit athirst, when they shall dwell in the gracious shadow of God, and His tender hand shall wipe away all tears from their eyes.

Four monographs, forming New Testament studies, call for notice at this point. In 1924 Peake gave two lectures on *The Messiah and the Son of Man* at the John Rylands Library.[1] In the first lecture he sought to establish the fact that Jesus believed Himself to be the Messiah; in the second he opened up the question of what this messianic consciousness involved. The reserve of Jesus in proclaiming his Messiahship lay in the essential difference of view between Jesus and His disciples as to its character. There is full justification for believing that Jesus connected the idea of the Son of Man directly with his passion. He may have combined with it the idea of the Servant of Yahweh. After a searching investigation for an interpretation of the title Peake arrives at the conclusion that 'we are safest if we start from the eschatalogical associations of the phrase, and recognize that extensions of the meaning were given to it by Jesus in consequence of His conviction as to what the vocation involved: while further extensions were due to the consciousness of his identity with the Son of Man'.[2]

Of this study Professor J. E. McFadyen, of Glasgow, wrote to Peake.[3]

... Written with all your customary lucidity, and with a simplicity which would beguile the unwary or the uninitiated into supposing that the problems were easy ones, your argument seems to me very cogent and very fair throughout. You always treat an honest enemy with the courtesy which is his due, and it seems to me your conclusion must stand, especially as the linguistic difficulty does not appear to be fatal.... I hope the discussion will reach a wider public; it is the kind of thing of which we have too little in English.

The following letter reveals the personal impact of this monograph upon

---

[1] *J.R.L.B.* January, 1924.
[2] Op cit., p. 30.
[3] J. E. McFadyen to A.S.P., 25 March 1924.

one who, as a classical scholar, had wrestled with the issues in the realm of his own experience.[1] Professor R. S. Conway writes:

... If it was a less vitally grave subject I should call it nothing short of brilliant, and it would be true in any case. The open and frank welcome or consideration you give to a great variety of theories, and the keen analysis of their bases and implications, wins one's entire confidence; and your own *method* of separating and *demonstrating* the steps you take in your argument is one of the most, if not *the* most splendid achievement of constructive enquiry that I have ever read. The result is—to me— a quite immeasurable access of light and *certainty* just where I have felt puzzled for years: and to relieve our Lord's character—*ut hominum more loquar*—of a doubt or suspicion, which, however unworthy, has often grieved me because I could only leave it as one of the mysteries still unsolved. Your insight has solved it—insight provided with your own amazing learning. ... You have made a lasting addition to our knowledge in a vital point, and I am deeply grateful to you, as one of the thousands who would like to call themselves Christian, if they were only less unworthy.

Three further John Rylands Library lectures are concerned with the subject of Paul the Apostle. The first entitled *The Quintessence of Paulinism*[2] gives a sketch of Paul's spiritual history, showing the rise of a theology created by and derived from experience in terms of a mystical union of the human spirit with Christ—'the most sympathetic and enlightening statement, in brief compass, of the teaching of St Paul'.[3] It was Dr Alexander Whyte, formerly of New College, Edinburgh, who, retired at Penn, in Buckinghamshire wrote to Peake:

I cannot tell you how much I have enjoyed your *Quintessence of Paulinism*. I am sending it to friends in Scotland.

In 1928 Peake produced a similar lecture, *Paul the Apostle: His Personality and Achievement*, in which he deals with Paul's contacts with paganism, his power as a controversialist, his pre-eminence as an organizer and his achievement in directing the Christian movement into world channels. Again, to quote Dr Howard:[4]

He struck with amazing force into universal history. There is probably no one else living who could pack into twenty-five pages the results of such wide

---

[1] R. S. Conway to A.S.P., 24 March 1924. Professor Conway held the Chair of Imperial Latin at Manchester University.

[2] *J.R.L.B.* October 1918. Reprinted in *The Servant of Yahweh and other Lectures* (1931) and in *Essays in Commemoration* (1958).

[3] W. F. Howard in *Methodist Recorder*, 6 September 1928. Cf. H. Wheeler Robinson in a private letter: 'I think it one of the best concise statements from a modern standpoint which I have seen'. J. Estlin Carpenter wrote from Oxford (30 June 1918): 'Perhaps this sketch—though in itself so finished—is only the prelude to a fuller treatment. All lovers of Paul will welcome a complete exposition from your faithful pen.'

[4] W. F. Howard, in *Methodist Recorder*, 6 September 1928. Cf. A. J. Grieve, 11 September 1928. 'It's a great service that you are rendering to us all in these ripe fruits. Long may the tree continue to bear them.'

reading and such long continued and profound thought upon the Pauline letters and the narrative in Acts.

A year later came a further lecture, *Paul and the Jewish Christians*,[1] in which Peake endeavoured to reconstruct the stages of the emancipation of Christianity from Judaism—a task of considerable difficulty. 'But for the clear insight of Paul into the grave issues which were at stake, the new religion might have been finally stranded in a backwater of Judaism.'[2]

These three lectures contain all that we possess of the larger work on Paul and Paulinism which Peake had hoped and intended to write—which undoubtedly would have proved to be his *magnum opus*. He sets forth his position as to Paul's message in the following sentences:

The secret of the spell which the theology of Paul has cast on multitudes is to be found in the illumination which it has brought to their own spiritual history. They have understood their bondage and their deliverance, their misery and their rapture, as they have entered into his despair or watched him as he passed from that strain of inward conflict and sense of failure to harmony of spirit and untroubled peace with God. A theology created by experience speaks with directness and power to those whose pilgrimage has taken them along the same way. The influence of Paul ebbs and flows along long stretches of history. It shrinks and seems as if it would vanish and then all suddenly it gathers volume and velocity, and the arid waste becomes a garden of God.[3]

IV

As an interpreter of the Bible it was inevitable that Peake should eventually move into the realm of biblical theology, criticism and textual exegesis having been the necessary instruments through which such a theology was to be constructed. It was on such a foundation that Peake rested his own theological position, a statement of which he set forth probably in 1907.[4]

This was the year in which R. J. Campbell produced *The New Theology*, and it was in view of this, and by request, that Peake set down his own theological convictions, in sixteen declarations as being his confession of faith. The following was the statement of his theological position:

1. The term 'new theology' is a misnomer. The positions included under that term are quite familiar.
2. The critical movement which has been going on for more than a century with reference to the Old Testament has, I believe, resulted in establishing the main conclusions of the dominant critical school, popularly associated with the names of Kuenen and Wellhausen.

---

[1] *J.R.L.B.* January 1929.
[2] Op. cit., p. 32.
[3] *The Quintessence of Paulinism*, p.3.
[4] In *The Tribune*, January 1907 and reprinted in *P.M.L.* 7 February 1907.

3. Since Christianity is a revelation in history, it cannot withhold its documents from critical investigation, and this applies not simply to the Old Testament, but also to the New.

4. It is no longer possible for us to base theology on an infallible Bible, nor even upon an infallible New Testament.

5. In spite of this fact Scripture, and especially the New Testament, remains the most important source from which Christian Theology is derived, authenticating itself by the power with which it speaks to the soul and its response to our deepest needs.

6. We walk by faith, not by sight. The search for an infallible authority of any kind is doomed to disappointment.

7. If theology is to be systematic it must be guided by a dominant principle. I find this principle in Christ's doctrine of God, and make the Fatherhood of God the regulative principle of my system of theology.

8. Since the recognition of distinctions within the Godhead seems to me the only adequate safeguard of the love and personality of God, I cannot agree that we have outgrown the doctrine of the Trinity.

9. I hold the doctrine of the Divinity of Christ in the strict sense of the term, regarding Him as the eternal Son of God who assumed humanity that He might reveal God and redeem man.

10. The pre-existence of Christ is an integral part of my Christology. Otherwise I could not hold in any real sense His Divinity.

11. Since I believe that God is the Father of all men, I recognize the kinship of man with God, but I cannot assert man's identity with God in any sense that seems to me tenable.

12. The historical problems as to the career of Jesus cannot be solved in isolation from our general view as to His personality. For the historical critic, as such, some elements in that career are much better attested than others—the Resurrection, for example, than the Virgin Birth.

13. Faith has no vital interest in asserting the Virgin Birth, since the Incarnation of the Son of God is our vital concern and that is secured as well with two parents as with one. The historical evidence for it is not strong, though it is sometimes unduly minimized, and probably the individual will decide the question for himself in accordance with his general sense of fitness.

14. The formula that Christ suffered instead of the human race seems to me untrue alike to Scripture and experience, except as a mere external description. The essential principle of the death of Jesus is that in it the Sinless One identifies Himself with the sinful race, sharing with it the consequences of sin and breaking its power for those who are willing to become one with Him in a mystical union. It is the supreme expression of the love of God and the supreme creation of His grace.

15. If the Incarnation was a real experience and not a fictitious appearance, the knowledge of Jesus must have been limited. In the realm of religious and moral truth His teaching, where we can reach it, is authoritative. There is, however, a borderland where the line cannot be drawn with precision. I hold that it is improper to invoke His authority to settle questions of historical, physical or critical science, unless these can be shown to be vitally involved in His religious teaching.

16. On questions of eschatology we have definitely broken with much in the

old-fashioned views. I think we have also come to understand more fully the extreme complexity of the problems involved. The important thing to my mind is to insist on the fact that we live in a very strict moral universe and that 'Whatsoever a man soweth that shall he also reap'. The difficulties in the way of dogmatic universalism are, I think, philosophical rather than exegetical, but some of these difficulties have been unduly exaggerated.

As we have observed, in the early decades of the twentieth century, the thoughts of many were greatly disturbed and uncertain owing to the impact of the new critical approach to the Bible, the pressure of rationalist forces, and in particular by the stirrings that arose from the Campbell controversy. It was natural therefore that, as a leader of Christian thought, Peake should step forth as an exponent of and a defender of the Christian faith.[1] It is here that we see Peake as a Christian apologist in a time of uncertainty and seeking. It was upon this background that he produced his timely volume *Christianity: Its Nature and Truth* (1908), in which we pass with him into the distinct field of apologetics. Peake wrote in his 'Preface':

It has long been the writer's conviction that more ought to be done to expound the truths of Christianity, and the grounds on which they may still be accepted. The task is especially urgent for the sake of the young people in our Churches, who are slipping away from the faith because they have been trained neither to understand nor to defend it.

Simple and popular in treatment, avoiding the abstruse and technical, the book is no formal treatise on systematic theology or apologetic, yet precisely the kind of writing required in view of the existing situation.[2] Peake was sensitive to the difficulties, and wrote in order to reassure believers who were disturbed by the questionings of a rationalist philosophy and a scientific criticism. The book was 'a rally-point for the faithful and a beacon to the wavering'.[3]

The successive chapters argue for the reality and necessity of religion, for the place of theology as well as morality in life; they present arguments against materialism, those for the existence of God, for the

---

[1] It was for this reason that he undertook public lecture work: (a) in a 1902 Sunday Afternoon Lecture in the Central Hall on 'Did Jesus Rise again?'; (b) in 1911, The Deansgate Lectures; (c) 'I believe in Jesus Christ', one of five sermons preached by five Non-conformists in St Ann's Church, Manchester, and published in *Our Common Faith* (1922), ed. D. Dorrity; (d) 'The New Testament Record', in *The Christian Faith*, ed. C. F. Nolloth (1922).

[2] Part of the book is a reprint of articles by Peake in the *Sunday Strand* written in 1907–8. The newly-appointed editor, W. Llewellyn Williams, wrote to him on 8 November 1906 expressing his wish for 'articles dealing with dogmatic theology if treated in a popular manner.... They might well be headed "Plain Thoughts on Great Subjects".' The letter continues: 'In thinking the matter over your name suggested itself to me as the name of the one man who could do the work in a way to command the ear of the very class I desire to reach. Your reputation for sound scholarship would give authority to the articles, and assure the readers that they might implicitly rely upon the soundness of the teaching'. In a letter (dated 19 June 1907) W. Robertson Nicoll wrote to Peake: 'Would you let us make a book of them? I think they would be exceedingly useful at the present moment.'

[3] *Manchester Guardian*, 19 December 1908.

Christian religion, for the Christian doctrine of the Trinity; the problem of sin; the Person and Work of Christ, his Divinity and Incarnation, his Birth and Resurrection, and then the book closes with an examination of the doctrines concerning personal salvation.

The book was an immediate success;[1] within six months fifteen thousand copies had been sold, and by 1911 it had reached its eighth edition. In 1910 a special edition was published in New York, and American reviewers were enthusiastic; in 1911 an edition was published specially for the Brotherhood Movement—a fact which gave Peake great satisfaction, for he believed that the Movement was lacking systematic teaching in basic Christian doctrine, and was in some danger of suffering through religious intolerance.

It was an even greater satisfaction to Peake when a request was made by Dr Hopkyn Rees, of Shanghai, on behalf of the Christian Literature for China, for the translation of the book into Chinese. Peake wrote on 1 July 1915:[2]

... It was an exceptional gratification to learn that you had translated it into Chinese. It was one of my earliest wishes, reaching back to the time when I was five years old, to be a missionary, and although the work I am doing is probably what I am best qualified to do, I have always had a certain regret that my work did not lie in the mission field. I think your letter has done more to remove it than even the fact that I have now many old students who are missionaries. I feel as if the circulation of the book in China may accomplish greater results than I could have attained by personal work, and at any rate joined to the work I am actually doing, it shifts the balance and makes me more content to have stayed at home. You will understand from this with what joy I give my consent to the publication, and it will be a red-letter day for me when I have the book in my hand, and know that in its new form it is doing the work.

Of this book Dr J. H. Moulton wrote whilst on a journey:[3]

... I have again got your *Christianity* with me for what little time the week-end gives. I am only slowly getting on, which is tantalising for the super-excellence of the book becomes more and more apparent. It is exactly the thing we need for a very large class indeed in these days, and I have had more than one chance of urging it personally on people of the kind I am thinking of. How you manage to write so much, of such quality, as you always must write, is a perpetual marvel. You are a sort of consolidated Grenfell and Hunt, with your Oxyrhynchus within your own head! But I must turn from author to book, and

---

[1] It is interesting to note that the leading article in *The Literary Guide and Rationalist Review*, March 1909) gives a long review of the book under the title: 'The Latest Phase of Christian Apologetics'. Whilst naturally against Peake's views it speaks of his book as 'the product of a well-trained, scholarly intellect, and is likely to enjoy a wide circulation. Dr Peake is preeminently a modern man, the ripeness of whose scholarship is unquestioned.... As a theologian he is to be highly commended for his sweet spirit and tolerant tone'.

[2] A.S.P., to T. Hopkyn Rees, 1 July 1915.

[3] J. H. Moulton to A.S.P., 22 November 1908.

read a bit to stimulate me for my morning's service—for a sermon on ὅσα ἀληθῆ κ τ λ the book should be a mine.

After reading the book, a copy of which had been sent to him by Sir W. Hartley, Sir Alfred Dale, Vice-Chancellor of Liverpool University, wrote in acknowledgement:

I have been reading Professor Peake's book with much interest. He always impresses me by his freshness and fairness. He has the additional virtue—not too common among theologians—of enabling you to see precisely what he means.[1]

As an example of Peake's theological acumen we may recall at this point his challenge to Dr James Denney early in 1904. A review of Denney's *The Death of Christ* (1903) in the *Primitive Methodist Quarterly* provoked that keen swordsman to reply in an article in *The Expositor* which was republished in his book *The Atonement and the Modern Mind*. The particular issue involved in the controversy centred on what Peake regarded as fundamental and vital in Pauline theology, and he was unwilling to see its rather contemptuous dismissal by Denney. Peake regarded the death of Christ as an act involving the whole human race and taught a mystical union of the believer with Christ. Denney had replied: 'This is presented to us as something profound, a recognition of the mystical depths in Paul's teaching. I own I can see nothing profound in it except a profound misapprehension of the apostle.'[2] Peake wrote a long article in *The Expositor* (January 1904) setting out his understanding of Pauline doctrine, and not seldom with rapier-like sharpness. Denney wrote a rejoiner in *The Expositor* (February 1904) on 'Adam and Christ in St Paul' and the controversy ceased.

This writing of Peake not only reveals his powers of incisive argument in controversy, showing his opponent that he was 'a foeman worthy of his steel', but we find precisely set forth the same position on the subject of Paulinism as he maintained in his writings years afterwards. The following passage illustrates both Peake's own conviction and the thrust of his argument.

I am thankful that we can start from the common ground that Paul has much to say of union with Christ. But while I, with many, believe this union is of a mystical character, Dr Denney affirms that the New Testament knows only a moral union. He is afraid that we may lose ourselves in soaring words, and thinks that the idea of a mystical union approaches the region of the unintelligible. There are elements in Paulinism of which one cannot write adequately unless he writes with rapture. . . .

---

[1] A. W. Dale to Sir W. P. Hartley, 10 October 1908. Dr Fairbairn wrote to Peake from Lossiemouth on 27 October 1908. '. . . As to the apologetic work on *Christianity: Its Nature and Truth* I will not attempt to say what I feel about it. I wish I could write as you do, as simply, as clearly and out of a full heart.'

[2] *The Atonement and the Modern Mind*, p. 98.

It strikes me in the first place as strange that if Paul meant a moral union merely, he should have hit upon such a term as 'in Christ' to express it. . . . When Paul says: 'I have been crucified with Christ' he may mean no more than that he has passed through an experience similar to that of Christ. But when he proceeds: 'And it is no longer I that live, but Christ liveth in me' it needs some very strange exegetical spectacles to distort this into a moral union. . . . The words 'he that is joined to the Lord is one spirit' are themselves very striking, and do not readily lead themselves to anything but a personal identification. In fact it is difficult to see how a mystical union could be better described than by this daring sentence. The context however definitely excludes the thought of a merely moral union.

On the issue of Denney's volume, *The Atonement and the Modern Mind*, Dr W. Robertson Nicoll, whose theological position was always conservative, wrote to Peake asking for a review-article for *The Expositor*, and his letter[1] includes an interesting observation on Denney's standpoint, together with his estimate of Peake's ability to produce a definite work on the subject of Paulinism:

I have great difficulty in understanding his position, but he seems to me to have an intensive dislike of all mysticism, and this a serious disqualification in writing of St Paul. I can thoroughly understand your feeling that to treat Paulinism properly one should have years to work in, but then after all, things have to be done as we best can under conditions of great pressure or they have a very awkward way of not getting done at all. . . . You do not need to quote experts to me to convince me of your competence to write about Paulinism.

Sometime later Peake met Denney, at a meeting of ministers in Manchester; they had tea together and Peake saw him off at the station. At a still later time, when Peake was in Glasgow to deliver an inaugural lecture to the Theological Society of the United Free Church College on the occasion of his being made Honorary President, although Denney could not attend the gathering, he kindly came to the Principal's house after his own meeting, and 'we had a very pleasant time together'.[2]

A further work in the theological field is Peake's lengthy essay on 'The History of German Theology during the Nineteenth Century', contributed to *Germany in the Nineteenth Century: Second Series* (1915), one of three closing lectures delivered in Manchester University largely through the initiative of Professor C. H. Herford, having as their object the attempt to promote more friendly feelings between Britain and

---

[1] W. Robertson Nicoll to A.S.P. 24 October 1903. Cf. a letter from Denney to Nicoll, 28 November 1903:'About the *Atonement* I have no desire or intention to say more at present, but I will be interested to hear what Peake says. . . . When a man maintains that there is something which may be described as a "mystical union", all I can say is that my mind does not follow him. I cannot conceive anything which transcends a moral union' (*Letters of Principal James Denney to W. Robertson Nicoll* (1920) p. 37).

[2] *H.R.* April 1921.

Germany in appreciation by British scholars of the part played by Germany in the development of modern civilization.

Peake's lecture begins with an analysis of Schleiermacher, then passes on to a consideration of Strauss and F. C. Baur and the Tubingen school, the concluding portion being devoted to Ritschl, 'the most epoch-making personality in the history of the nineteenth century'. There is shorter reference to representatives of the Liberal school, the Confessional theologians and the Mediating school. An opinion often expressed at the time was that too much regard was paid to German theology. The lecture forms a corrective of that false view, and Peake affirmed that 'our own theology, when it has not been too deeply limited by insularity to learn from Germany, has in the past greatly profited by its teaching'.[1] Few scholars at home knew German criticism and theology in its length and breadth better than Peake, and there was none more truly an English theologian and critic. He possessed a clear vision of the whole field, and had discerned the essential things.

A letter from Dr J. H. Moulton corroborates this estimate of Peake:

Many thanks for your Lecture, which I read with the utmost interest. I am quite ashamed to have to confess that I actually did not know the lectures were published, much less that they had got into a third edition. Your lecture is entirely characteristic, and takes one's breath away by the evidence of gigantic reading. How you can possibly manage to swallow such vast quantities of German theology and criticism without spiritual indigestion, I cannot imagine! I am sure nothing short of penal servitude with only Schleiermacher to mitigate the rigour of solitary confinement would ever induce me to read such stuff, and even then I think I should take it in very small doses. How you find time to do such things beats me altogether, and you have got such a grip of it all that you are able to criticise these fellows as well as to give an account of them!

V

Two further pieces of writing claim brief notice—and each in its own way is an example of Peake's ability as an interpreter.

In 1908 he published his 'Aids to the Devotional Use of Scripture', which consisted of three small books entitled: *The Christian Race; Election and Service; Faded Myths*. These were a collection of devotional studies which had appeared in the pages of the *Primitive Methodist Leader* in 1906–7. In the Introduction to the first of these books Peake states his reason for entering into the field of devotional writing:[2]

---

[1] Op. cit., p. 184. In 1916 Peake addressed a large meeting of ministers in Manchester on 'Ought we to reverse our estimate of German theology?' It was a further example of Peake as a Christian apologist. 'All truth must be accepted for its own sake wherever found and all untruth rejected whatever company it might chance to be keeping.' *Methodist Recorder*, 13 April 1916.

[2] In his *Memoir* of his father the Rev. L. S. Peake is inclined to think that it was because of a letter written to Peake some years earlier by W. Robertson Nicoll that Peake decided to turn

The task of the professional student of the Bible is not exhausted when he has dealt with its criticism and interpretation, or even with its theology. He is a debtor to his own age, and especially to his fellow Christians, and it falls within the sphere of that duty to make the Scriptures more helpful to them as a means of grace. In doing so he will recognise the value of the results he has reached in his scientific investigations. But he will keep steadily in view that his chief purpose is to deepen and expand the religious life of his readers.

The Christian Race is a series of expositions on the early verses of the twelfth chapter of the Epistle to the Hebrews which have in them the quality of a personal confession and entreaty. In *Election and Service* the harsh tenets of Calvinism are set aside and a true doctrine of election propounded.

We were chosen before the foundation of the world. Even in the distant eternity that lies behind us we were present to the mind of God, the object of His love, the creation of His predestination.... It is a wonderful thought that God, out of the tangle of human life, should constantly weave the beautiful and harmonious pattern of His own eternal design, taking up into it and subordinating to it the crossing, clashing, twisted threads of our individual action. It might seem that a million chances would inevitably frustrate God's purpose.... But God's wisdom comes out in this—that He leaves us freedom, and yet gets His own way.[1]

Faded Myths is different in character and theme. Recognizing that there are myths in the Bible, by Peake's masterly hand the reader is enabled to trace through the folk-lore and nature myths the origin of the symbolism associated with the dawn, the storm-cloud or the 'mutinous sea', and to discover the core of truth to which they point.

These three small volumes reveal how it was possible to unite expert scholarship with the truths of the spiritual life.

In 1926 Peake published his last book: *The Life of Sir William Hartley*. The names of Hartley and Peake had been so long associated that it was fitting that the biblical scholar become the biographer of the merchant prince. It was a fine tribute to the work and character of one who had been a life-long friend, an obligation which, although the work inevitably involved the stealing of time from Peake's proper field of work, could not be withstood. The story is told with a simplicity and directness which

---

his hand to the writing of devotional literature. The letter is dated 21 May 1898. 'You know I am old-fashioned ... and I do strongly sympathise with you up to the point of endeavouring to support critical questions and theological questions as far as possible, and allowing a free discussion on criticism. At the same time you must pardon me for saying that I do think it a mistake that you take no opportunity in writing to show that you hold the great truths that have made Primitive Methodism. If I had not known you except from your articles in the *Primitive Methodist Quarterly* I should have considered you a man with no definite religious opinions whatever, in fact as open-minded as Robert Elsemere. I know this would be very wrong and unjust, but still the others would think as I do... You must not be cross with me for saying this.'

[1] Op. cit., pp. 40–1.

enables the reader to see the man as he was; the portrait is true to life. With masterly skill Peake marshals the facts and shows with great vividness the manufacturer, the model employer, the princely philanthropist and the far-seeing ecclesiastical statesman. In the closing chapter Peake estimates the personal qualities of the man he knew so intimately, and the reader is left with the impact of a great and noble personality, the dynamic of whose life was a profound Christian experience. The quality of the work may be summed up in the following sentence, written by one who knew well the subject of this biography:

The book is brief, but ample. Dr Peake was perfect master of his material and wasted no words. In his own lucid and felicitous way he has painted what all who knew Sir William must acknowledge to be an authentic portrait.[1]

This is the most fitting place at which we should recall Peake's vast and varied contributions to dictionaries, to learned journals, and to the religious press both at home and abroad. It is impossible to survey in any measure of detail the amazing output, but the bibliography at the end of this present volume indicates in some measure the extent of Peake's contributions. From his pen came articles in the *Dictionary of National Biography*, the *Encyclopaedia Britannica*; the successive volumes of Hastings's *Dictionaries* of the Bible; the *Encyclopaedia of Religion and Ethics*; the *New Standard Bible Dictionary*; *Chambers' Encyclopaedia*. Numerous articles are to be found in learned journals: *The Primitive Methodist Quarterly Review* and its successor *The Holborn Review*; *The Expositor*, *The Times Literary Supplement* and *The Expository Times* and others. To the religious press he contributed voluminously, especially to *The Primitive Methodist Leader*, in which he also conducted a weekly correspondence column on biblical matters, by which he answered questions sent to him by a host of readers. In addition to all this he was the constant writer of book-reviews, a survey of which indicates the enormous range of his reading. Finally we should note how greatly skilled Peake was in the preparation of bibliographies, some of which were contributed to books written by other authors; some written for his own writings and lectures; some at the request of education authorities; and some for the general use of students and other readers in the biblical field. His numerous publications at intervals on 'Recent Developments' in both Old and New Testament research bringing up to date the literature on the Bible, available in languages also other than English, were widely circulated. All this indicates the vast extent of his acquaintance with the available material on a world-wide scale.

[1] Edwin W. Smith in *H.R.*

CHAPTER SIX

THE EDITOR

I

WHATEVER may be regarded as the essential qualities of a successful editor it is certain that Peake possessed them all in a marked degree for his editorial labours and achievements were outstanding.

In 1905 as Dean of the Faculty of Theology in the University of Manchester, Peake edited a volume of *Inaugural Lectures delivered by Members of the Faculty of Theology* during its first session 1904–5 to popular audiences. This symposium bore eloquent testimony to the breadth of the newly formed Faculty, and in his 'Preface' Peake pointed out that each lecturer had been free to take his own course and 'though the standard of popular treatment fluctuates, the lectures should be judged as intended for those who, while interested in theology are not theologians. The University sinks below the level of its privilege and duty unless it hears the call to share the gains of scholarship with those whose life runs in other grooves'. He goes on to quote a remark of Harnack: 'The theologians of every country only half discharge their duties if they think it enough to treat of the Gospel in the recondite language of learning and bury it in scholarly folios'. This judgement of 'one of the greatest masters of the science' seems to have greatly influenced Peake, for from this time onward he felt it to be his special vocation to popularize the historical study of the Bible. Peake himself contributed a lecture to the volume on 'The Present Movement of Biblical Science'—a significant designation at that particular time and in that context.

In 1925 Peake edited a volume containing fifteen essays by different authors, who worked independently, yet in accordance with a general plan laid down by the editor, and who undertook the work at the request of the Society for Old Testament Study of which he was President. Its purpose was twofold: 'to check the suspicion that the Old Testament has been discredited and that modern culture can with impunity neglect it'; to explain the position of Old Testament study at the time when it was written. Its contributors were in the foremost ranks of English Semitic scholars, and for the selection of them Peake assumed responsibility. He also wrote the important Introduction and contributed the essay on 'The Religion of Israel from David to the Return from Exile'; in addition he supplied a detailed bibliography for the book as a whole.

In the judgement of one reviewer: 'Professor Peake deserved high praise not only for his own share as editor and essayist, but also for the distinct success in gathering round him such a band of able contributors, every one of them so admirably equipped for the task assigned to him.'[1] A further notice of the book—which was very widely commended—declared: 'It is seldom that collective work succeeds in maintaining such a high standard of accuracy, completeness, interest and value. This is no doubt largely due to the efficient editorial hands to which the work was entrusted.'[2]

One who was a distinguished member of the Society[3] but not a contributor to the volume wrote: 'If our praise is superlative it is because we feel that any reader who possesses himself of this book, together with the admirable one-volume *Commentary* on the Bible, is more or less completely furnished for the understanding of an imperishable literature.'

In the same year, 1925, along with Dr R. G. Parsons, Peake edited the British edition of *An Outline of Christianity: The Story of our Civilization*, a work in five volumes, profusely illustrated. The American edition was published in the hope of combating the ignorance and irreligion of the masses by the presentation, in an attractive form, of the story of Christianity. Mr R. H. Paget of America, who had pioneered this proposal, was desirous of serving the British people in a similar fashion, and came over to this country to explore the possibilities. He wished to discover two editors, one representing the Church of England, the other the Free Churches. On the ground of advice received in America, he approached Peake as to acceptance of the editorial responsibility, and although reluctant to undertake the work, after an examination of the typescript of the American edition, Peake agreed. Dr R. G. Parsons,[4] who was Peake's colleague at the University, also agreed, as representing the Church of England.

In planning the British Edition it was found that, while many of the articles in the American edition could be retained, it was necessary to add other articles to be written by British scholars. The work proved far more

---

[1] *The Jewish Chronicle*, 12 February 1926.
[2] *The Modern Churchman*, 1926.
[3] C. R. North in *Methodist Recorder*, 1 April 1926.
[4] In November 1926, Dr Parsons was consecrated Bishop of Middleton. In acknowledging a letter of congratulation, written to him by Peake, he said: ... Many people seem to think they ought to have made me a Bishop earlier. Had it happened sooner it would either have prevented or cut short our co-operation on the *Outline*. This might have been good for the *Outline*, but my loss, as I can now realise, would have been irreparable. My happy experiences with you have been one of the most valuable influences in my education. I am proud to have some share at Wells and elsewhere in the making of priests, but you have had a great share in the training of a Bishop! I hope you will not have to regret your responsibility.

arduous than at first seemed would be the case; there was a large amount of re-arrangement, and a heavy correspondence, and for some two years the two editors met at least weekly for a long afternoon—two to seven o'clock. It should be said that the publishers, who took responsibility for choice of illustrative material and proof reading, lightened the burden. Over a hundred authors, all of whom were leading scholars in their fields, contributed to the work: the writers were drawn from the most diverse schools of thought, and controversial issues were therefore raised from every point of view. Peake was responsible for four articles in the work: 'The Preparation for Christianity in Israel'; 'The Criticism of the Old Testament'; 'The Genius of Methodism'; 'The New Testament assembled'.

There were those amongst Peake's friends who were doubtful about the wisdom of his undertaking this immense editorial responsibility, realizing that it inevitably withdrew him from the very major work to which he was committed, and there is no doubt that Peake himself regretted the invasion of his all-important time. However, it was because of his passion to secure the maximum spread of the truth of Christianity, at whatever cost to himself, together with his concern for a closer drawing together of Christian forces, that he committed himself to the task. Peake always put faith in any endeavour to popularize modern ideas as a means of enlightenment and progress.

Reviews of the work were many and without exception favourable. 'The Editors deserve great praise for their success in welding so many diverse contributions into a whole so that the noble story unfolds from stage to stage with the inevitableness of a great design.'[1] Again: 'It is an admirable book to recommend to the intelligent reader who wants to study the beginnings of Christian history in the light of the best modern scholarship, without the confusion of technical phraseology or the apparatus of critical investigation.'[2]

II

It will be generally agreed that the one-volume *Commentary on the Bible* was Peake's greatest and outstanding editorial achievement. Published in 1919, after suffering delays mainly owing to war conditions, it was the result of six years of patient and exacting toil.

The origins of the *Commentary* are interesting. As far back as 1912 the publishing firm of T. C. and E. C. Jack of Edinburgh expressed the desire that a handbook of reference on the Bible should be produced to find a place in their series of Reference Books, which was widely successful. In that year Dr E. Griffith-Jones, Principal of the United Independent

---
[1] *The Guardian*, 12 November 1926.
[2] Dr W. F. Howard in the *Methodist Recorder*, 19 September 1926.

College, Bradford, agreed to accept the post of general editor of such a handbook; two others, one for the Old Testament and one for the New to be appointed. For the latter, Dr A. J. Grieve, of Bradford College (afterwards Principal of Lancashire Independent College, Manchester) was chosen to supervise the New Testament; for the Old Testament Peake was approached,[1] in October 1912, and after a careful interview he intimated his willingness to serve, and indeed stated that he himself had contemplated a book along somewhat similar lines.[2] Dr Griffith-Jones had intimated to the publishers, even prior to his approach to Peake, that for reasons of health, he would be glad to be relieved of the editorial responsibility which he had promised to undertake, thus leaving the firm at liberty regarding the matter of the general editorship. It was thus that Peake accepted the invitation to become editor-in-chief, Dr Grieve willingly agreeing to co-operate in the task.

By the spring of 1913 Peake had secured a large list of contributors to the proposed volumes, and Mr Edwin C. Jack, one of the heads of the publishing firm, was able to write: 'I am delighted with the scheme. You are making a much more authoritative book than I had hoped to be able to get, and you are putting it through more promptly than you led us to expect. I am glad that you still hope to be able to write a portion of the book yourself'.[3] Through the months that followed details were settled, but the onset of the war changed the situation. 'This war will turn our plans upside down. We dare not publish much this year.... We are so completely taken by surprise I cannot yet decide upon our policy with regard to the Commentary.'[4] Nevertheless, despite difficulties, the work proceeded quietly, though the prolonged illness of Peake's secretary, Miss Elsie Cann, and his own illness in 1915 added to the delay. It was not until 1919 that the work was completed. It bore the title: *Peake's Commentary on the Bible*—a title for which the publishers were responsible, and which Peake himself eventually accepted.

The team of contributors numbered sixty-one, and Peake had succeeded in enlisting the co-operation of practically all those who stood in the first rank of Old and New Testament scholarship; he had also secured the help of 'secular' scholarship where that could throw light on biblical studies, and there was the widest denominational representation. As editor, Peake was successful in the matter of assignment of work to members of his team, so that the overall impression was to present the main critical position in regard to the Bible, alike for both Old Testament and New. Peake himself wrote about one-eighth of the work, and in order to secure complete co-ordination also made numerous additions to the work of other contributors, so that nothing of importance should be

---

[1] E. Griffith-Jones to A.S.P., 28 October 1912.
[2] T. C. and E. C. Jack to A.S.P., 20 November 1912.
[3] Edwin C. Jack to A.S.P., 23 April 1913.
[4] Ibid., 6 August 1914.

omitted. Such additions were enclosed in brackets and initialled: over the wide range of subjects nothing escaped Peake's own notice. Editorial work on the bibliographies was considerable, again in the interests of completeness of information for the reader. In addition to the general planning of the work and the distribution of space, the articles and commentaries were read in manuscript and at every stage of the proofs, a process which involved a very considerable correspondence with the authors on matters requiring reconsideration. Peake was also responsible for the massive index, which extended to some sixty-eight three-columned pages of small type. To this book of more than a thousand pages, closely reprinted with double columns, Peake gave immense care for the perfection of the work, and this is indicated by the fact that as editor he worked through the whole volume ten times before its publication.

The opening paragraph of the 'Preface' reveals the fact that in this case, as in so many others we have noted, Peake recognized the need of the religious situation and sought to meet the condition: the time was ripe for such a work:

The present work is designed to put before the reader in a simple form, without technicalities, the generally accepted results of Biblical Criticism, Interpretation, History and Theology. It is not intended to be homiletic or devotional, but to convey with precision, and yet in a popular and interesting way, the meaning of the original writers, and reconstruct the conditions in which they worked and of which they wrote. It will thus, while not explicitly devotional or practical, provide that accurate interpretation of the text through which alone the sound basis for devotional use and practical application can be laid. It has been the desire of the promoters that it should be abreast of the present position of scholarship, and yet succeed in making the Scriptures live for its readers with something of the same significance and power that they possessed for those to whom they were originally addressed. While it is intended in the first instance for the layman, and should prove specially helpful to day- and Sunday-school teachers, to lay preachers, to leaders of men's societies, brotherhoods and adult classes, and to Christian workers generally, it should also be of considerable use to clergymen and ministers, and in particular to theological students.[1]

The *Commentary* proved phenomenally successful, and it would be difficult to estimate its far-reaching influence. We find record of it being used in theological colleges as far apart as Canada, Australia and New Zealand; amongst Italian pastors ('several who read English have already purchased it'[2]) and there is a request from Portugal for copies; it found its place for degree courses in the University of Calcutta: and on the

---

[1] The Commentary was several times reprinted, and in 1936 a small Supplement, edited by Dr Grieve, was published in order to record the principal developments in biblical studies since 1919. In 1962 the whole *Commentary* was revised and reset under the editorship of Dr Matthew Black and Dr H. H. Rowley. It still bears the same title—*Peake's Commentary on the Bible*—an indication of the esteem in which Peake's work is held. The paragraph quoted above is set down in the new *Commentary*, as indicating the continuity of ideal and purpose.

[2] E. W. Smith, in Italy, to A.S.P., 28 December 1920.

shelves of countless ministerial studies through the homeland. Professor Ashida of Japan wrote asking for permission to translate it into Japanese, to which Peake gave ready agreement.[1]

The success it achieved was a source of great satisfaction to Peake himself. As early as August 1920 he wrote to Mr E. Jack:

... As you know I undertook the work in the first instance with great hesitation owing to the pressure of other things, but undertook it nevertheless because I saw that, if I could succeed in getting the kind of book I had in mind, it might well prove one of the most important steps ever taken in bringing home to those familiar with English all over the world the results of modern Biblical scholarship.

Its publication brought particular delight to two of Peake's former teachers at Oxford. Dr Sanday wrote from Christ Church, Oxford, on 11 October.

My dear Peake,
I am writing in the midst of confusion and almost in the very act of changing houses.... I am reducing my library, and parting with books pretty freely right and left.... But I shall hold on tight to the one-volume *Commentary* which reached me two or three days ago. I must not delay any longer to thank you for *your* share in it, and to offer my heartiest congratulations. No one else could have done it, and still less could any one have done it nearly so well. It is a triumph of organisation, and a great public service—full of good things.... You have a fine record to look back upon, and may rest on your oars a bit with a clear conscience.
        Yours with very sincere regard and affection,
             W. Sanday

From Mr T. C. Snow, his early classical tutor in the old Oxford days, Peake received the following, written 17 November 1919.

The book has come. What a magnificent present! I cannot at all understand how it can be done for the money, even if it was set up before the war, as I suppose a good deal of it was. Of course, I have not had time even to look through it; but I can see plenty of things in it that I have long wanted.

It suggests one thing very powerfully, that now that it is finished, it might be a signal for slacking off a great deal of work. You have done your duty to your generation, and you ought to re-mould your scheme of life, with a great deal more leisure in it. I am rather afraid when I hear of the College and the University and the *Review* all going on together—'Are they all unevadable?'
                 Yours faithfully,
                  T. C. Snow

A postscript was added by Mrs Snow:

Thank you so much. You would like to have seen Thomas' delight in it on its arrival this morning.... E. Snow.

[1] A.S.P. to Professor Ashida, 7 July 1924: '... It is a pleasure to me to express my cordial consent to your project, and I shall be glad if you succeed in finding a publisher. If so, I should be glad, when it is finished, if you would kindly send a copy to me.'

The importance of the work cannot be better summed up than in the following excerpt from a review:[1]

> We know of no other work that so closely and compendiously sets out the results of modern critical study, and yet so convincingly manifests the permanent spiritual value of the Bible. It ought to be the constant companion of theological students, teachers and ministers, and of those who without expert knowledge desire to read the Bible with the understanding, so that they may gain that divine wisdom which it has always conferred on the devout and patient student. Such a book as this has been long wanted.

Remembering that the traditional view of the Bible still persisted strongly it is of course not surprising to find that the *Commentary* had to face some opposition, despite the fact that its critical position was in no way extreme. Sometimes, as in the following example, the challenge was by private letter to Peake, expressing a personal opinion. To such letters Peake always replied at length with great courtesy and understanding.

> ... Will you accept it as a compliment if I say that if you had not become a Professor of Theology, you would have excelled as a King's Counsellor? ... The souls of men are today being saved in multitudes in the revival movements in all parts of the world, but I have yet to learn that teaching which discredits the Bible and charges the Son of God with liability to error can produce such fruit—the fruit for which Christ died. ... I can conceive of no more dangerous and deadly work than mutilating and adapting the revelation of God until it becomes congenial to those who are guided by the wisdom of this world. ... I regard your teaching concerning the Bible as pernicious and I believe that it has wrought incalculable harm both within and without the Christian Churches, but I hope I have never questioned the honesty of your motives, however incomprehensible they may be to me.[2]

There was also much more public utterance sometimes even vituperative.

> This is an extraordinarily clever, but not a safe book. Professor Peake's troop of writers have all had leave given them to be Higher Critics before a crowd of humble enquirers. ... Professor Peake himself is a strange compound in the matter. He has a name for being a great Higher Critic, and I believe does his best to live up to it, but the Primitive Methodist local preacher will crop up![3]

Again:

> Peake's *Commentary* is now well known, and it is notoriously the summation in one volume of almost every destructive view of Scripture which human genius has yet invented.[4]

[1] *Times Literary Supplement* 16 October 1919. It is interesting in passing, to record that a lady, in whose house at Conference Peake had been a guest some while before, was on board ship on voyage to America. She asked the cabin-boy to bring to her some interesting book from the ship's library. He returned promptly carrying a large volume, and gave it to her, saying: 'This is a grand book, Miss.' It was a copy of Peake's *Commentary*!

[2] B. J. Greenwood to A.S.P., 1921.

[3] *The Journal of the Wesley Bible Union*, August 1920.

[4] Ibid., March 1927.

Yet again:

Such men as Dr Peake . . . are doing Satan's work far more effectively than the blatant infidel of our parks and commons. These men, while professing to be followers of Christ, and taking the pay of the Churches are really undermining His authority through their attacks on the Written Word, for be sure of one thing, the Written Word and the Person of our Lord stand to fall together.[1]

But these attacks, whether by private letter or public statement did not seriously trouble Peake, not least because of his sense of humour. Now and again, he entered into a vigorous counter-attack when serious issues were at stake.

It is interesting to record that in the theological training of the Methodist Church in Australia, the *Commentary* speedily found its place, opposition notwithstanding. At the Methodist Conference of 1920 held in Sydney, despite a certain pressure from traditional elements, the work was introduced as compulsory reading for all probationers. Dr W. G. Torr, an old Oxford friend of Peake's wrote: 'It was opposed as all *new* things are by some high and dry Tories in ecclesiastical statesmanship, and it was with a glow of satisfaction I spoke of your worth and work.'[2] In 1923 the same writer told Peake that for the last three years *Peake's Commentary* had been a fruitful theme in the religious press, in pamphlets and in books. The issue came to a great debate in the Methodist Conference at Adelaide in 1923, and the following is a report of the occasion:

The spirit of the debate was of a very high order—only one minister who was 75 years of age spoke against it. All our professors and lecturers favoured its retention. I kept myself till the last and urged a unanimous vote in favour of 'Peake'. There was a solemn hush as the vote was taken and we rose and sang the Doxology. It was a triumph for modernism. . . . Our Conference vote was a great triumph for the truth and thousands will thank God![3]

Two cases of misunderstanding regarding the *Commentary* were unfortunate in that they received public expression; the one related to an earlier one-volume commentary which had appeared in 1909; the other in relation to a commentary which was in the process of preparation, and which appeared in 1928.

The editor of the earlier commentary (reprinted in 1913) was J. R. Dummelow, an Anglican clergyman, who on the appearance of *Peake's Commentary* wrote to Peake, accusing him of using what he regarded as

---

[1] *The Life of Faith*, 13 January 1921.
[2] W. G. Torr to A.S.P., 15 August 1920. 'This Conference deems it necessary to place on record its conviction that many statements in *Peake's Commentary* are not in agreement with the Christian faith as held by the Methodist Church, and are calculated to undermine the faith of the students in the Bible as the inspired Word of God.'
[3] Ibid., 29 May 1923. A similar record is found in a letter from Principal L. E. Bennet of King's College, Brisbane: '. . . Had a great debate on *Peake's Commentary*. It was held to be among the greatest days in the General Conference for years past, and it was a great victory for the liberal party in the Church. They secured an almost unanimous verdict.'

his 'original inventions', namely, prefatory articles and notes without the biblical text. He assumed that Peake's book owed its idea and form as a complete Bible commentary to the pattern of his scheme. Peake made a somewhat spirited reply and at some length:

> I do not owe either idea or form to your work. The request was made to me by the publisher.... The work had been planned on these lines before they even heard of your Commentary and I think they had not more than heard of it when they asked me to edit a volume for them.[1]

Unfortunately the matter, which should have remained as a private discussion became public by a letter written by Dummelow, withdrawing with apologies, his remarks as to Peake having 'appropriated my two inventions' being printed in the *Guardian*. So the controversy ended. It should be noted that Peake himself had written earlier an appreciation of Dummelow's *Commentary*.

More serious was the misunderstanding that arose in the early stage of planning a *Commentary* which appeared in 1928 under the joint editorship of Bishop Gore, H. L. Goudge, and A. Guillaume, bearing the title *A New Commentary of Holy Scripture including the Apocrypha*. In *The Times* of 3 January 1925, part of the annual letter to the members of the English Church Union recording the work of its Literature committee appeared, written by the secretary, the Rev. Arnold Pinchard. Being a private letter for the members it should not have appeared in the press. It declared 'the first and most immediate project' of the Committee to be 'the production of a one-volume commentary ... which shall be truly and soundly Catholic'. Unfortunately the letter contained the following statements:

> There are at present two one-volume commentaries on Holy Scripture which are accessible—one of these [Dummelow] is wholly out of date and far behind the point of advance which modern knowledge and criticism have reached: the other [Peake] while not lacking in scholarship, is written by a Nonconformist in the very spirit of Nonconformity,[2] and is permeated through and through with an atmosphere of sheer modernism. For want of a Catholic Commentary on the Scriptures, this book now holds the field, and is even being recommended by bishops' examining chaplains to be read by ordinands in preparation for their examinations.

Naturally Peake was prompted to reply[3] in the interests of truth, and he wrote an incisive letter in which he pointed out the facts, namely that Peake himself had written not more than one-eighth of the volume; that there were twenty-two Anglican contributors, and, had Professor Driver lived to write his promised contribution, there would have been twenty-four; also that several other Anglican scholars of international reputation

---

[1] A.S.P. to J. R. Dummelow, 11 December 1919.
[2] On 6 January Mr Pinchard wrote a further letter in which he altered his phrase to 'edited by a Nonconformist in the very spirit of Modernism.'
[3] *The Times*, 17 January 1925.

had been approached, but, though in cordial support of the enterprise, they were unable through pressure of other duties to consent; that so far from 'conceiving my task in the spirit of Nonconformity' Peake had intentionally invited an Anglican expert on The Church and the Ministry to write *Ephesians* and *Colossians* 'because of the prominence of the Church in these epistles'. Peake concluded his letter:

... I am much interested to hear of a 'Catholic' Commentary; and so far as such a work increases the interest of its students in the Bible, and promotes its scientific study, I shall cordially welcome it. But in the study of Scripture the terms Protestant, Catholic, Anglican and Free Church seem to me wholly irrelevant. The biblical student, if he is worthy of his vocation, will approach the Scriptures, not to force them by extension on the rack or by savage mutilation into a bed of Procrustes, Roman or Protestant, 'Catholic' or 'Evangelical'; but denying his prepossessions and crucifying his prejudices, humbly to ascertain the actual facts. This is a study which transcends our confessional differences, and unites in close ties of Christian fellowship students in different ecclesiastical organisations. There is no cause which is nearer to my own heart than that of Reunion: and it would have been in my own eyes an unpardonable apostasy if I had edited a commentary on Holy Scripture, our common possession in a sectarian spirit.

Several members of the English Church Union, including Dr H. L. Goudge, one of the editors, and Dr C. Harris, the Chairman of the Literature Committee, at once repudiated 'this grotesque misrepresentation' implied in Mr Pinchard's letter, and by letter tendered profound apologies to Peake. It may also be recorded that on receiving a copy of *Peake's Commentary* in 1919, Bishop Gore himself had written: 'I hope to make much use of it: I have already made some.'

When the *New Commentary* appeared Peake wrote a lengthy critique of it[1] and 'whilst it must be recognized that the *Commentary* in its ecclesiastical and doctrinal standpoint is definitely Anglo-Catholic', yet he declared that 'the level it reaches is often high, and an immense amount of valuable information and exposition is here brought together. And those who cannot accept the theological and ecclesiastical position for which the *New Commentary* stands, may be glad to have so competent and authoritative a statement of it.'

III

The intellectual movement within Primitive Methodism in the 1850's found expression in the establishment of a journal, *The Christian Ambassador*, which was founded in 1854, and some years later took the title of *The Primitive Methodist Quarterly Review*. In 1910 under the editorship

---

[1] *H.R.* April 1929. pp. 223-30.

of the Rev. H. B. Kendall, the connexional historian, it became *The Holborn Review*.

As far back as 1891 Peake had contributed an article on 'The Synoptic Problem' to the *Quarterly Review*, and in February 1892 he was asked to undertake the editorship of the Literature Section, which had become vacant through the departure of the Rev. J. Day Thompson for Australia. The General Editor, the Rev. Colin C. McKechnie, wrote to Peake:

> ... In view of the unhappy break I have been wondering whether you could be induced to take that section of the *Review* into your hand. I fancy the work would suit your taste, and I feel sure you would manage it in a way that would give general satisfaction and contribute to the credit and efficiency of the *Review*.

Peake accepted the invitation and so entered upon the editorial tasks in this particular field which he was to carry during the next forty years. Here began his work as a book-reviewer, a work which was to be one of his important contributions to critical and theological study, and by which he was to be the guide for multitudes of readers, both lay and ministerial.

When in 1910 the journal became *The Holborn Review*, Peake conducted this particular work, and at the retirement of the editor in 1919 he accepted the invitation to become editor of the whole journal. Of this acceptance he wrote:

> ... I have done so with misgivings and some reluctance, because the amount of time and labour involved will be very considerable, and I shall probably have to set aside some other plans which I was hoping to carry out. The call of the Church, and particularly of the ministers weighed a good deal with me, and my long connexion with the *Review*, and the work I have done for it for nearly thirty years make me anxious about the future.... I have always considered the *Review* as one of our chief educational institutions and it gives us an intellectual standing among the churches which we could not have without it. It has been a very remarkable thing that for more than fifty years we have been able to carry on a Review of this character, while much larger and wealthier churches have had to abandon similar enterprises.

Peake introduced several new features which certainly increased its circulation. Previously very small payment had been made to contributors, who were almost entirely among the Primitive Methodists themselves; now, in order to make it possible to invite outside writers of eminence to provide contributions, Peake raised a fund privately, and thereby added distinction to the *Review*. From time to time he prepared series of articles in celebration of centenaries; thus, on the centenary of George Fox he secured seven articles from authorities on the subject. Early in 1923 he introduced a 'Study Circle' in the form of questions followed by suggestions for further reading. The most distinguishing features, however, were the sections on 'Current Literature' and the 'Editorial Notes'. Of these reviews of current literature more than half were written by Peake himself, and they revealed the enormous range of his own reading, as well as his soundness in the method of reviewing. The 'Editorial Notes' were made possible because of Peake's wide contacts with scholars and movements both at home and abroad. As an editor and reviewer, Peake was apt to be unusually autobiographical, and many of the continental theologians were his personal friends; taken together these *Notes* form an index to British reaction to these movements. Again and again in Peake's correspondence it is declared by those who wrote to him, that these two sections in the *Review* were those to which readers turned first and that many purchased the journal for the sound guidance offered by the long and numerous reviews in its pages from his pen. In this particular the periodical maintained its original design and purpose, namely, to serve as a guide to the reading and study of the ministers, preachers, and seriously-minded people in the denomination. A selection of these editorial notes, containing sketches of the scholars and leaders, most of whom were known personally to Peake, was made in 1938 by Dr W. F. Howard in *Recollections and Appreciations*.

Two examples will suffice in illustration of the regard in which the *Holborn Review* was held.

Mrs E. Herman, author of *The Meaning and Nature of Mysticism* wrote:

It is always a delight to read the *Holborn* which strikes me as quite the best review of its kind. I always look forward specially to your own book-reviews. The *Review* deserves to be far more widely known than it is.[1]

The following extract from a letter written by Tokio Matsumoto, a Methodist minister and Professor of New Testament in the largest theological school in Tokyo, is interesting as an illustration of the far-reaching influence of Peake's work:

You will doubtless be surprised to receive this letter from a stranger like myself. But your distinguished name and the numerous books on the Bible you have written have long been familiar to me, and I feel quite natural to write to you even so suddenly. . . . I feel I am related to you in at least three ways: in being a Methodist minister, in being a Professor of New Testament, and in being an editor of a theological review. Your books have been of great benefit and instruction to me as well as to many others here.

Now I have undertaken to write to you to ask if you will not kindly consider a proposal which I want to make, namely: I would very much like to start an exchange of magazines with you. I mean your splendid *Holborn Review* and our *Shingaku-Hysron* (Theological Review). . . . We are very anxious to get hold of our sister magazine so rich and valuable in content. We think you might be interested to possess a theological review which is not only the only one Methodist magazine in Japan which at all pretends to deal with the theological

---

[1] E. Herman to A.S.P., 2 October 1922.

and biblical questions in any scientific and thorough fashion, but also one of the only three quarterlies which are being issued by the Christians in Japan.

By exchange of magazines like this will be significant as expressing sentiments of fraternity between the Methodists in England and in this country. We do want to keep in touch with you and your scholarly achievements, and also to be reminded by you in matters of faith as we struggle to penetrate into the inner life and deep significance of Christian faith as revealed in the Bible and in our age.... With apologies for 'my broken English and hurried writing', this moving letter closes with the hope that there may be a meeting between them. 'How I wish to sit under *your* feet for study and inspiration some day!'[1]

It is interesting in passing to note that *The Congregational Quarterly*, founded in 1923 under the editorship of Dr Albert Peel, traced its beginnings to a meeting with Peake on a holiday visit to Appledore in Devon, and later to weeks when they met at summer pastorates in Keswick. Peake had many things to share with his younger friend and encouraged the idea of a learned yet popular Congregational quarterly journal. Dr Peel later declared that a great deal of the success of the venture was due to Peake.[2]

The problems which an editor has to face are not seldom considerable, and in this respect Peake's experience was no exception. The following excerpts from his letters not only reveal some of these, but also the way in which he dealt with those who were involved. He could be firm and direct, yet not without characteristic humour and grace.

To a contributor whose manuscript was difficult to decipher he wrote:

I suppose it has taken me five times, at a low estimate, the time to decipher the cuneiform, Hittite and heiroglyphic script with which your paper is so plentifully adorned, than an article written in English script would have taken. To help the printer I have transliterated a good deal more than you yourself had done. I specially want to write a meditation for you which would be fairly extensive, and probably last some weeks! If you exercised your conscience faithfully on it, it would create a revolution in your hand-writing, and you would feel that illegibility is not an eccentricity to be pious about, a trifle to be dismissed with a shrug of the shoulders, but a downright vice and a source of vice in others. A good deal of the stuff I had to read through a magnifying glass, not because it was in itself so microscopic, but because the differentiating elements which were imperceptible to the naked eye did often reveal themselves under a glass of higher power than my spectacles. If I were your father-confessor I should put you under an inflexible penance to devote so much time

---

[1] Tokio Matsumoto to A.S.P., 15 March 1927. Many years after this letter was written Dr Matsumoto called on the present writer at Hartley Victoria College, Manchester, desiring to visit the place where Peake had taught. He was a sad and ageing figure: he told me that both his wife and children had died at Hiroshima, and that he alone had survived.

[2] Cf. Albert Peel to A.S.P., 8 December 1922. 'Passed the last sheet of the *Cong. Quarterly* for press this morning, for which Yahweh be praised! However do you manage it quarter by quarter! I fear we are far from approaching the standard of the *Holborn*, so you need not worry about competition.'

every day to writing slowly enough to secure that every letter was so formed as, whether beautiful or otherwise in appearance, to be differentiated from every other letter. Moreover you would at the end of the time never write two words together so that they looked like one word, nor run two letters so that they looked like one, or telescope seven letters so that you can only count four. I do think you owe it to your correspondents and to compositors, who are after all God's creatures like the rest of us, and especially to over-driven, over-worried, over-tired editors to learn to write.... One picks one's way painfully from stepping-stone to stepping-stone, working one's imagination hard and practising divination, and finally succeeding in piecing the thing together bit by bit. But it's a horribly slow process, and one needs to draw heavily on the reserves of Divine grace before one is through!...

You would yourself be greatly surprised at the end of a month, and your correspondents would bless the unknown influence which had so radically transformed you; the editors would read your manuscript joyfully, while there would be joy in heaven over another sinner returning from the error of his ways; there would be joy and much less blasphemy in the printer's office!

To another contributor who had been too severe in a review, Peake wrote:

I wonder whether you could find it in your heart to mitigate a little what you say about S......, I mean perhaps in expression rather than in substance. I have in fact taken out 'very muddy' and substituted 'somewhat cloudy', which expresses your meaning in a somewhat heavenlier form! And is there anything you could say in appreciation?... I am returning it in case you feel you can handle him as if you loved him, while you string him on your hook. I didn't read a line of the book myself, and am not quarrelling at all with your judgement: but I'm afraid in the list of casualties he will appear among the 'very seriously wounded'.

To yet another contributor whose tendency was to be late in sending in his manuscripts, Peake wrote:

Please work off the reviews as soon as possible. I only once heard Dr Torrey preach and he struck me as essentially a commercial traveller for God with a first class line to offer! The best thing about his sermon was his text, which showed a touch of genius in its collocation of two passages: 'The Holy Ghost saith, Today; the fool saith tomorrow'. I pass on the text as a word in season!

CHAPTER SEVEN

THE PREACHER

IN THE light of his early religious background, and his own personal Christian experience, it is not surprising that Peake turned his thought to the subject of preaching as a service to be rendered to the cause of Divine truth. As we have already noted, from time to time he entertained in his mind the question of entering into the ordained ministry, but events steadily brought the conviction that that was not to be his life-vocation. Nevertheless the opportunity to preach, as a local preacher in the Primitive Methodist Church, still remained to him. The issue began to crystallize in the early days at Oxford.

Soon after his arrival in Oxford in October 1883, he made the acquaintance of the Rev. James Crompton, the minister then in charge of the Oxford Circuit. On the Friday following his arrival Peake called at the home of Mr Crompton, and on the Monday the latter took him to see places of interest in the city; the following morning they went on the river. Thus began a friendship which was to have important consequences, for it was through Mr Crompton's influence that Peake became a worker in the Sunday School and a local preacher on the circuit plan.

The first sermon that Peake preached was at a small village chapel at Murcott, about twelve miles from Oxford, on Sunday, 2 March 1884.[1] In a letter Peake describes the occasion:[2]

Some time ago Mr Crompton and I made an arrangement to go together to Murcott the first Sunday in March—yesterday. So we drove over yesterday morning—beautiful drive—and got there for dinner. Then came the dread ordeal. I had carefully prepared the outline of a sermon on 'Come unto Me, all ye that are weary etc....' and two following verses. I took no part in the service till after the lesson; then gave out the second hymn, and that over, I took my text. Horror of horrors! I stopped short in a couple of minutes. I called all my faculties together, and told my congregation of the fact that this

---

[1] In a letter to Peake, dated 1 October 1928, Dr Theodore H. Robinson wrote: 'I saw my mother incidentally. She tells me that your first sermon was preached at Murcot! Why didn't I know this before! It must be 40 years ago since I went to that quietest of all English hamlets. It is not at all unlikely that my grandfather was in your congregation that day!'

[2] A.S.P. to George Peake, 3 March 1884.

was my first time, entreating their sympathy and prayers, and then I went on. I got through the rest of it pretty well, though not very fluently, and concluded after about three and twenty minutes of speaking.

Although Peake himself was much disheartened, Mr Crompton expressed his sense of satisfaction; in the evening Peake preached 'with considerable freedom' on the text, 'Come for all things are now ready: and they all with one consent began to make excuses'. He spoke for some eighteen minutes and made discovery of himself as to the manner of preaching—the contrast between the two experiences finally led him to adopt the method of extempore speech.

The years that followed showed how complete was the success he achieved. Again and again it is noted how, even in treatment of intricate subjects in his lectures and addresses, he could speak for an hour or more in faultless English without a single note before him. To a preaching service he would come with his mind stored with divine truth, and leave the utterance to the guidance of the Spirit step by step.

During the Easter vacation of 1884 his preaching experience became 'considerably enlarged' by appointments in his home circuit, and on his return to Oxford he preached at Pembroke Street Church, the head church of the circuit, on 'And his servants shall serve him; and they shall see his face'. Of this important occasion he wrote:[1]

As far as practical experience goes I have lost much of the nervousness I had before preaching, though I never felt much while I was preaching. I have also gained some of the fire I lacked. As a rule I find it better not to use notes. Perhaps they are useful as a safeguard; but my easiest times have been those undoubtedly when I have had no notes.

On 2 September 1884 Peake received the following letter from the Quarterly Meeting of the Presteigne Circuit, in Radnorshire, where his father was the superintendent minister:

You are respectfully informed that the following Resolution was passed at the Quarter Day: *Minute 20*: That Bro. Arthur Samuel Peake has sanction to preach and take appointments. Signed on behalf of the Quarterly Meeting.

John Davies: *President.*
Philip Davis: *Secretary.*

It is not surprising that as a young preacher Peake encountered problems and difficulties. One such was the quality of his voice, a matter which gave his brother some concern, and we find him giving advice to Peake in a letter at this time:[2]

There is one thing which you will I think have to look to carefully, that is your voice and delivery. Be careful to get into the way of speaking every word clearly

---

[1] A.S.P. to George Peake, 3 May 1884.
[2] George Peake to A.S.P., 10 May 1884.

and distinctly. Don't speak too fast ... much of the effect is lost in rapid speaking.

Peake was able to give his brother some assurance after preaching in the large Pembroke Street Church: 'My voice is considerably better than I anticipated. Since I wrote to you I discovered that I could be well heard all over the chapel, and it was a large one and by no means full'.[1] He so definitely mastered this problem that in the after years he could be heard with perfect clearness in large assemblies numbering some two thousand or more people.

Peake tells us that his greatest difficulty, however, was to overcome the temptation to personal vanity. This is declared in a letter to his cousin Annetta.[2] He wrote:

I have lately discovered a most subtle and dangerous temptation. It is this: when I have been preaching and had a good time I feel elated, as though I had done some great thing, and the devil makes capital out of it. And not only that, but others come and praise me to my face. I cannot retail all that I have heard them say but one or two instances will suffice. Our chairman at Stanton Long Tea-Meeting, when I had done speaking, told father he ought to be very proud he had a son who talked so easily and so nicely; he wished he could. Then Mr Skett gets up and talks about my speech, that I had given them an epitome of ecclesiastical history, and what an intellectual treat it was! This, though very kind, was certainly injudicious. But the worst part is yet to come. I sat in my seat and felt pleased and flattered. It was very sinful, I know, 'but the flesh is weak....' I know so far from taking any glory to myself I should give it all to God, and account myself but as an unprofitable servant. But this temptation, which is one of the most dangerous to which I am subject, imperilling all communication between God and my spirit, is one of the most difficult to battle. Help me with your advice or cheer me with your sympathy, but *above all* pray that I may escape the wiles of the devil who seeketh to take me captive at his will. I should like to make my life useful to others, but in the very act of doing it, I find a snare.

One thing is certain, as the after-years abundantly proved, Peake's character as a preacher was marked by the deepest humility, recognizing as he did the solemnity of the task to which he was committed.

Although it was Peake's custom to use extempore speech in preaching, it was his way to set down in brief form and outline beforehand the main trends of his thought for any discourse, and some of these manuscripts have survived together with a number of verbatim reports of his sermons. These are valuable as revealing on analysis the type of his discourses. Two features are common throughout. First, his preaching was always Christocentric in its content. All his sermons moved steadily to the climax which

---

[1] A.S.P. to George Peake, 20 May 1884.
[2] A.S.P. to Annetta Peake, 18 April 1884. Quoted in L. S. Peake, *Memoir*, op. cit., pp. 88–9, to which I owe the reference. The incident is also recorded in a letter: A.S.P. to George Peake, 3 May 1884.

was to be seen in the Person of Christ. If he preached from the Old Testament it was always in the light of the Old Testament as a preparation for the message of the New. The whole discourse steadily focused itself upon Jesus Christ as the goal of his preaching. Again, in a letter to his cousin, Annetta,[1] he declared in his early days what he believed to be the principle at the foundation of all his preaching ministry:

I think I might sum up all my creed in that one word, Christ, and all that is good in my own religious experience. I don't care to get beyond that because as St Paul has told us and as many have proved it true, Christ is 'all and in all.' Our preaching in the future will have to be the preaching of Christ, and not the preaching of pet doctrines. That is, I shall not preach sanctification, but Christ *made* sanctification to the believer. 'Jesus Christ and Him crucified' *must* be the theme of our ministry if it is to be of success. We must not enter into fine-spun argument about this or that point of belief, but we must show Christ to the people. ... It is one of the points on which I feel very strongly.

The second feature of Peake's preaching was its simplicity. Those of us who have listened to him were influenced by his eloquence, but it was the eloquence of simple and unadorned speech; in every discourse there was a steady development of argument, step by step, set forth in clear and faultless English, without ambiguity or excess of words, and with amazing accuracy of emphasis. On this matter of directness and simplicity in preaching Peake expressed himself strongly. Following a visit to Oxford by Dr Antliff, a leading Primitive Methodist preacher, he wrote:[2]

Dr Antliff has grasped the true idea of preaching, that the preacher is not in the pulpit to proclaim to the admiring, or it may be disgusted, throng, that he is learned, inasmuch as he knows the Greek alphabet and the first declension of Latin nouns, but rather to proclaim how existing relations between God and man may be changed or bettered, and make us forget the preacher in what the preacher says. ... I am afraid our preachers, the younger men especially, are great sinners in this respect. But if they learn more every day they will at last, we may hope, become capable of expressing great ideas in pure English.... It is a matter on which I feel strongly. One of the safeguards of religion in the pew is simplicity and directness in the pulpit; and that it was which lent power to the old Methodists, and again to the Primitive Methodists.

The following extract from the conclusion to a sermon preached at the Parish Church of St Ann's, Manchester, in 1902, illustrates these features of Peake's preaching:

Ultimately the question always comes back to this: What do we think of Jesus Christ? What in the very essence of His being was He? Was Jesus Christ the highest and greatest thing humanity has been able to produce in personality and character, in spotless perfection and moral beauty? Was He the greatest achievement of mankind in that sphere as Shakespeare is the greatest in the

---

[1] Quoted L.S. Peake, *Memoir*, p. 92.
[2] A.S.P. to George Peake, 4 July 1885.

sphere of poetry? Are we to approach God, and ask for his judgement on man to be determined by what the human race has in Jesus been able to produce? Is Jesus our ultimate word to God, or is He something entirely different, not humanity's creation but God's last and best gift to man? Is He God's word to man or man's word to God? That is the ultimate question of the faith. Our answer is given with some conviction that Jesus ultimately belongs to the side of God, and not to the side of man; that in the very basis and essence of his nature He belongs to that Godhead whom we adore as the Trinity in Unity. In infinite pity and gracious love, He took our humanity upon Himself: He knew what our experience was from the inside; He understood it to its farthest reaches and its finest sensibilities. And thus understanding it, He has brought to us through His Incarnation and His redemptive work, that perfect peace with God, and that solution which answers for us our deepest and greatest problems, and gives us a certainty and a victory in this life and ultimately the hope of a blessed immortality.

In the early years as a young preacher he was much sought after during his vacations from Oxford, particularly by the country chapels in Shropshire and Herefordshire, and of course afterwards his field of service became extended far and wide. In the Manchester years he preached on special occasions in the pulpits of denominations other than his own—Carr's Lane, Birmingham; the City Temple, London; to the Assembly of the Congregational Union; for the British and Foreign Bible Society; in Anglican churches and cathedrals on the call of Christian Unity. For some years in succession he took services throughout the month of August in Keswick. However, on account of the pressure upon his slender physical reserves, and especially after his illness in 1915 he was compelled under medical advice to limit himself in the task of the preaching he loved so well.

It would be impossible to gather the results of Peake's preaching ministry, but they were far-reaching, and seem to suggest that in the main this ministry was twofold. His discourses brought mental illumination and spiritual comfort. Two examples will suffice to show the depths of this ministry—both from members of the congregation entirely unknown to him. Following a sermon at Carr's Lane, Birmingham in 1907, a lady wrote this letter to him:

I feel I must write and thank you for the sermon you preached on Sunday morning at Carr's Lane. You cannot know how much it is helping me. The thought of Moses' patience, of faith for forty years, makes me bear a trial which sometimes has made me rebellious. I have my youngest boy under-developed in brain. I myself know that I have the power within me to do a great work which I commenced before the trial came. I am being constantly urged not to 'smother the gift', and yet as you said on Sunday, it is not the fight that is hard—but the *inaction*, and the keeping quiet when 'the fire burns within'. We have him at home—and he is quite happy and improving slightly, but I cannot see my way to do otherwise than I am doing. You have helped me—to make the way easier and the path plainer.

From a hearer in Liverpool, unknown to him, in 1914 came the following:

Will you pardon me for expressing my deep appreciation of your most inspiring ministry last evening? It is good to be lifted on to the mountain occasionally, nor does it spoil us for the heat and stress of the valleys; we face them once again with fresh stimulus.... Your helpful thoughts have been returning again and again through the busy hours of this day, and will long dwell in my mind as a source of strength and cheer. With renewed thanks and every prayer that you may long be spared to revive the drooping spirits of those who have to face the grim facts of life, and to set them in heavenly places.

From the pen of one who, then a student in Hackney College, London, came the following in 1911:

The reason I write is because I have always wanted to tell you that it was largely owing to two sermons you preached on 'The Call of Moses' that I felt compelled to take up the preparation for what I hope will be my life's work—the ministry of the Gospel of Christ. Previously I was in an architect's office, but I often half-hoped to take up the work of preaching. I *hoped* but after your sermon on 'Esteeming the reproach of Christ greater riches than the treasures in Egypt', I felt *compelled* if the way were possible, to take up this new course, and I told my father on the following Sunday evening and Dr Jowett some weeks after .... I suppose men are called to this great work in many different ways, but I often feel glad that I can look back to one Sunday that was a day of crisis which turned the tide of my life's work.

Such examples could be multiplied, and there must have been many of which we have no record at all.

CHAPTER EIGHT

MOVEMENTS TOWARDS REFORM

FROM his early years Peake had a strong humanitarian concern arising out of his vital religious experience. A deep social sensitiveness marked his outlook on the world, and this gave him a sense of being committed to the support of all involved for the betterment of mankind. Thus beyond the demands of his academic life he found himself answering the call of human need wherever he found it and he was therefore a disciple of reform as far as lay in his power and opportunity to fulfil it.

I

Within the life of the Church Peake was haunted by the question: What is to be the religious condition of the Churches and what the spiritual condition of England in, say, twenty-five years from now? To him the signs in many respects were ominous. If Christians really believed in their religion as the most precious thing they could give to their generation, then it should be presented as effectively as possible. The beginnings of preparation for such effective presentation must be found in the life and work of the Sunday School. In this field he saw the need for reform, both as to substance and method.

This necessity for reform was thrust upon him soon after his arrival at Oxford, when he accepted an invitation from the minister, the Rev. James Crompton, to take a class of boys in the Sunday School at Pembroke Street. Of that experience he wrote to his brother George[1] in a letter which not only gives a picture of many a Sunday School eighty years ago but sheds light upon Peake as a youthful reformer, and points to the course of action he was to take in the work of reform in later years.

I was at school the Sunday before last and last Sunday. On the former of these two days we sang, prayed, then names were called over, then sang again, and at last teaching began. I was getting on capitally when closing time came, and we endured an address from the Sunday School visitor. After the usual

[1] A.S.P. to George Peake, 7 December 1883.

compliments, that of all the eight or ten schools he has lately visited, ours was the best arranged, he went on to tell us he had noted one defect, and that was we didn't use the International Lessons in our bible classes! That was not of the pleasantest for Sunday No. 1 and he went on to show us how interesting the lesson was and of course, I suppose, profitable (it was the tale of the fight between Goliath and David!), and most of his interesting discourse was taken up with proving what was perfectly obvious, that David was grown up at the time of the fight. I dare say you will agree with me that St Luke is far more fitted for promiscuous reading in a Sunday School than any account which might incite the already too much developed fighting instincts of the boys. We sang again once or twice and concluded. That's their ideal of a Sunday School!

Last Sunday it was even worse. I went down and we sang, prayed, roll-call and sang again, and at length I discovered they had the insane custom down there of sacrificing the last Sunday afternoon in the month, lesson and all, to a prayer-meeting. I was thunderstruck. Fancy, when I had a lesson for them, to have it put aside by a prayer-meeting! Well, one or two prayed, then a hymn, then the superintendent said something and some ignorant girl recited in a flat, dull manner, at her own request, some hymn about hearing instruction young and "twill save you from ten thousand snares', etc.! I dare say it's not altogether unfamiliar to you. The superintendent—who by the way, is a meek and mild sort of man and all the better in some respects for it—having commended her, asked some fellow, a local preacher, I presume, to speak to us. He came up and gave us a speech which was remarkable for nothing but its length, notwithstanding which I happen to remember one thing that he said, viz:- that he had not prepared a speech so he had nothing grand to tell us, which was perfectly true, though there was no necessity for us to be reminded of it. Well, at the end of it, for it did come to an end at last, the superintendent gave out a hymn and so we concluded. I should most certainly not have wasted my time by going down if I had known that such a mad custom existed. I shall set my face against it, and if it isn't altered, I shall have first Sunday in a month free.

International Lessons are all very well for teachers who don't prepare their lessons, because the teacher's assistant is a very good crutch for them, but I shall certainly not use them.

My class I like well; they are docile and ignorant, so we shall get on well together, I hope. But I must have my own way in teaching them. It's ridiculous to have one's time cut so short by such an idiotic way of opening: and in time it is all too short. I make very great personal sacrifice because they have no reliable teacher for the first class boys, and I would do more, but I must not be hampered in my work by stupid prejudice. The boys are glad to be taught well, as it is a rare circumstance for them, and I am resolved to teach them well, and reforms must be made. The second hymn is a wicked waste of time, and the roll-call might well be done by each teacher in his or her own class. But according to the usual system of teaching, time is not so valuable. A quarter of an hour means some couple of chapters more read, but a quarter of an hour means a great deal more than that with me. My ideal would be for the boys to meet me separately. I should pray two or three minutes with them, call their names and begin, and after lesson go to the last hymn and prayer with the rest of the scheme. I am afraid the teachers will want some considerable education before they get to that. I must be content to advance by degrees. All things come to the man who waits bravely. The first steps will be to abolish roll-call and the second hymn, then the monthly prayer-meeting. Perhaps they will then be prepared to let me have what I want, and what eventually I will have.

It is interesting to record that Peake's criticisms were not without effect; the reforms he desired in this Sunday School took place not long after his protest.

This early experience of the inadequacy of the work being done in Sunday Schools left a deep impression on Peake's mind, and in 1905 he wrote a series of nine articles in the *Primitive Methodist Leader* on the subject of Sunday School Reform, which in the following year were published under the title *Reform in Sunday School Teaching* (1906), a book which received a warm welcome from many quarters, showing that it expressed the thoughts that were simmering in many minds, though few could have expressed them more powerfully and with greater authority.

The chief part of the book was an attack on the International Lessons Committee and a bare exposure of the system by a skilful marshalling of evidence against it. Peake acknowledged the force of the idea of an international system, namely, that it represents the world-wide sympathy in Sunday School work, and he notes the large development of literature which had grown up around it, but declared that, as a system, reform was required. His criticism was concerned with the practice of invariably basing the lesson on a brief section of Scripture; the mistake of spreading the lesson over the whole school; junior classes should be occupied with more elementary subjects, the senior with more advanced. 'The present system is rather a closed circle; whenever a boy joins it, he has the whole school with him, and round the circle the whole school tramps together' (p. 28): a detailed criticism of the method of selection employed—'switching back from Gospel to Genesis'—leaving a most confused impression on the mind. Constructively Peake urged that longer portions of Scripture should be given with the aim of teaching what they contain rather than taking small selections as texts for the teacher's own ideas; the adjustment of passages chosen to the ages of scholars; the institution of training classes for teachers, and school libraries for both teachers and scholars. Students in theological colleges should also receive training.

Much of what is in the book is now taken as commonplace in Sunday School work, but the book has to be seen in the light of the time when it was written—the necessity for reform in this sphere of Christian work. It was the stirring of the waters and it had a distinct influence upon the new approach which followed shortly afterwards. The system of the International Lesson became greatly improved; lessons were graded according to the age of the scholar; the scheme was so remoulded as to give a picture of Christianity in its historical setting. Peake himself took a leading part in the preparation of the new scheme.

Believing the work of the Sunday School to be so vital for the future of religion in the country, as well as in the upbuilding of the Churches, Peake never allowed his interest to diminish. Frequently he spoke to conferences of teachers on the work, and himself served as President of the Manchester Sunday School Union. The reason for his challenge to the participation in the work was stated quite clearly when he addressed an assembly of the National Sunday School Union in 1906:

> It is because of my deep-rooted conviction that the work of the Sunday School is doing for England, and still more the work that it might do for England is the most important work that could be done, that has caused me, in a busy and crowded life to turn aside and speak of what I feel to be the grave defects of the present system of instruction.[1]

II

As we have already observed Peake's early years in Oxford brought him into touch with movements for social betterment which were finding expression in a group of men—'The Oxford Socialists'—and his sympathy with the movement caused his father some searching of heart. In a lengthy letter[2] to his parents, Peake sought to justify his position.

A socialist is not necessarily an infidel. An Oxford Socialist is hardly likely to be one. Murder and plunder are no more connected with socialism than noise is necessary in a religious meeting. True many socialists are infidels, but not infidels because they are socialists, but because they are too vulgar to know any better. An Oxford socialist is one who takes a deep interest in the welfare of the people. The church parson of a hundred years back would not be a socialist. The more *socialistic* a religious man is, in the proper sense of the term, the more good he is likely to do because he will look upon other men as being his brothers. I think decidedly that if Christ had lived at this day he would have been an Oxford socialist. The way he treated the Pharisees and Sadducees and the publicans and sinners is a proof of this. Christ didn't recognise class distinction, but people seem to do so now. I should call Gladstone, Bright and Chamberlain decided socialists, as was the author of *The Bitter Cry*. We claim a right for every man to think for himself, which our opponents deny. Of course, in a proper society, murder and plunder would be impossible, because society protects itself. The action of a true socialist is to set society upon a proper basis. In such a society the chances of murder and pillage would be much less than in present society. We can't make people religious by an Act of Parliament, but we can make a state of society in which religion would be made more attractive owing to the loss of class distinctions. Of course *property* cannot be touched. It's simply ridiculous to think of such a thing. But we can make laws to raise the moral conditions of the people. We can make laws to lessen drinking and other forms of misery. We can make laws to put people in better homes and keep them clean: we can lessen disease and dirt a hundredfold.

[1] Supplement to the *Sunday School Chronicle*, 10 May 1906.
[2] A.S.P. to Samuel Peake, 2 February 1884.

Till the country is in a perfect condition and society rests on a proper basis, socialists must be at work. It's quite natural to suppose that the conservatives will try to keep the people under their thumb. It's impossible. They will rise sometime or other and assert their rights. Is it not better to give them, and that peaceably, than that they should take them by force? But before they can make use properly of their rights they must be taught. This is the province of the religious and the educated, and this is what is needed; men who shall teach the masses the broad truths of Christianity, saturate their lives with them, and then it will not seem so bad a thing nor so terrible for them to gain their rights, for they will know how to use them and to use them well. If however men will be so blind as to think that the volcano will not burst forth at some time or other, and will not lend a hand to help to train the masses, they cannot hope, in the general wreck of an uneducated revolution, to escape unhurt. Our rulers would know no religion, because they had never been taught, and the state of the country would be desperate indeed. But a Christian socialist is one who sees that the masses must one day have their place and tries by all means in his power to make them a God-fearing religious element of society. Joseph Arch was you know a Methodist preacher, but that does not hinder him from being a socialist. We want them to make a right use of their power when they get it.

Peake's idealism found origin and reinforcement in certain events which occurred at this particular time.

The first of these was the reading of a book entitled *The Bitter Cry of Outcast London*, through which he felt called to devote his life to work as a clergyman in the Church of England in the slum areas of London, despite the frailty of his health at that period. He recorded his convictions in a letter to his cousin Annetta.[1]

One would think that one's health and strength were to be weighed against human souls. There are many reasons to induce me to take such a course. Their abject misery and utter godlessness, their immorality and pursuit of every form of vice, their ignorance and destitution, all make it necessary that some effort should be made to raise them into the condition of religious, virtuous and healthy Christians. I will send you either in this letter, or a future one, a copy of *The Bitter Cry of Outcast London*. You will read it carefully and ponder on the startling revelation contained in it. Then ask yourself if you are any longer unwilling to let your brother devote himself to the work. The Gospel must do these people good, and if the Lord permits me to live but five years among them, when my university life is over, will not these five years have been well-spent? There will be much fruit assuredly if I can but work hard enough and keep humble and full of faith.

Another event that strengthened Peake's concern for a better social order was the movement to secure Home Rule for Ireland, led by Mr Gladstone and the Liberal Party in 1886. A letter written to his brother[2] shows not only his indignation at the sufferings of the Irish, but also his

---

[1] A.S.P. to Annetta Peake, 18 April 1884. Quoted in *Memoir*, pp. 58–9.
[2] A.S.P. to George Peake, 13 April 1886.

MOVEMENTS TOWARDS REFORM 149

thoughts as to the value of the political element in the effort to secure social reform. He wrote:

Are four-fifths of a nation to be debarred from their rights for the sake of a paltry minority with no patriotism but for their own pocket, and no toleration but for their own religion? The union was obtained by men who sold their country to a tyrannical and oppressive Prime Minister. It has been kept by us and maintained by such means as would in England have long ago goaded the people to a revolution. The Irish have been more long-suffering, but the day of reckoning has come at last. If we as a Protestant country had been governed by an Irish administration, with Mr Biggar at its head, with a troop of servile Irish Roman Catholics, who would alone be eligible for office to oppress us, if the name of an Englishman had been flung about by them as a bye-word, and our liberties trampled on in the dust, do you not think that we should have revolted? And that is how Ireland has been treated in defiance of all laws human and divine that had a particle of justice and uprightness in them, and that is what Mr Gladstone proposes to alter. That Home Rule will come I firmly believe. It is better to give it in time of peace, than make Ireland our enemy in time of war: and as a matter of justice it should have been given long ago.

A further stimulus to Peake's concern for social issues was the reading of General Booth's book, *In Darkest England and the Way Out* (1890), and in a letter[1] he discloses his distress at the thought of suffering humanity.

I am much struck with the book. I think the scheme is admirable. I must try and send him a subscription when I am a little richer. I do feel deeply the horrible disgrace that attaches to us as a nation for allowing such a frightful state of poverty and misery to exist. If Christianity means anything at all it means that we should say that our brothers and sisters should not live under conditions which make happiness and sobriety and virtue quite impossible. Years ago I proposed giving up my life to work in the East End. I think now that I was not meant for that work either by physical or mental constitution; but I do want very much to be preserved from any callous indifference to the welfare of my fellow-men who live in such hopeless destitution as many of them do. The scheme is based on sound commercial principles and will have no tendency to pauperise those who receive benefit from it. . . . One thing I feel sure. Indiscriminate charity will never do any good but only harm . . . What is wanted is not that money or food should be given, but that work should be given to the unemployed. And the work should not be stone-breaking or oakum-picking, but useful interesting work, and, if possible the work a man is best able to do.

The severe winter of 1890-1, when the weather was so bitterly cold that an ox was roasted on the Thames at Oxford, gave Peake further concern for the sufferings of the poor. In another letter[2] he wrote to Miss Sillman about this:

If the frost continues I fear it will mean much more terrible suffering and

---

[1] A.S.P. to Harriet M. Sillman, 29 December 1890, quoted in *Memoir*, p. 63.
[2] A.S.P. to Harriet M. Sillman, 7 January 1891. Quoted in *Memoir*, pp. 64-5.

destitution than you or I have any conception of. I do wish something could be done. It seems dreadful sometimes to me that I should be well-housed and clothed and fed, while people who are far better and more deserving than I am should have to suffer all the rigours of a severe English winter with all the loss of work that it implies, and without the alleviation of food and warmth at all adequate to their need. Really life is so sad and full of bitterness that my wonder is that people cling to it so passionately as they do; life can be hardly worth living under the conditions to which thousands of our fellow-countrymen are subject, yet the patience of the poor, their long-suffering with oppression, is to me more wonderful still. The heroism shown by innumerable people in humble life, who never dream that their conduct is other than natural, is truly amazing. When I set myself by them I feel humbled. I do hope to do something to help. Feeling so sorry is useless unless one helps them oneself. I do want each of us to feel that we are not here on earth just simply for our own selfish pleasure, but set here by God himself to do a definite work. He is our Master; we are His stewards. The poor are Christ's representatives. He has identified Himself everywhere with the down-trodden, the suffering and the outcast. Inasmuch as we do good to one of these we do it to Him. We serve God by helping our fellow. I feel intensely that privilege implies responsibility. If I am more learned, more wealthy than my neighbour, I am so for his sake and not chiefly for my own.

It should be remembered that this moving letter is all the more significant because it was written shortly after Peake had received the Merton Fellowship, with all its financial and other advantages. Throughout his life Peake held the stewardship of money as a sacred trust, and though removed from direct participation in humanitarian work, he never ceased in generosity toward such movements, as well as by direct personal assistance to those whom he knew were in need.

III

Other social issues claimed Peake's interest and support in terms of reform.

Peake was a life-long total abstainer and as early as 1886 began to address 'Blue Ribbon' Temperance meetings in the neighbourhood of Presteigne. Educated at home in a completely teetotal atmosphere, his convictions were firmly based. He wrote:

What I accepted on trust from others secured my strong adhesion when I was able to think for myself, and I have never wavered in my conviction as to the truth of our principle and the necessity of our propaganda.[1]

By his address and counsel he brought encouragement to the movement for reform, and gave generously to the work. He was for years a vice-president of the Manchester, Salford and District Temperance Union and

---

[1] Article in *The Alliance News and Temperance Reform* on 'My Settled Antagonism to the Liquor Traffic: A Personal Confession of Faith'. 17 December 1911.

also of the Lancashire and Cheshire Band of Hope and Temperance Union. When he died in 1929, the officers and committee of the latter organization recorded its appreciation of his support:

Again and again he cheered and helped us in difficult days; by the graciousness of his speech and thought he encouraged and inspired all of us. His beautiful scholarly life will long be treasured among us and an abiding influence to better service for the little ones.

The strength of his conviction on this social question is illustrated by two incidents.

In 1907 a meeting of Manchester citizens assembled in the Free Trade Hall to make strong protest against the projected appointment as Lord Mayor of the city of one who was a brewer and owner of many tied houses in the municipality. At this meeting Peake was one of the chief speakers, and he spoke in trenchant terms.

I do not oppose the man as such. I know next to nothing of him. It would make no difference were he everything his most generous adherents proclaim him to be. He is a mere accident of the situation. The better the man the more pleased I am to have a straight fight on the principle.... We do not oppose because of political or ecclesiastical difference; in such a matter barriers of this kind do not exist.... We have to oppose him because the trade by which he lives is incompatible in the best interests of the city over which he is asked to preside.

Many years later, in 1928, when President of the National Free Church Council, Peake preached in the Albert Hall, Manchester, and made the following statement typical of his conviction on this subject:[1]

In my earlier years I have frequently been thrown into company where I should be, perhaps, the only teetotaller; often with men of very brilliant intellect, and some of them famous. I am quite prepared to say from experience that if I want a company where talk is brilliant, where capital stories are told, where there is a constant flow of merriment and good humour, I know of none equal to a company of ministers. That I say quite deliberately. I am a layman myself, but I have been in the company of ministers over and over again, and I have heard remarks quite as brilliant, quite as humorous, even higher than any I have heard when alcohol was freely flowing all the time.... I have heard social workers down in dark areas speak with passion of the way in which at every turn the beneficent ministries they have exercised are being held up and hampered by this thing.

It is no use saying my influence does not count. We all count for something, and our influence is a thing of which we shall have to give account at last at the judgment seat of Christ. This is a question we all have to face. I decided it long ago for myself. I had no hesitation whatever in deciding that every atom of influence I had should be thrown on the side of Temperance. To me every

---

[1] Quoted in *Memoir*, pp. 309-10. In 1929, in moving a resolution to thank Professor Gilbert Murray, who had been a guest lecturer at the Primitive Methodist Conference, Peake recalled how in the far-off Oxford days the two of them had taken sides with the Blue Ribbon Movement and had worn the colours as undergraduates in the University.

man's duty to become a teetotaller was absolutely clear. I do not judge others who take a different view. But I do beg of them to ask whether they may not be using their influence in a way for which they may blush when they stand before the judgment seat of Christ.

From that absolutist position Peake never withdrew.

Other social problems touched him deeply. The menace of gambling met with his challenge, along with other and important figures in public life; he gave his sympathetic understanding to those working on the question of housing: the condition of defeated Germany wounded him deeply and along with others he urged the necessity of a policy of rescue from starvation. In 1921, in a review of Stephen Graham's book *Children of the Slaves*, he made a vigorous attack on the mob-violence and the cruelties against the negroes in the Southern States of America:

To take pleasure in inflicting atrocious pain points to a depth of depravity which we associate with devils. . . . We should be glad to think that the United States will take her place in the moral leadership of the world: but with what effective voice can she speak while the smoke of negro burnings goes up to God and the innocent blood of her victims cries to Him from the ground?[1]

Peake was a member of C.O.P.E.C. in 1924, and also of the Continuation Committee which met in Manchester. No movement for social betterment was beyond his interest and support.

IV

There is no greater illustration of Peake's humanitarian concern than his attitude to the treatment of the conscientious objector during the First World War. Setting his face against what he believed to be an injustice, he stepped out of his academic world to plead that justice should be done. Not only did he add his signature to protests against ill-treatment, but in the autumn of 1917 wrote a series of eleven articles in the *Primitive Methodist Leader* under the title, 'Who is offended and I burn not?' In the spring of 1918, under pressure from many quarters, but particularly from Professor Gilbert Murray and Mrs Hobhouse,[2] these articles were published in book-form under the title *Prisoners of Hope*—a phrase taken from Zechariah 9:12. In the early part of 1916 he had written to the press twice on the subject, and had also drafted a lengthy resolution dealing with all sides of the question, and this had received the unanimous approval by the Primitive Methodist Conference in June of that year. The situation having become more serious, Peake realized that he must raise the question again; the opening of a new era of persecution for religious

---

[1] *H.R.* April 1921.
[2] A.S.P. to C. P. Scott, 5 April 1918: 'That judgment, based on a much fuller knowledge of the situation than I had, removed my hesitation.'

and ethical convictions was a challenge which those who had concern for justice could not evade. He wrote:

Two motives prompted me: keen sympathy with the victims, though I did not share their views; and a desire that my own Church should be loyal to its ancient convictions, in spite of all temptation to surrender them for the duration of the war.... A special responsibility lies on those who disagree with the conscientious objectors to plead for justice, and try to explain a point of view which they do not share.... Those who believe in the righteousness of this war, but in whom the flame of freedom and of love burns with unweakened intensity, ought not to shirk the odium of pleading an unpopular cause.[1]

The first part of the book examines the counts brought against the conscientious objector. To the charge that in refusing to defend their country the conscientious objector is declining one of the fundamental duties of citizenship, Peake replies that if a man believes his country is guilty of a crime against God and humanity, it is his duty as a Christian to obey his own conscience rather than co-operate in the crime which his conscience condemns. 'Unless he can hold that the will of God always coincides in the cause of his country, it is obvious that a conflict between the lower and the higher duty will inevitably arise, and he must accept the higher.'[2] To the assertion that there is no excuse for men who will not help the country in some other way, Peake points out that 'to help the country is an ambiguous phrase', and that in war-time it takes on a new meaning: to objectors it really is a euphemism for 'helping the country to win the war'. The distinction is not an easy one:

It is allowed that conscience may forbid them to beat the German directly; but it is not realised that it equally forbids them to beat the Germans indirectly. There is nothing in principle to choose between the man who kills, the man who will not kill but makes munitions or invests in War Loan to enable others to kill, the man who releases another that he may kill, the man who prays for victory which can be won only by killing, or preaches sermons designed to lead others to go and kill.[3]

To the view that it is base for objectors to accept the privilege of their country and yet refuse to shoulder the obligations to defend it, Peake gives the examples of Jeremiah and the early Christian martyrs, who were sure that their best way of serving their country was to protest against its policies.

To the criticism that the objector remains in safety at home while others are exposed to the horrors of modern warfare, Peake replies that these men are not alone in this position; there are many men of military age, earning large wages and in occupations where they are exempted;

[1] *Prisoners of Hope*, pp. 5, 11. Just prior to the writing of the book Mrs Hobhouse had published her book *I appeal unto Caesar*, which dealt with the problem of extremists who refused alternative service. Peake's book examined the whole problem.
[2] Op. cit., p. 19.
[3] Op cit., p. 39.

even amongst the soldiers themselves there is great disparity as to privation and peril.

To those who challenge the claim of the individual conscience to receive consideration at all, Peake declares that there is no such thing as a collective judgement on this matter. A large body of opinion may recognize that war may be right; but also 'an influential and intellectually and morally reputable minority which insist that all war is wrong'; history shows that majorities are no more infallible than minorities. Peake's warning is against any attempt 'to cheapen conscience'.

If we teach the youth of the country that conscience may be lightly set aside in deference to the general drift of opinion, we need not be surprised if, with the thoroughness and logical consistency of youth, they push our teaching to conclusions at which we shall stand aghast. No extemporised ethics to deal with an inconvenient situation will offer us a stable foundation for the morality of the future.... The man who utters a sneer at conscience is fooling with moral explosives.

In the remainder of the book Peake discusses the legal situation and the treatment which was being meted out to the conscientious objector. He exposes not only the incompetence of the tribunals, but also their terrorizing methods in forcing a man to act in violation of his own conscience: he challenges the gross injustice of punishing a man more than once for the same crime, and releasing a man after his sentence had been served, and then re-arresting, bringing to trial, and sentencing to a second or even a third term. Peake concluded with a passionate appeal for reform and remedy.

What then ought to be done? Obviously the pledge of the Government should cease to be treated as scraps of paper, and a people that honours its engagements to religion should honour its own promises, which so greatly eased the passing of the Military Service Act. Obviously these men, however objectionable, should get their legal rights and cease to be treated more severely than criminals. And I put it to those who dislike and despise the objectors that, if they count it a mere trifle that they should suffer, and are glad that for them the way should be made exceedingly hard, it is not a light thing that Britain should be false to her word or callously refuse to rectify a patent wrong.[1]

In an appendix Peake gives an account of typical cases dealt with by the tribunals, and cases where men had died under the treatment they had suffered in prison.

Following the publication of the book, Peake received an immense outburst of approval from many quarters, and there is no doubt that his protest played a significant part in an increasing endeavour to remedy the tragic situation. Stephen Hobhouse—who had served a term of imprisonment—wrote: 'You have understood and described the position of the "absolutist" objector to conscription more successfully than even

[1] Op. cit., p. 96.

some of our closest sympathizers and pacifists could do.'[1] Professor C. H. Herford wrote: 'It is a powerful argument and your position as at once a decided supporter of the war, an orthodox Nonconformist, and a specialist in Biblical Exegesis, give your urgency of the case against persecution rare and peculiar weight.'[2] Professor John Skinner, of Westminster College, Cambridge wrote: 'I could not desire to see the case for freedom of conscience more forcibly and eloquently stated than you have done it.'[3] Dr J. Estlin Carpenter spoke of it as 'a clear and calm exposure, full of quiet and penetrating force—a brave plea'.[4] But perhaps the greatest appreciation of Peake's courageous effort in his impassioned call for justice is expressed in a brief note from Dr J. Rendel Harris:

My dear Peake,
I have read your book through at a sitting. It is the best and greatest thing you have done; lucid and lovely. The Lord bless you in it and for it.[5]

From the wife of one of the men to whom Peake had made reference came this word:

As the wife of one of the men mentioned in your book I appreciate your courage in speaking for an unpopular cause, especially knowing you do not share their views.

We have given some considerable time to an account of this work of Peake's as it illustrates very strongly his intensity of conviction upon any cause for social justice that he espoused, and shows the keenness and thoroughness of his engagement in undertaking any task for reform.

[1] S. Hobhouse to A.S.P., 27 July 1918.
[2] C.H. Herford to A.S.P., 12 April 1918.
[3] J. Skinner to A.S.P., 14 April 1918.
[4] J. Estlin Carpenter to A.S.P., 19 April 1918.
[5] J. Rendel Harris to A.S.P., 19 April 1918.

CHAPTER NINE

THE ECUMENICAL CHURCHMAN

ARTHUR SAMUEL PEAKE was a man of deep ecumenical sympathies, which deepened with the passing of the years. In a letter written in his undergraduate days there is early evidence of this. Two years after going to Oxford he wrote to his cousin Annetta:[1]

I can never be satisfied till we have gained an organic unity. This unity will never be gained till we consent to sink difference of belief and make Christ the foundation on which we build.... For myself I don't care to be called either Methodist or Church of England, or Protestant, or any name except Christian.

The essence of that youthful enthusiasm never forsook him. It was on this ground that he gave abundance of time and effort to the cause of reunion in all the after years.

Although Peake cherished this wide outlook the fact is that he remained throughout a convinced Free Churchman. Inheriting this position from his early training, as we have already noted, he left Oxford more deeply rooted in Free Church principles than when he began his course. His loyalty to this conviction is seen in his long-standing association with the National Council of Evangelical Free Churches, founded in 1892, participating in its committees and addressing its assemblies throughout the years. He was a member of the representative Committee that produced a Free Church Catechism in 1899, and at the Bridlington Assembly in 1928 he became President of the Council itself.

The Federal Council of the Evangelical Free Churches also claimed his allegiance. It was founded in 1919 as an official and deliberative body and Peake was associated with every stage of the consultations and negotiations leading up to the creation of the Council; he diligently attended every Assembly and was a member of the small Continuation Committee which dealt with matters between the annual meetings of the Council itself.

These facts indicate that, although throughout his life Peake had the widest ecumenical interests, there was never any deviation from what he

---

[1] A.S.P. to Annetta Peake. Quoted in *Memoir*, p. 159.

regarded as fundamental Free Church principles which he strongly upheld.

I

Peake's address[1] as President of the Free Church Council, delivered at the thirty-third Annual Assembly in 1928, is valuable because it reveals at one and the same time not only his strong Free Churchmanship but equally his wider vision concerning the future of the Church. It bore the title *Pray for the Peace of Jerusalem*, and gave a wide conspectus of the things that to his view were involved in the reunion of the Christian Churches.

Peake was chiefly concerned with questions regarding the doctrines concerning the Church and the Ministry, both of which were vital to his position as a Free Churchman on the one hand and the possibilities of wider reunion on the other.

He held the most exalted view of the Church and its functions—a doctrine which he had learnt from his study of the Epistle to the Ephesians many years before. It was that the Church is made up of those who are united to Christ by faith which is primary, and that the Church, in fellowship with its Living Head, has authority to shape its own institutions and to create the ministry it needs.

In discussing the Church we are in the region of first principles and an appeal to the classical documents of our religion is altogether in place. They set before us a very lofty ideal. The Church is the Body and Bride of Christ, and the Holy Temple of God. Its members constitute one organic whole, a Body of which Christ is the Head; He is the principle of its unity; His life fills the whole organism and animates and controls all its members; His life-blood courses through its veins. It is the organ through which He functions in this lower world and exercises His gracious ministry. It is His Bride, the cherished object of His illimitable love, redeemed at the cost of His life; sadly stained and scarred at present, but destined for eternal fellowship with Him when He has presented it to Himself, pure and radiant, free from spot or wrinkle or any such thing. It is the Temple in which God dwells, which He hallows by His presence, wherein He is worshipped, and where He and man can meet. Its unity should be marred by no schism, its loyalty compromised by no illicit love, its altar desecrated by no willfulness or self-love. Such is the noble churchmanship of Paul; such and no meaner should be our own.[2]

On two matters in the life and organization of the Church, Peake expressed his conviction with firmness—the sacraments in the life of the Church and the relation between Church and State. Concerning the former he declared:

---

[1] The address is reprinted in *Plain Thoughts on Great Subjects*, ed. L. S. Peake (n.d.) ch. 2: *Essays in Commemoration* (ed. J. T. Wilkinson) 1958. pp. 143 f.
[2] Op. cit., pp. 8–9.

While I deprecate the tendency to pit one form of worship or means of grace against another, I recognise the place of the two sacraments in the life of the Church. But I cannot concede the dominant position often claimed for them. I am profoundly impressed with the difficulties which surround the New Testament references. The problems of exegesis and of lower, higher and historical criticism present a tangled thicket through which we must cut our way to what truth there may be at the centre. Can matters so vital as is asserted have been left by God in such obscurity and uncertainty? Moreover the sacraments were just the features in Christian worship to which non-Christian interpretations and accretions would most readily be attached. Yet so many precious associations have gathered around the Holy Communion, and experience has dominated its spiritual value, that we may justly accord it an honoured place in our worship. . . .

We joyfully recognise the real Presence of Christ in the Sacrament of Holy Communion. For He is both the Giver and the Gift. It is His pierced hands which break for us the bread of life. It is Himself that He gives to the believing soul. But His Presence is in the Sacrament as a whole, not localised in the elements, to which it would be better that the term 'sacrament' should not be applied. If this is recognised, there would in itself be no objection from a strictly Protestant point of view to taking the elements from the Lord's Table to the sick. But when it is believed that the Real Presence is localised in the elements, and abides there even when the congregation of the faithful has departed, it is not illogical to say that Christ, actually present in the elements, may be, and ought to be, adored. It is this which constitutes the peril of continuous reservation. But the Real Presence must be more spiritually interpreted, and it ought not to be regarded as different in kind from that which the Christian experiences in prayer and other acts of devotion. I do not deny that the Eucharist has its own specific value. But this is not to be found in any change which takes place in the elements themselves.[1]

The question of the relation between Church and State had just been emphasized in consequence of the rejection by the House of Commons of the Deposited Prayer Book in 1928. Peake's views on the issue of establishment were entirely clear.

It is to me quite incredible that the Free Churches would consent to form part of an established church. . . . It is part of our Christian duty to render the State our own unstinted service and loyal obedience where this does not clash with our highest loyalty. We must render to Caesar the things that are Caesar's; but there is a realm where Caesar's writ does not run, a sphere which he has no right to invade. There is and can be only one Head of the Church. The prerogatives of the ministry may have their importance; but the crown rights of the Redeemer are far more sacred to me than the right of any ministry; they touch me to the quick. But what is the present position? The Church suffers the indignity of having by its constitution a secular monarch as its official head. He may be a Christian, neither in belief nor practice. . . . We put the indignity on our sovereign of forcing him to belong to a particular church, and to different churches in different parts of our island. He cannot freely choose the communion to which

---

[1] Op. cit., pp. 10–11.

he could belong; nor can he refrain from belonging to any if his personal convictions are out of harmony with Christianity. We may even compel him to violate his conscience as the price of accepting his crown. Nor can the church be free to take unflinchingly the Christian line since it is fettered even though it is not paralysed, by its entangling alliance with the State. No church can do its work aright unless it possesses complete spiritual autonomy. It cannot allow the secular power to determine its beliefs, its organisation or the form of its worship....

The State ought to be colour-blind to all religious differences. Citizenship is the only status which it can properly recognise.... Nor can a religion consistently seek to impose its own specific beliefs on the community. The conscience of the agnostic should be as sacred to us as our own. We are simply entitled to claim the benevolent attitude of the State to our philanthropic work and our attempts to elevate the morality of the people.[1]

Peake thought, however, that it would be better for disestablishment to come from within; or that it should come in the course of political development rather than out of religious controversy. Precipitate action on the part of the Free Churches might easily embitter a growingly happy relationship between the Church of England and the Free Churches, whereas with patience the ideal might be realized perhaps through common consent.

Peake was convinced that the principle of development must be allowed in the matter of the organization of the Church, and therefore this must be regarded as something fundamental in the life of the Free Churches. It is a false view that a form or organization is necessarily right because it corresponds to a primitive mode.

Our interest in early Church organization is antiquarian. Congregationalism and Presbyterianism can, it is true, appeal to the apostolic age with better right than monarchical episcopacy, but no appeal to the first century can lawfully determine what our own organisation should be.... No form of organisation has any intrinsic divine right. The living church has the competence to create its own organisation and to modify it by retrenchment here and expansion there as new occasions arise and new needs have to be met.[2]

From this delineation of the ideal of the Church, Peake proceeds to state his conviction regarding the nature and functions of the ministry.

It is vital to insist that only when we have given its rightful position to the Church can we safely formulate any doctrine of the ministry. As a High Churchman I view with deep repugnance and distrust any theory of the ministry which tends to lower the conception of the Church. The unbalanced exaltation of the ministry may lead to the depression of the laity, the denial of universal priesthood and the consequent depreciation of the Church as a whole. The cure for high clericalism is High Churchmanship; the antidote to extravagant claims for a section is an exalted conception of the whole body. Apart from the Church

[1] Op. cit., p. 11.
[2] Op. cit., p. 8.

the ministry is nothing at all. It possesses significance only as it serves the Church and enables it to function more effectively. The ministry has nothing which the whole body does not possess, though functions which belong to the Church as a whole may be fitly exercised by a special order. But should the body be totally deprived of its ministry, it can replace it out of its own resources.

The minister must have his own individual call from God. But the commission to exercise his office must come to him through the Church. The head does not act without the body. The minister may not go over the head and behind the back of the Church to Christ. His vocation must be tested and proved by the Church. He is called to be a prophet and a priest. But the ministry has a prophetic and priestly character only because the Church already possesses it. For purposes of order and convenience these functions are normally exercised by special organs. But there is no hard and fast line which divides minister and laity into fixed and rigid orders. The Church possesses in its own divinely given and inalienable resources, the means, as it has the right, to exercise these functions apart from these organs. The minister may rightly rely on Divine grace for the fulfilment of his vocation; and since he leads a separated life, wholly consecrated to his sacred task, he is equipped with special grace for that purpose. But this grace is in no way different in kind from that which any worker in the Church may confidently claim. It is no mysterious spiritual essence with which he is once and for all inoculated at his ordination. It is just the Divine help constantly vouchsafed and adequate to every need. 'As thy day is so shall thy strength be.'[1]

The question of ordination was a serious problem, inasmuch as differences of interpretation were responsible for raising barriers in Christian practice. The Free Church ministry, though allowed to be a real ministry[2] was not regarded as qualified to celebrate the Eucharist in the Anglican rite. To Peake the essence of what is conveyed in ordination was clear—'the authority to administer in the ordaining body'. If this interpretation were recognized then those who were already ministers in the respective churches need nothing more than reciprocal authorization to minister throughout the united Church.

These excerpts from Peake's Presidential Address make plain his loyalty to the principles of Free Churchmanship, and yet at the same time reveal that wider outlook towards the reunion of Christendom which to him was a cherished ideal. It is here that we see Peake standing forth as an ecumenical statesman and administrator.

In the course of his address at Bridlington, Peake made an open confession of his concern for the wider Christian unity.

I stand with those who deplore our divisions and desire with all their hearts that the shattered unity of Christ's Church might be restored. I think of our separation as 'unhappy divisions', though I recognise that under present cir-

[1] Op. cit., pp. 9–10.
[2] G. K. A. Bell (ed.), *Documents on Christian Unity* (1925). 'Memorandum on the status of the existing Free Church Ministry presented on behalf of the Church of England Representatives'. 6 July 1923, pp. 158–9. 'We regard them as being within their several spheres real ministries of Christ's Word and Sacraments in the Universal Church.'

cumstances some combinations would be unhappier still. I would have a unity in which the greatest elasticity should be not simply permitted but welcomed. Every variety of organisation, every shade of belief consistent with loyalty to our central affirmations, every type of worship congenial to our varied temperaments, should find in such a Church its legitimate home.[1]

With typical caution he seeks to offer counsel regarding the approach to this problem.

Let us remind ourselves at the outset that our protests against positions we believe to be false, however necessary such protests may be, almost inevitably narrow us. We tend to push them into the centre instead of keeping them in their place. Then our emphasis is wrongly distributed, our presentation of the perfect orb of truth is distorted. We may regard views and usages as matters of principle, when we are really invoking that sacred name for our prejudices or our habits. There are indeed fixed principles, permanent characteristics which must abide through all flux and change. But Free Churchmen may make the mistake of the Bourbons if, forgetting that all life involves development, adjustment to environment, they insist, as a matter of principle, on retaining their organisation in its traditional form.[2]

In this matter of the wider union Peake was convinced that the Church of England was of pivotal importance, and that a union between the Anglicans and the Free Churches was probably the most immediate step. He recognized, however, that the Anglican Church had affinities with the Lutheran, the Reformed and Evangelical Churches on the one hand, and with the Eastern and Latin Churches on the other. This situation at once demanded extreme caution on the part of the Church of England lest the relations with the Eastern and Latin Churches should be endangered. Peake believed also that the Free Churches should be equally cautious lest relations with non-episcopalian Churches elsewhere should become imperilled.

He had also a clear conviction as to the problems involved in any attempt in the direction of union with Rome, believing that, in the Roman view, the only possibility was submission to the Roman Church as the one true Church of Christ on earth: the real issue lay beyond the realms of any discussion.[3] The whole Roman position was staked on the truth of the dogma of papal infallibility[4]—the weakness of which Peake expressed in a passage which has now almost become classical in its statement:

It is suspended by a chain of hypotheses of which very few are raised above a narrow margin of probability while several are improbable in the last degree. If Matthew 16:18 is authentic; and if by the 'rock' Peter is intended; and if the

[1] Op cit., p. 7.
[2] Op cit., p. 7.
[3] It would have been interesting to find the reaction of Peake to the attitude of the Roman Church since Vatican Council II. He would have discerned the limitations and weaknesses of the new situation, but would have rejoiced greatly in the new approach.
[4] Encyclical Letter (*Mortalium Animos*) of Pius xi, 6 January 1928. See *Documents on Christian Unity* (ed. G. K. A. Bell) 2nd Series. pp. 51-63.

passage implies the infallibility of Peter; and if Peter ever resided in Rome; and if residing there he was its bishop; and if he passed on his prerogative to later Bishops of Rome; and if he did not pass them on to the Bishops in other places where he resided; if indeed there was any monarchical episcopate in Rome till decades after his time; and if the explicit utterances of Jesus did not forbid such a claim; and if it was not incompatible with much in the New Testament record—then, and then only could one consider Roman claims. . . .

If, inspired by a new and sweet humility and a regard for the results of unfettered exegesis and historical research, Rome should renounce her claims to supremacy, her boast of infallibility; if she would revoke all the profane anathemas, repent before the world of her ghastly record of atrocious persecution, and undertake a drastic reform from within, how gladly we should welcome such a triumph of divine grace! But divine grace does not act without the co-operation of the human will; and the will for so splendid a recantation, or indeed any recognition that she owes it to humanity, is, we must judge, entirely absent.[1]

As to the Eastern Churches, Peake also felt that reunion was at best a very remote possibility, though there was some hopefulness in the fact that discussion of such matters was not rejected, and also that the Eastern Churches, though somewhat paralysed for progress by an immovable attachment to the Seven General Councils, were not bound by any decree of papal infallibility. For the Anglican Church to look in the direction of Rome was to look for the impossible; to look in the direction of the Eastern Churches was at most a hope that implied a very far prospect: on the other hand to look toward the Free Churches was to envisage a real possibility of accommodation. It was the recognition of the significance of this opportunity that determined the theme of Peake's Presidential Address.

In his thought upon reunion at home Peake regarded the Federal Council of the Evangelical Free Churches as supremely important for the examination of the problems involved.

In this matter of home-reunion Peake realized that the chief difficulty arose in connexion with the ministry of the Church. Whilst it was admitted on the Anglican side that the ministry of the regularly constituted Free Churches was a true ministry within the Church of Christ, yet from the Anglican point of view, episcopacy must be retained in any united church, because to abandon it would not only be the surrender of something which all valued highly and some indeed regarded as essential, but it would break one of the chief links with the Eastern and Roman communions. The position was qualified, however, by the proviso that it must be constitutional and not prelatical, and combined with elements of con-

---

[1] This passage received critical comment in *The Catholic Times*, 13 April 1928, to which in a long letter Peake made reply in further explanation. The conversations initiated by the Archbishop of Canterbury and Cardinal Mercier (at Malines, 1921–2) had shown how immovable the Papacy was and how far some Anglican scholars were prepared to go towards Rome. See *Documents and Christian Unity* (ed. G. K. A. Bell) 1st Series, pp. 249–65; 2nd series pp. 21–35.

gregational and presbyterial order. Along this line Peake saw the possibility of removing the major difficulty.

To an episcopacy so limited, provided no theory that episcopacy is of the essence of the Church is demanded, I should personally have no objections. Church order is for me a matter of expediency and not of principle. I could live and work happily under any form of church order except a despotism. The existing Anglican system needs strengthening and reform; but recent non-episcopal developments suggest a recognition that episcopacy has its own value.

We may note two instances of the depth of Peake's conviction on the subject of reunion. His response to the *Appeal to All Christian People* issued from Lambeth in 1920 was wholehearted. He wrote:

Its importance is universally recognised alike for its temper and the actual proposals it makes. The proposals themselves may be unacceptable; but the surprising advance in spirit ought to receive the warmest and fullest welcome, the most cordial and ungrudging recognition. There ought to be no reserve in recognising the entire sincerity of the approach to the Free Churches and the desire to heal the breaches in the visible unity of the Church. There is one point to which I desire to call special attention, and that is the deep conviction of Divine guidance which filled the assembly, the consciousness of the presence and influence of the Holy Spirit.[1]

As Peake presented the implications of this historical declaration to the Conference of his own Church in 1921, we see him once again stepping forth as a leader of thought and action.

The first and last feeling that should be in our hearts should be one of unreserved recognition of the spirit and temper of the Lambeth Appeal. It is a Christian document from beginning to end ... a new note is struck. ... In this appeal there is the real presence of Christ who himself is calling us along this path. ... Our immediate duty is not to think about ultimate terms of reunion, but with the utmost warmth of spirit to reciprocate the temper that lies behind this appeal. From this great movement a new era is beginning for all.[2]

The resolution of commendation of the *Lambeth Appeal* was carried unanimously.

In the following September, the Federal Council appointed a Committee of representatives to meet those of the Anglican Church, and from it a sub-committee of four bishops, two Anglican theologians, and six Free Churchmen, under the chairmanship of the Archbishop of York, was appointed to continue discussions. Of this sub-committee Peake was a member. Seventeen meetings were held with the purpose of exploring the territory: there was no mandate for negotiation.

Peake declared his own attitude with the utmost clearness:

---

[1] *H.R.* (1920), p. 392.
[2] *P.M.L.* 20 June 1921.

Our first duty to those who are separated from us is not to refute but to understand them. Of all qualities in this connexion that of sympathetic imagination is most to be prized, the quality which enables us to step out of our own theological and ecclesiastical prepossessions and to survey the situation from the standpoint and with the eyes of those from who we dissent. Nor must we ever forget that the Church is no human institution merely but a Divine creation. It is the Body of Christ, the sensitive and responsive organ through which He functions on earth. It is the Bride of Christ, chosen by Him before the foundation of the world, to be His own, bought with a price, redeemed at the cost of His blood, cleansed by His Spirit, destined at last to be presented to Him in her radiant glory and free from spot or wrinkle or any such thing. It is the Temple of the Holy Ghost, not meant to be rent by schism and defaced by unseemly rivalries. We are not abandoned to our dimness of insight, defect of wisdom or perversity of will. And where we can see no outlet, God may find the way.[1]

In 1926, following the discussion of the intervening years, the Conference of the Primitive Methodist Church made an official reply to the *Lambeth Appeal*, and it was to Peake that the drafting of the documents were entrusted. It forms one further illustration of Peake's far-reaching sagacity and administrative wisdom.

To some who were outside official contact with the discussions, it seemed that there was undue delay in the matter of response from the side of the Free Churches. Thus the Dean of Durham, Bishop J. E. C. Welldon, wrote to the *Manchester Guardian* in 1922 expressing his concern. With typical insight Peake gave reconciling assurances in a letter in reply:

It is idle to indulge the hope of a swift settlement, even where goodwill is present in the amplest measure. The path to union is steep; we shall need courage to surmount its obstacles and vigilance to avoid its pitfalls. All the resources of Christian statesmanship will be taxed and our reserves of patience will be strained before we have reached the end of the way. The leaders must persuade the rank and file to follow them, and they must count on opposition and still more on apathy. The wounds which separation has inflicted in the Body of Christ cannot be quickly healed.[2]

The second instance is seen in Peake's association with the Conference of Faith and Order held at Lausanne in 1927, of which he was a member. He regarded this Conference as 'the most important event in the religious world for many a long day'. In commending its importance he declared:

The great thing at present is to create the right atmosphere and acquire a sympathetic insight into points of view other than our own.... We must all be prepared to examine our first principles afresh, and see whether they are wholly matters of principle, or whether they may not be rooted in custom, tradition or even prejudice. We rightly expect that others should do this; we cannot evade

---

[1] From an Address, 'The Reunion of Christendom', given to the Unity Meeting of the Wesleyan Conference at Sheffield in July 1922. (*P.M.L.* 3 August 1922.) The Final Report of this Joint Committee under the title 'Church Unity' may be found in *Documents on Christian Unity* (ed. G. K. A. Bell), 2nd Series (1924).

[2] A.S.P. Letter to the *Manchester Guardian*, 10 March 1922.

the challenge to do it ourselves. The trouble with all reunion movements is that there is on both sides a solid body of opinion obstinately entrenched in the conviction that its own position is impregnable, and viewing any attempt to criticise its own presuppositions and conclusions or strive impartially to appreciate the truth held by the other party as selling the pass. . . . This may be a far-off divine event, but we should cherish it as an ideal and work toward it with the courage which will not know when it is beaten, the faith that can stand the shock of repeated disillusion, and the patience which holds on in spite of every set-back.[1]

Such was the spirit of the man who moulded the thought of his own communion and beyond it, as the issues of a World Church began to unfold and take shape. It is perhaps fitting that this account of Peake's labours for the wider union of Christendom should close with a tribute from the pen of the Archbishop of Canterbury (Dr Lang), expressed in a letter to Mrs Peake following her husband's death in 1929:

We were thrown very closely together for some years in the Conferences which were held, and over which I presided at Lambeth on the great though difficult theme of Christian Union. Of all those who took part in these Conferences he was the one who seemed most anxious, whilst maintaining his own principles, to understand and sympathise with the point of view of others. Again and again at difficult moments it was his openness of mind and breadth of brotherly sympathy which enabled us to continue. He seemed always to bring into these discussions, not only knowledge and sympathy, but also a quite special loyalty to the Mind of our Lord.

III

To the early impulses towards understanding and co-operation between the Methodist denominations, Peake soon gave allegiance. As early as 1905 Peake wrote the following letter to the *Primitive Methodist Leader*:

For the ultimate union of the Methodist Churches I long earnestly and I greatly desire that we should not stand outside the present movement. I see no reason why such distinctive mission as we are possessors of should not be as successfully prosecuted in a larger Church: and if we have something to give others, it is well they should receive it; and on the other hand it is good for us to receive what they have to give.[2]

In particular he attended the meetings of the Methodist Assembly in 1909, which was formed to increase fellowship and stimulate action, although no reference was made to organic union. Peake contributed to the occasion and afterwards he wrote:

The movement thus happily initiated must be carried forward. . . . No good can come of any attempt to force an organic union; rather we should seek all

---
[1] *H.R.* 1927. p. 511.
[2] *P.M.L.* 3 August 1905.

opportunities of fellowship and co-operation that we may be prepared for an easy and natural union when the time is ripe.

In 1913 the Wesleyan Conference appointed a committee to explore the possibilities of uniting the various branches of the Methodist Church in Britain, but the war prevented its implementation. In 1918, however, at the three denominational Conferences resolutions were passed appointing a Committee to take up the work, and submit proposals to the Conferences of the following year. The two smaller churches—Primitive Methodist and United Methodist—passed the resolution unanimously, and at the Wesleyan Conference only, two opposing views were registered. Shortly afterwards in Manchester at an informal lunch of representative Methodists of all branches, Peake spoke on behalf of the Primitive Methodist Church. This may be regarded as his public entry into the movement.

During the first stage, Peake's contribution lay in exposition of his own convictions on the whole subject, and by so doing he gave important leadership. He was certain that union, both in spirit and organization, was the ideal of Christ for His Church. The great similarities between the Methodist Churches far outweighed any differences. Moreover the whole Church suffered in the eyes of men because of its divisions, and a united Church would provide a new instrument for evangelization as it confronted the forces of evil in the world. Further the concept of reunion was becoming more widespread, and he was convinced that a Methodist Church united in one organization would be an important factor in the promotion of a still wider union.

Naturally certain principles governed Peake's work for this cause. He constantly urged the necessity of being willing to surrender prejudice to principle, not least when self-interest tended to assert itself or when an impasse had been reached. Further, with any suggestion that negotiations should be brought to an end he urged that the will of the people must be ascertained through their representative courts before such suspension could be morally justified.

Amidst the impatience that was inevitable because progress was often slow, again and again Peake indicated the solemn and serious responsibility of taking any decision to abandon the scheme, and pleaded that, if in the end a refusal had to come, it should not be those of his own Church who incurred such grave decision. His place and attitude in these negotiations bring to mind the entreaties of Richard Baxter at the Savoy Conference in 1661, as he stood between the two parties, the one side having to be restrained in their endeavours and those of the other side to be persuaded into conviction. Throughout the negotiations Peake appealed above all for elasticity both in doctrine and organization.

The first flush of widespread enthusiasm for union was followed inevitably by intensive criticism. Between the years 1920 and 1925 Peake gave time and energy to a leadership that again and again was to prove decisive. By patient explanation he pointed out that, although there might be differences in the distribution of emphasis, yet the lines of division, whether theological or ecclesiastical, by no means coincided with the lines of denominational cleavage. Above all he deprecated 'the manufacture of differences which had no substantial existence', and urged that the particular type of evangelism which belonged to his own denomination was no longer the monopoly of Primitive Methodism, and had for a long time ceased to be specially characteristic of that group.

Nowhere more than in the framing of the doctrinal standards for the united church did Peake show greater sagacity. He confessed that he would have preferred a doctrinal statement of a more general kind, and the omission of any reference to Wesley's *Notes on the New Testament* and *Sermons* from such statement,[1] but he recognized that behind this reference there lay a sense of the value of continuity, and also a constant reminder of the heritage of the Evangelical Revival. Moreover in the phrase 'generally contained' he felt there was an adequate safeguard against anything beyond a general acceptance of this evangelical position. He urged the significance of the natural loyalty felt by the Wesleyans for their great founder, and he reminded those of his own denomination that their own declared articles of faith were in part obsolete. His discussions of these doctrinal issues became decisive for many, and were described at the time as 'historic'.

A further instance of Peake's sagacity is seen in his exposition of the nature and office of the ministry. His interpretation went far to dissolve the fear of sacerdotalism which undoubtedly existed in the smaller Methodist denominations on the one hand, and the fear of a lowering of the ministerial position which existed equally in the larger group. Much of the discussion centred in the proposal that the Pastoral Session of the Conference in Wesleyan Methodism should continue as part of the new order. Although hesitant at first—for in Primitive Methodism there was no organization composed exclusively of ministers—Peake became convinced of its value, and accepted it as part of the scheme. His commitment went far to turn the scale in favour of its inclusion.[2]

In the larger church there was some measure of opinion which tended to suggest that the Wesleyan Church held a higher conception of its ministry than was the case in the smaller groups. This view Peake most strongly repudiated as being entirely false. He wrote:

So far as the ministry is concerned there is a real difference in practice and no doubt a certain difference in emphasis. But the difference can hardly be des-

---

[1] The following indicates some ground for Peake's hesitancy on this point. 'It is obvious that Mr Wesley's exegesis of the New Testament which was confessedly derived from Bengel, has frequently to be rejected. His whole exposition is radically unsound.' See art. 'Methodist Union: The Doctrinal Statement' (*P.M.L.* 19 February 1920). Peake recognized that Wesley's interest was 'not a speculative but a practical interest'.

[2] *P.M.L.* 9 November 1922, art. by A.S.P. on 'The Ministerial Session'.

cribed as essential. I think, if I may be quite frank, that some ministers are in danger of emphasising the ministerial function and prerogative more than is normally good for them, and are exposed to the temptation of unduly depreciating the laity.... On the other hand it is possible that when lay co-operation is more extensive, this may react on the estimation of the ministers. But that is hardly my experience. At any rate when I heard it explained in the early days of the Union Committee that the Wesleyans did not regard their ministers as 'the paid agents of the Church', I asked myself in amazement what Methodist people entertained so grovelling a view of the ministry. It was, with more than half-a-century's experience of Primitive Methodism, being myself a minister's son, entirely unfamiliar to me. The description of it as the highest calling open to a man, the most sacred vocation, one not to be taken, save on the warrant of a Divine call authenticated by the call of the Church—all this was familiar to me.

But if any Wesleyan is in such ignorance of the principles on which our conception of the ministry rests, then it is high time that he began to learn, and from no tainted source, the real truth about us. I repudiate with hot indignation, as one whose life is dedicated to the training of the ministry, the opinion that we value it so lightly. But I reiterate that we cannot safely define the ministry until we have cleared our minds with reference to the Church. It is possible to elevate the office by contrast, as some non-Methodist Churches have done; to depress the laity that the ministry may be exalted. Be it ours to have a high doctrine of the ministry just because we have a high doctrine of the Church, to regard the ministry not as possessed of any priesthood which it does not share with the laity, but to recognise that that priesthood finds its fittest organ and most intense expression in the activities of those who are wholly dedicated to its service. If anyone thinks of a grace different in quality, which is not the possession of the whole priestly body, I repudiate this as wholly at variance with the New Testament teaching on the Church. And in this I rejoice to believe that the vast body of Wesleyan opinion is with me.[1]

Peake had earlier reinforced his position—which he had stated clearly in an ordination charge in 1921—by showing the agreement between his own view of the ministry and that expressed by an eminent Wesleyan scholar, Dr G. G. Findlay.[2]

In the various functions of her ministry the Church does but specialise and concentrate in particular organs the powers which exist diffused through the whole membership. Christ's people are a spiritual people, filled with the Holy Ghost; and every one of them has spiritual qualities and spiritual duties. Preaching, teaching, public prayer, the care of souls—in all these the ministry has a principle and directing part, but not an exclusive property. Even in establishing the sacraments and committing them to His apostles our Lord Jesus does not prescribe their administration by a definite order of men.

Peake's strong and patient interpretation did more than any other factor to assuage the deep tide of feeling on both sides. It should be remembered that at this particularly crucial stage in the movement some eight hundred

[1] *P.M.L.* art. 'Methodist Union Opposition'. 8 June 1922.
[2] G. G. Findlay, *The Church of Christ as set forth in the New Testament* (1893) p. 36. *P.M.L.* 7 July 1921, 'Methodist Union: The Ministerial Office Defined'.

Wesleyan ministers had signed a manifesto against union,[1] in April 1922. To this Peake replied in a lengthy article which was printed in all the Methodist papers, and his criticism made a powerful impression that went far to dissolve the bitterness that had become engendered. These references are not made now in any sense for the purpose of reviving unhappy battles of long ago, but simply to indicate how crucial was Peake's influence in dissolving the bitterness that had arisen because of these things, and which, if unchanged, might well have caused the collapse of the whole union movement.

We should also recall the emergence of a movement of opposition which took place in 1923. There were some in the Primitive Methodist Church who had regretted the absence of any organization for criticism of the scheme, despite assurances that were given that minority views were being fully considered, although it was declared: 'Our people may feel fully assured that the representatives of the Primitive Methodist Church on the United Committee are pressing their views to the utmost.' But some were doubtful, and a year earlier some in the United Methodist Church shared these opinions. On 24 January 1924 there was also public advertisement for such an organization, which really represented a vote of 'no-confidence' in some of the leading representatives on the United Committee. The newly-formed group was known as 'The Primitive Methodist "Other Side" '. It was declared that its organization had been delayed 'in the hope that such action might be rendered unnecessary by the strong insistence of our representatives on the things for which as a Church we have stood'. Centred in London, the chief criticisms of the 'Other-Side' were in regard to the Ministerial Session and the privileges of the layman which were being endangered.[2]

During this most critical period Peake's influence was also felt in yet another matter, namely, the question of the Sacrament of the Lord's Supper.[3] He preferred that the service should be conducted by a minister, and that on several grounds: it conformed to the normal pattern of Christendom; the minister stood in close pastoral relation to the congrega-

---

[1] *M.R.* 27 April 1922. The Manifesto referred to 'the valuable historic individuality of the Wesleyan Church, and continued: 'We believe that the obliteration of the Wesleyan type would inflict a real loss upon the Universal Church.... We hold that the viewpoint of Wesleyan Methodism is essentially different from that of the other Methodist Churches in regard to doctrinal standards, the sacraments, forms of worship, the ministry, party politics and other matters of first importance. The proposed scheme of union involves a large accession of those whose sentiment and training will inevitably lead further and further away from the Wesleyan tradition and usages.'

For Peake's reply see *M.R.* 8 June 1922; *Methodist Times*, 8 June 1922; *P.M.L.* 8 June 1922; *United Methodist*, 8 June 1922. For Dr J. E. Rattenbury's rejoinder see *M.R.* 15 June 1922. For Peake's final reply see *Methodist Times*, 22 June 1922; *M.R.* 23 June 1922.

[2] A pamphlet was issued under the names of T.R. Auty, M. H. Bainton and W. Usher, bearing the title: *Methodist Union: The Case against the Scheme*. Details regarding the development of this movement are found in the *P.M.L.* from 12 July 1923 to 3 April 1924, *passim*. See also full discussion in R. Currie, p. 269. *Methodism Divided: A Study in the Sociology of Ecumenicalism* (1968).

[3] *P.M.L.* 10 April 1924, 'Methodist Union and the Sacraments'.

tion; he was likely to conduct the service in a smoother manner than a layman less accustomed to the practice. Nevertheless he believed that there was no New Testament evidence that declared that a layman could *not* perform the office in the absence of a minister. He also knew that within the Methodist structure there were many small country churches that could only be visited by a circuit minister on rare occasions, and therefore he felt that for such congregations this meant a denial of reasonably frequent participation in the Sacrament. He therefore advocated that laymen, duly appointed for the work, should be set aside as representatives of the Church. They could be local preachers, though not necessarily so, for he believed that this duty was closely allied to the pastoral ministry of the class-leader. Such advocacy arose out of Peake's conviction that it is for a living church to create its own congregation and to modify it or expand it as new conditions arise and new needs have to be met.

In the required background of this concern for matters theological and ecclesiastical during this critical period, Peake's great contribution again was the upholding of patience and goodwill within his own Church, at a time when the negotiations were not seldom prolonged and even wearisome. He wrote significantly:

If the negotiations are ultimately wrecked may the responsibility not lie at the door and be a burden on the conscience of the Primitive Methodist Church! If the great refusal has to be made let it not be said that it was we who have made it.[1]

In 1925 the scheme was referred to all three Conferences for sanction, with the requirement of a seventy-five per cent majority to be secured.[2] The Conferences of the Primitive Methodist and the United Methodist Churches voted strongly in favour, the vote of the former, when Peake moved the resolution, being ninety-three per cent. In the Wesleyan Conference, however, the vote fell short of the required majority. The scheme was therefore referred to the Drafting Committee to report to the Conference of the following year. Again it was Peake who by his spirit of conciliation proved to be invaluable. Two amendments were adopted by the Committee; the first concerned doctrine and emphasized the claim of Methodism to belong to the Church Catholic; the second concerned the administration of the Lord's Supper and was designed to secure more elasticity, and, in particular, more frequent observance. Previously it had been decided that each of the three Churches should, for the time being, continue its own practice: it was now decided to adopt the suggestion which Peake had recommended, namely, that if no minister could be present, the Quarterly Meeting was empowered to elect a suitable layman to administer.

[1] *P.M.L.* 20 November 1924.
[2] For an excellent and detailed account of the development of Methodist Union proposals see R. Currie, *Methodism Divided: A Study in the Sociology of Ecumenicalism* (1968), ch. 8, 'The Making of the Methodist Church'.

At the Conference of his own Church, Peake declared that he himself had had the privilege of drafting these amendments for the Committee, and stated that the first amendment brought the new Methodist Church into line with the great affirmations of the Church Catholic, and that behind the second there lay the vital principle of the priesthood of all believers, and its adoption would strengthen the place of the Sacrament in the life of the Church.

At the same Conference Peake spoke to the main resolution about Union, reminding the assembly that a very critical moment in the history of the negotiations had now been reached. Again he declared that it would be a tragic decision if Primitive Methodism reversed its previous policy of support. The voting resulted in 162 for and 26 against the scheme. Such was the judgement after eight years of endeavour. Unfortunately once again the Wesleyan Conference failed to secure the required majority.

In the Conference of the following year, 1927, Peake was once more entrusted with the moving of the resolution; and once more, with typical caution, he declared that any future step could be dangerous, and that an impatient attitude could not be justified. This time the voting issued in 190 for and 22 against. Yet again, however, the Wesleyan Conference failed to obtain a sufficient majority.

At the Conference of 1928 the subject was presented for the tenth time, and it was to Peake that the piloting of the debate was committed. He appealed once again for the spirit of patient understanding, and reminded the assembly that they were legislating for future generations; it was nothing less than the struggle of the Methodist Church for future efficiency. The voting resulted in a majority of 89 per cent—after ten years of debate!

There is no question that the persistent triumph throughout the years was due largely, if not entirely, to the strong, quiet, and persuasive influence of Peake, whose advocacy had its influence also upon the other Methodist communities.

The same year, 1928, the Wesleyan Conference procured the required majority, and early in 1929, Peake was appointed as one of the number to give evidence before the Parliamentary Committee in connexion with the Methodist Union Enabling Bill.

In August of that year Peake died. The land he had so wished to enter he saw, but entered not. The consummation he so devoutly wished he never experienced.

Two contemporary testimonies can form a fitting estimate of the immense importance of Peake's work for the cause of Methodist Union—both from eminent leaders in the Wesleyan Church.

Dr Wilbert F. Howard wrote:

Writing as a Wesleyan Methodist I must testify to the great influence which

Dr Peake's handling of the Union question had upon many in my own Church. There were not a few on our side who feared that the two smaller Churches, in their traditional dislike of clericalism, would hold in too light esteem elements in our usage which our own experience has shown us to be of utmost value in the development of a strong and healthy churchmanship. Others of our number hesitated to press for a high doctrine of the Church lest they might seem to be advocating sacerdotalism—a heresy as repugnant to Wesleyans as to Primitive Methodists. It was here that Dr Peake's lofty conception of the Christian society raised us up above the comparatively petty differences of denominational customs and usage. As he expounded the New Testament doctrine of the Church he drew together men of diverse temperaments and traditions. If reunited Methodism holds up to the world in its teaching about the Body of Christ, the noble doctrine which Paul set forth in his Epistle to the Ephesians, we shall owe this more to Dr Peake than to any other man.[1]

The following came from the pen of Dr J. Scott Lidgett:

The great qualities of Dr Peake's character did as much as his eminent intellectual gifts and scholarship to make this great achievement possible. To unreserved consecration, high courage and loyalty to truth, he added a sincerity of spirit, sympathetic insight and untiring patience. The weight of his convictions was always accompanied by sweet reasonableness of temper, and by the balanced judgments of wisdom. Hence the results at which he arrived were expounded with lucidity, upheld with courtesy and gentleness and brought to acceptance by careful and conciliatory presentation. In maintaining his own he put himself at the other man's point of view.

All these qualities were displayed in Dr Peake's great contribution to the cause and triumph of Methodist Union. During its long drawn out proceedings the United Committee had to encounter at times serious dangers and possible crises. It surmounted them all, and did so, not by mere bargaining or artificial arrangements, but because 'the unity of the spirit in the bond of peace' was steadily preserved. And no man did more to secure, by God's blessing, this great result than Dr Peake. Here his clear vision of the end, his tenacity in pursuing it and his patience in overcoming obstacles, were conspicuous and uniformly successful.[2]

The torch which Peake had kindled in the early years by his reading of the Epistle to the Ephesians he carried unfalteringly to the end, and we may well remember a line of Browning he himself loved to recall:

Mine be some figured flame, which blends, transcends them all.

[1] *H.R.* 1930, p. 32.
[2] *H.R.* 1930, pp. 38–9.

CHAPTER TEN

THE MAN AND HIS ACHIEVEMENT

IN THE foregoing chapters we have sought to give some outline and analysis of Peake's life and labours. An attempt must now be made to look more intimately at his character and achievement.

I

The most immediate and overwhelming impression is that of the massive quantity and vast range of Peake's work. This was the source of constant amazement to his friends.

I am amazed and ashamed by your industry. How with all your lecturing you keep so wonderfully abreast of discussion in both Testaments, and find time to conduct such elaborate lucid and intensive discussions—to say nothing of the frequent public lectures in various parts of the country, passes my comprehension.[1]

His industry was indeed phenomenal. He much enjoyed telling the story of the American writer who wrote one article with his right hand, another with his left, dictated a third to his secretary and, in order to lose no time, rocked the cradle with his foot.[2] In a letter to his friend, Professor John Skinner, he wrote: 'My life is like that of an acrobat who has always one ball in his hand and five in the air'.[3] Again, at a time of 'almost unprecedented pressure' he writes:

I have long felt the appropriateness of Matthew Arnold's, 'A second wave succeeds before we have had time to breathe'. But really it's not a second wave, but a whole procession of 'waves and billows that have gone over me'.[4]

Yet another: 'I am not snowed under: I am buried many fathoms deep under an avalanche'.[5] The following letter in answer to a pressing request

---

[1] J. E. McFadyen to A.S.P., 10 November 1913.
[2] *Memoir*, p. 304.
[3] A.S.P. to John Skinner, 25 May 1923.
[4] A.S.P. to Leslie D. Weatherhead, 31 December 1925.
[5] A.S.P. to T. H. Robinson, 11 November 1925.

for a date for a manuscript holds a mirror to the man's extraordinary involvement, and is so complete a picture that it justifies its inclusion in these pages:[1]

Consider my situation. In term time I have my University and Hartley College work, which in their combination are very exacting, and even in the vacation there is a good deal of examination work and often committees. In addition to that there is the editorship of the *Holborn Review*, which I assure you is no sinecure, and I have, as you know, to write a great deal for it. I am Vice-chairman of the John Rylands Library, and Chairman of the Book-Committee. I am President of our branch of the Classical Association and also of the Primitive Methodist University Union. When I can do so I write an article for the *Leader*. I lecture once a year for the John Rylands Library, which would be a mere triviality if it did not generally pledge me to print something much more elaborate for the *Bulletin*. A good part of my time at Keswick was spent in dictating 'The Roots of Hebrew Prophecy and Jewish Apocalyptic' and I have another lecture (or rather two lectures) to put together on 'The Messianic Consciousness of Jesus'. Then for many years my Commentary on Isaiah 40–66 has been promised and I can scarcely get time at it at all. On the top of this programme I have all sorts of time-robbing and strength-wasting and temper-wearing (that is if my temper were different) engagements, each perhaps insignificant in itself, but in their cumulative weight a heavy and exhausting load. The burden of correspondence is very heavy: often a whole morning will go on my letters. Then, of course, nobody would even have thought of me as destined to blossom into an ecclesiastical statesman; but I have had a great deal of work to do of one sort or another for Methodist Union, and I am on the little committee which meets frequently at Lambeth in connexion with the *Lambeth Appeal*. The Federal Council and the Society for Old Testament Study also cut into my time. And much of this work has to be done, however one is feeling, and all the time the doctors are warning me to retrench and conserve my energies, and to give up the ruinous policy of living on my reserves.

I think I have given you data enough to get some kind of idea of my situation. Matthew Arnold put things quite appropriately at the close of Empedocles' long speech:

> *I say: Fear not! Life still*
> *Leaves human effort scope.*
> *But, since life teems with ill,*
> *Nurse no extravagant hope;*
> *Because thou must not dream, thou need'st not then despair!*

Usually in his study immediately after breakfast, he rarely returned to bed before twelve o'clock midnight; during the vacation he would often work fifteen or sixteen hours a day without relaxation save for his meals. On one occasion a friend was mildly remonstrating with him on the pace at which he was working. Peake remarked quietly, 'I simply can't help it: the work must be done'. Then he proceeded to tell the following story, the moral of which is obvious:

---

[1] A.S.P. to Arthur Hird, 13 December 1922.

Once upon a time a man was telling a naturalist of a scene he had witnessed in a field. A badger being chased by a dog, the poor creature was so hard pressed that he ran up a tree for shelter. 'But', interrupted the naturalist, 'that won't do, for a badger cannot climb trees'. 'I don't care whether he can or not,' said the man: 'this badger simply couldn't help it; the dog worried him so'.

The possession of a remarkable memory was of great help to Peake in his work. Whilst at Oxford he had attended a course of lectures with the purpose of improving it, and later he took a course in Pelmanism with the same object, but the authorities declared that the papers he sent in were so high in quality that they were unable to do anything to help him. In a church service he seldom found it necessary to use a hymn-book and if he read carefully twice or three times a poem in which he was interested as for example Browning's 'Johannes Agricola in Meditation' he could afterwards recall it at will. This quality of memory enabled him to possess a knowledge which was encyclopaedic in its range.

It is fortunate that Miss Elsie Cann, who was Peake's faithful and devoted secretary for almost twenty-five years, has left us some impressions of Peake's work in his study.[1] This may best be expressed in her own words.

Generally speaking Dr Peake worked easily, and seldom made any drastic alteration in what he dictated, though occasionally he would begin an article over again if he was not satisfied with it. He was not unduly disturbed if people came into the room while he was working, though latterly if he was interrupted he found it more difficult to pick up the threads again, especially if he was dictating anything that required concentration. I remember one morning at Freshfield, when visitors were staying there, we had so many interruptions that I began to make a list. In just over an hour they amounted to seventeen. One of the intruders was Dr Peake's little nephew (then six) who came running in saying he just wanted a rock in uncle's rocking-chair! Many men would have been exasperated at being disturbed so often, but Dr Peake simply said we must make the most of our time when they had all gone out. This was of course an exceptional day; we were not usually disturbed so frequently. But I remember on another occasion—possibly during a coal-shortage—his eldest son could not do his lessons with the two younger boys in the room, so they had to come in to study, and Dr Peake had to try to dictate while they were running their trains across the floor. He was the most patient as well as the most kind-hearted and self-sacrificing man I have ever met.

He could be absolutely relied on, and if he had promised a book or article to the publishers by an appointed date, he would work extra late in the evening or on into the morning to complete it. When he was writing his New Testament *Introduction* he had to finish dictating it lying on a sofa: afterwards he had rather a serious attack of brain-fag and had to take a month's rest. He was just as considerate and easy to work for when he was not feeling well.

In the early days I used to take down the letters and articles in shorthand,

---

[1] E. Cann. art. 'Dr Peake in his Study'. *P.M.L.* December 1929. Reprinted in *Essays in Commemoration*.

but for many years Dr Peake dictated straight to the typewriter. This saved a great deal of time, and had the advantage that he was able to read what he had written as he went along. In the winter I used to work the typewriter on a revolving chair by the fire, which could be twisted round to him at any moment.

Dr Peake always opened his own letters and perferred to dictate the replies, and with the exception of formal invitations and letters asking for subscriptions he seldom handed anything over to me to deal with myself. If he received a letter the contents of which he thought the writer would prefer no one else should become acquainted with, the reply would either be dictated in language which would convey nothing to me, or a letter would be sent in his own handwriting however busy he might be. Letters asking for advice on theological subjects or with reference to the purchase of books or the study of these always received careful attention. If by chance there was a letter of complaint to be written it would be so admirably worded that one would hardly recognise that any fault was being found, but Dr Peake would usually succeed in getting the matter that needed attention put right, without giving offence or hurting any one's feelings.

Book-parcels were always opened with keen interest, whether they were books he had ordered or books that had come for review. If three or four parcels came at once I should be allowed to cut the string and clear away the packing, but he always liked to discover what was in the parcel himself; he would often make a guess at what they contained before opening them!

Dr Peake had a second study at the top of the house, with book-shelves all round. He spent most of his time in the downstairs study, but if he was at work on a commentary, he preferred to write upstairs so that he could leave his work on the desk with the books he needed to consult open around it, and he would go up there when he could spare an hour or two from his regular work. His commentary on *Jeremiah* was written in this way, entirely by his own hand, and typed out afterwards, though he was in the habit of dictating his other books. At the time he was taken ill the desk in the upstairs study was covered with the books he was using in preparation for his commentary on Isaiah for the *International Critical Commentary* series. He had been working on this a good deal in the early part of July 1929, and had been hoping to get forward with it very considerably during the summer vacation.

Mrs Peake and the three boys were never well in Manchester during the winter and it was on medical advice that they should live near the sea for a few years to establish their health that, in 1912, Peake took a house at Freshfield, near Southport. This involved considerable strain in travel and made it much more difficult for Peake to do his work. It meant that he was away from his library; review-books and other material had to be carried to and fro a good deal, and much time was involved in catching and missing trains for which connexions were often difficult. His secretary writes:

If I was with him and we just missed the train by half a second, having the barriers shut in our face, I used to feel very indignant, but he always took it very philosophically, and would just put in the twenty minutes or half-an-hour looking at the book-stall, and perhaps buying a detective story or two!

The household returned to Manchester in 1920, to a house in Whalley Range, near the College. It was smaller than that at Freshfield and this created some problems of accommodation, particularly regarding his immense library, and books had to be distributed to the room at the College and at the University. His secretary gives a glimpse of the crowded and booklined room.

In spite of the fact that the study at Albert Road never looked tidy, Dr Peake was really very methodical. He usually had a good many pieces of work on hand at once, and he had several nests of drawers which varied in size; here we used to keep the work that was in progress. These drawers were added to from time to time, till we had about fourteen sets. Two or three were devoted to the *Holborn Review*, one to the Free Church Council, one to the *Times Literary Supplement*, one to Lambeth, another to lecture-notes, and several to letters. I had one drawer labelled 'autobiography'. Several friends used to express the wish that Dr Peake would write an autobiography,[1] and I often tried to persuade him to do this, but he always felt that he had more important work waiting to be done. I made the suggestion that all the time that was devoted to work after ten in the evening might be utilized for this purpose, but I could not get Dr Peake to consent to this. Twice when we were away on holiday he did spend a little time dictating some incidents of his childhood.

It would be wrong to suppose that amidst all the massive labours Peake went on without intermission for some brief holiday, but even such occasions were not aloof from work. If he were going away for any length of time he usually packed a box of books—some for work, particularly on wet days which would not then be wasted. After supper he would settle down to the work awaiting to be done. The index to his book on *The Bible* was largely done in Cornwall; the index to the *Commentary* was begun while on holiday in Goathland, on the Yorkshire moors. In the spring of 1929, on a Mediterranean tour, letters were sent on to anticipate his arrival at Constantinople; in the train between London and Folkestone he dictated an article for the *Times Literary Supplement*, and similarly through the voyage, in a corner of the *Ausonia* or at the place where he stayed.

Remembering that all this astounding labour was carried through by a man with a frail physique, it is not surprising to find that again and again his friends were concerned for his survival and constantly uttered their warnings against overwork. J. H. Moulton wrote as early as 1908: 'I am very much concerned by what you tell me, the more so as it is only

---

[1] e.g. the following letter from Dr H. McLachlan, Principal of the Unitarian College, Manchester: (23 July 1925) '... I have been frequently struck by the extraordinarily interesting personal notes in your editorials in the *Holborn Review*, and I want to urge you (if necessary) to shape all this material with an account of your own life, so as to provide your many pupils and admirers some day with your autobiography. It might not be published for many years, or never in your lifetime—that you would naturally determine for yourself. What I want to say is that I am convinced that you could give us a very charming and illuminating record. The preparation of it might prove a pleasant recreation in the midst of serious biblical research—not to say as a diversion from lectures, committees *et hac omne genus*'.

what I feared. You know you are not a Hercules, except mentally, and you will persist in behaving as if you were.'[1] Again in 1915: 'I am greatly grieved to hear what you say about yourself. I had not realized that you had been overdoing it again in this serious way. We really must not have any more of this. . . . We want to conserve you for the things which only you can do.'[2] Even more forcibly in the later years:

I am greatly distressed at the news. It is not in the least surprising, for I have seen you heading straight for disaster for a long time past. I know what you will say. You will accuse me of being a pot, even if you are a kettle! But there is a difference. I play tennis, and you don't. It all means that if your precious life is going to be kept going till you have done all we want out of you—and that means a good long time—you must absolutely slow down and restrain output. You must be perfectly obedient and let the work simply go.[3]

One of his own colleagues wrote to him in 1924:

One could wish that you could—and would—take a little more rest from your incessant work during the vacation. I fear these wishes fall on deaf ears, but some of us who care a great deal for you have a feeling that you are not always fair to yourself.[4]

We have already noted that in Peake's boyhood and youth there had been a lack of robust health. As the years passed, however, he grew stronger, and in particular enjoyed cycling, devoting a number of his holidays to tours in North Wales and the Lake District. He withstood the stress of the Oxford years on the whole remarkably well. In the latter part of 1902, however, he had to undergo a serious operation for the removal of a cyst attached to the liver, and this debarred him from almost all physical exercise, and he had to spend long periods lying on his back. This experience left a permanent mark upon his health. In 1915 as the result of prolonged overwork he had a severe breakdown, from which he did make recovery, but received the warning from his doctors that he should not expect to be so fortunate a second time, should a breakdown occur. With amazing tenacity of purpose and dogged persistence, however, the work went on, more and yet more, as he became the more involved.

There were indications, with the approach of his sixtieth birthday in 1925, that the burden was becoming perceptibly more weighty. Even as early as 1921, being advised by the doctor to take a rest, and under this suggestion proposing to go to Ambleside, he wrote to his secretary:

I am *very* tired. It doesn't suit me at all to be on my feet much now. My legs get tired much as they did in 1915 though of course I am a long way from being as bad as I came to be. I hope to rest a good deal up at Ambleside; to walk

---

[1] J. H. Moulton to A.S.P., 30 May 1908.
[2] Ibid., 10 March 1915.
[3] Ibid., 20 September 1915.
[4] J. T. Brewis to A.S.P., 24 July 1924.

very little and go about on coaches, or boats or wherever I can sit and take the fresh air without effort. I hope they will have a deck-chair with leg-rest at Gale Mount: if not I must try to buy one, as it makes *all* the difference to the rest one gets, or at least to me.... I must not write any more. I had to have a long rest in the chair before I was fit to write this.[1]

It was early in February 1925 that he wrote to a friend:

I watch the years race by with scarcely anything to show for them as they go, and wish that I could find some leisure and regain health enough to make use of it; but I'm afraid both will be denied me until it is too late. I shall be sixty this year, and at present I feel nearly worn out. Things would be different if I were not doomed to be like the acrobat who has all the time five balls in the air and one in his hands.[2]

To another friend came these words in a letter in which he requested to be relieved of a particular task:

I still get tired far too easily: so I hope you won't mind seeing the matter through its remaining stages. I am sorry to feel so comparatively useless, but after all it is not to be wondered at, in view of the distressing fact that I shall by sixty next November, and that I must work while it is day.[3]

The following extract taken from a letter which he wrote to his eldest son, on 20 September 1925 shows the intense strain under which Peake was working in the last years of his life. He wrote:[4]

The doctor is not satisfied with me. He says all the good I got from my holidays I have worked off already, and he thinks I cannot go through the winter (he means without a breakdown) unless I get some more holiday. I asked if weekends would do: he is dubious but thinks they might be tried. I think public life for me is really over, as my other work is more than enough for my strength. At sixty we haven't the old resilience, and if we hit the floor we can't bounce up again as we did in the old days.

Some two years later, when he was approached regarding his becoming President of the National Free Church Council, there were at once those who tried to dissuade him from accepting the office, but after full medical consultation and the assurance that his duties would be kept to a minimum, under a strong sense of duty he accepted the call and was duly initiated in 1928. As his son declares, it was sometimes remarked that he looked tired, and that he was sometimes using notes in the pulpit—in one case even full manuscript; it was clear that he was not well. Nevertheless he showed no sign of an immediate collapse, and went on with his manifold duties.

[1] A.S.P. to E. Cann, 13 July 1921.
[2] A.S.P. to Mr Derbyshire, 14 February 1925.
[3] A.S.P. to E. Marjorie Davies, 7 March 1925.
[4] Quoted in *Memoir*, p. 302.

II

Perhaps any glimpses into Peake's family and home life can be most fittingly recorded here in the words of his son, the author of the *Memoir*, in a choice chapter in that book, from which these excerpts are taken.

My earliest memory of my father goes back to the days of his first operation when I used to go in to his study where he was lying convalescent in the house at Wellington Road, Manchester, and sing to him about the beautiful bird in the gilded cage. My father always had a horror of cruelty in any of its forms, and especially the cruelty that kept birds in cages or that enjoyed hunting merely for hunting's sake. Perhaps his idea in teaching me this simple song at the beginning of life was to instil the same principle into me.... It has not been possible to trace the author of the song, but as my father was in the habit of making up short verses himself, it was not unlikely that he wrote it. The verse runs:

> *It's only a bird in a gilded cage,*
> *A beautiful sight to see:*
> *You'd think she was happy and free from care:*
> *She's not, though she seems to be.*

Two points about the verse demand a passing comment because they formed part and parcel of father's philosophy of childhood. Though the child is meant to regard the subject as a painful one, every attempt is made to see that his feelings are in no way harrowed. The picture that he is to condemn is a picture which at first sight strikes him as being beautiful. By not stating the definite reason why the bird was unhappy the child is led to ask questions, and so draw the moral for himself.

The only other memory of my very early childhood is that of my father conducting family prayers—also in the old study at Wellington Road. When we were children it was his custom to take family prayers each morning after we had had breakfast. These always consisted of a short passage from Scripture (frequently a story), two prayers from the Church of England Prayer Book, the Lord's Prayer and the Benediction. Though a great believer in extempore prayer where the pulpit was concerned, he always maintained that some of the prayers in the Anglican Prayer Book seemed to have been inspired beyond any other written prayers that he had ever come across, and on the simpler of these we as children were brought up. Later we were taught a prayer of our own which we learnt at his knee.... To him it seemed most natural that father and mother should create the right atmosphere by kneeling together in family worship.

Three days in the year stood out with prominence—Gunpowder Day, Christmas Day, and Sunday.

On Gunpowder Day father always had a magnificent array of fireworks which he used to send off in the back garden much to our delight. He himself would enter into the fun and frolic with all the enthusiasm of a child.... Christmas was nearly always spent at the farm of our uncle and auntie in Shropshire, and Christmas Day was the one day in the year on which father never reckoned to do any work. The whole season was always made a royal one for us boys. The old farmhouse, with its long passages, its panelled walls, its dim-lit hall, its fields, ponds and pine-trees, often covered with snow and frost, was one in which all the romance of Christmas could be fully and fitly celebrated. When games were played, he always entered into them with characteristic vigour: 'Hunt the Thimble', 'Hide and Seek', and above all, 'Blind Man's Buff' being his apparent favourite.

On Sunday afternoon he would gather us round the fireside, and read to us sometimes hour after hour. *The Pilgrim's Progress, The Holy War, The Fairchild Family, Sandford and Merton, Uncle Tom's Cabin*; stories from the Old and New Testaments were read through in this way. Every now and then he would break off and question us on what he had read, and when he came to the moral of any story it was always his method to make us discover it for ourselves. He was also a great believer in the value of pictures as a method of religious education. He had a number of Bibles, beautifully illustrated, which he would show us from time to time, telling the story behind each picture as he turned the pages over. . . .

Another thing on which he laid great stress was the importance of music. Not being a musician himself he purchased a gramophone to give us an idea of tune, to introduce us to some of the best singers, and to instruct us in some of the hymns that he wanted us to learn. The instrument gave us endless pleasure, and my mother once remarked that father never bought anything for the house for which he had been more thoroughly repaid. Indeed in all these activities she took an equal share, for she was essentially a home-maker.[1]

One thing that brought great pleasure into the household was Peake's immense fund of stories, dealt out not only for the enjoyment but for instruction. He was a great lover of fairy stories, and expressed the hope that his children would never grow too old to appreciate a fairy tale, and one of the last things he did before he was taken ill was to buy a fresh supply for his grandchildren.[2] He also enjoyed books of travel, partly because he liked stories of adventure, partly because he felt it would help towards a better understanding of other folk. Hence the children were always well-supplied with books by such writers as Ballantyne, Kingston, Stevenson and others.

As we have seen in his early years, Peake lived amongst the Shropshire hills, and the walks through the country-side certainly strengthened him physically. His son describes his affection for the hills of Shropshire as 'one of the most touching elements in his character'.

He would never pass them in the train without calling for silence from his children, during which he would point out the hills one by one concluding with the remark: 'I knew what beautiful scenery was when I was a boy'. It almost seemed as though each rock and stone had been graven upon his memory. . . .

---

[1] Op. cit., pp. 292–6.
[2] A master of Murchiston School, Edinburgh, asking guidance from Peake regarding books on the Bible wrote: 'One of my earliest recollections is of some delightful books about Jack the Giant Killer which you gave us about twenty years ago in Oxford. I don't suppose I shall ever forget them, and I have never seen the like since.' H. S. Young to A.S.P., 22 June 1908.

In a letter to my mother, written in the early autumn of 1890, he gives us a brief description of one of his many rambles. William and I went for a walk up the Ashes Valley this morning. It lies between two of the Stretton hills of the Long Mynd range, a romantic spot with a brook flowing down it. We came to a little bit of a waterfall, but that scarcely gives a right impression, as the water does not fall sheer, but down the stones. We amused ourselves putting stones across it half way down so as to catch the water and throw it up and over like an open fan formed of a thin sheet of water. This looked very pretty. And so we left it. William having got his feet wet, and I, I daresay, with my cold, none the better for it.

One of his favourite pastimes as a boy consisted in skimming pebbles across a lake or river and counting the number of times the stone bounded from the surface.[1]

This is perhaps the most fitting point to recall that in his later years in particular, Peake's chief recreation was the reading of detective and adventure stories, of which he had a wide knowledge. The following letter[2] gives us in a glimpse his keen interest in this kind of writing:

Many thanks for your kind letter, and for the abridged *Life of Gladstone* which is very good. Of stories my most desperate need at present is Austin Freeman, *The Magic Carpet*. It strikes me that Dornford Yates's *Blind Corner* must be very much my style as treasure-hunt stories always greatly appeal to me.

A letter written about three weeks later records:

I read Austin Freeman's *The Magic Carpet* and Dornford Yates's *Blind Corner* with great enjoyment. Austin Freeman's short stories are ingenious, though I think that the long story gives his type of talent better scope. *Blind Corner* is very good indeed.... I see, among your three-and-sixpennies, you have *The Supreme Adventures of Mr Shutterby Cobb*, which I have never heard of, and also somebody or other '—*Detective*', by Oppenheim. I can't remember the full title.

P.S. The title of the Oppenheim I couldn't remember is *Nicholas Grade: Detective*.[3]

III

Of Peake's personal qualities that which most impressed others was his genuine humility, as abundantly expressed in his private correspondence and in published accounts. Dr Hewlett Johnson, Dean of Manchester, wrote concerning him:

---

[1] Op. cit., pp. 307–8.

[2] A.S.P. to Arthur Hird, 28 March 1927. On one occasion, when in Blackwell's, Oxford, he was looking in the shelves for a supply of these stories, a shop assistant, unaware of who he was, asked if she could help him to find what he required. She handed several to him always to receive the same reply: 'I have read that'! Finally, rather naïvely she said to him: 'Sir, don't you think it is time you read something more serious?'

[3] Ibid., 15 April 1927.

He was indeed a wonderful and beautiful character: wonderful in the range and depth of his learning; beautiful in the splendid humility and simplicity with which he carried all off. His learning adorned his simple, rarely simple Christian life. That is why we loved him and treasured him.[1]

That this quality in him was profoundly sincere is illustrated by the following extract from a letter which he wrote to the writer of a long and appreciative article on the occasion of the celebration of his twenty-one years at Hartley College[2]—a letter which only a man of true humility could indeed write:

I do not know how to thank you for your character sketch.... I feel that were I half as good as you depict me, I should be far better than I am. Your words encourage me to hope that the ideal you have rightly divined may have been sometimes more nearly reached, or perhaps I should say, less miserably fallen short of, than in my self-distrustful way I am apt to think. I stand such words better than some people, for such self-knowledge as I have prevents undue elation, while they come to me like healing the wounds of self-criticism, and as an assurance that one's failure is, it may be, less than one had been tempted to surmise.

And as self-revelation your sketch is beautiful.... To say that it is very hard to make out why so many should write and speak with such warmth sounds too much like mock humility, but I am quite honestly puzzled by it, not only when I look at myself, but when I look at the qualities and gifts of others. I can't help thinking that somehow a kind of legend has grown up about me, and in spite of everything I do to reduce it, people go on crediting me with very much more than my due.

On the occasion of a large meeting in the Free Trade Hall, Manchester, when Peake got up to speak, the vast audience rose to its feet, and burst into applause which lasted for some minutes. Peake stood with bowed head, entirely overwhelmed by the tribute thus paid to him and for a while remained unable to speak.

Allied to this humility of spirit was Peake's quality of simplicity. Dr Albert Peel, Editor of the *Congregational Quarterly*, wrote concerning him: 'With a truly Himalayan range of learning and with marvellous powers of exposition, he had the simplicity and the naivete of a little child.'[3] It was this quality in him that appealed to children and found immediate response.[4] He was fundamentally a lover of simple things—in dress, diet, recreation—and this was his general attitude to life. The more public worship expressed itself in simple form—in hymn, in prayer, in sermon—

---

[1] Hewlett Johnson to Mrs Peake, August 1929.
[2] A.S.P. to Emily Jones Davies, 6 December 1912. The article referred to is printed in *P.M.L.* 5 December 1912.
[3] Quoted *Memoir*, p. 313.
[4] A little girl of eleven, in the junior branch of the Trinity Hall School, Southport, wrote home to her parents: 'We were very lucky to have Dr A. S. Peake, the Prime Minister, this morning. He is very nice; personally I think he is a darling. I forget what he preached about but it was very nice'.

the more was he moved by it. He did not care for liturgies, anthems, the chanting of the Lord's prayer; he was content with the old classic hymns set to familiar tunes. For him worship was the simple attitude of the child in the presence of the Father, direct, uncomplicated and unadorned. He himself had learned to express profound truths in simple terms.

Peake possessed a fine sense of humour, delicately balanced. As we have already observed, he had a fund of stories and a particular ability to use the right story for the circumstance, and could meet a situation always with the apt remark. On one occasion when he was due to lecture at the Rylands Library he did not appear at the appointed time. After a quarter of an hour's waiting it was announced that he had met with an accident but would arrive shortly. He came about half an hour later, and quietly explained that he had cut off the end of his finger not long before. The chemists had failed to stop the bleeding and he had been to the doctor to have the finger dressed. 'Happily,' said Peake, with a smile, 'It wasn't the end of my tongue'—and at once proceeded to deliver a brilliant lecture! In his letters there are flashes of humour of which the following, written to his sister-in-law, who was an ardent Christian Scientist, is an excellent example:

May 9th 1923

My dear Chloe,
  You will remember that the author of the seventy-third psalm says:
But as for me, my feet were almost gone
My steps had well-nigh slipped.
The Psalmist was more fortunate than I was, for with me a fortnight last Thursday morning it was not a case of 'almost' and 'well-nigh', but of 'altogether' and 'completely'. On the mental delusion known as a pavement outside the hallucination of mortal mind called St Pancras Station, the dark projection of my imagination known as my body experienced the error that it was pitching forward, the result being a bad strain in that materialisation of my consciousness known as my right leg. I imagined myself several times during the day to be careering through space in what I believe deluded mortals call a taxi and in the corrupt imagination of my heart I have seemed to myself to have been limping badly. I am thankful to say that the mists of error seem to be thinning; as the ordinary victim of illusion would say, the leg is much better. I noticed your emphatic approval when Dr Hutton said that some people didn't require coddling, they wanted shaking: and you will be delighted to know that I got a very severe shaking when I tripped into that error, and it took me some time to regain my mental equilibrium.
With our best love to you all
Yours affectionately, Arthur S. Peake[1]

Peake was exceedingly quick at repartee when the occasion required it. Here are a few examples amongst many that might be quoted. In his earliest teaching at the College a student, introduced for the first time to the idea of documentary analysis in the Pentateuch, exclaimed: 'But Sir,

---

[1] Quoted from *Memoir*, p. 317.

do you not believe the Pentateuch is Mosaic?' to which came the answer: 'A mosaic.' Again, having given in some detail a theory propounded by a German professor, Peake observed in concluding, 'But, gentlemen, he has no support'. A rather shallow student, not noted specially for his modesty, said: 'Well, Sir, I'll give him mine'. When the laughter of the class had subsided, Peake quietly commented. 'He still has no support'. On another occasion in the class-room the students became restive when the dismissal bell had rung, and Peake, wishing to complete the subject, carried on with the lecture. When the shuffling of feet became too pronounced to ignore, he mildly looked up and said: 'Gentlemen—I have yet a few pearls to cast before—I finish!'

Another outstanding mark of Peake's character was his kindness to others, allied with which was an innate courtesy. His devoted secretary Miss Cann, spoke of him as 'the most patient as well as the most kind-hearted and self-sacrificing man I ever met'. On the occasion of the meetings of the National Free Church Council at Bridlington in 1929, the secretary of the Women's Council in making her annual report likened some of the officers in the Free Churches to particular Bunyan characters. Afterwards Peake said to her: 'Of all Bunyan's characters I should like best to have the name of "Help".'[1] It is by that name that many remembered him and still do. The letters which he received bear abundant testimony to this personal quality. To those, ministerial or lay, at home or abroad, who required help for their studies, courses would be at once indicated and lists of books sent in detail in a personal reply. Cases of personal need, whether through sickness or financial stringency were always sympathetically considered and aid afforded. To one who was going out as an army chaplain he wrote:

I am glad and proud that you are going. I pray earnestly that you may do a great work and be restored to us for many years of service. I treasure your words. I am thankful to know that you feel I have been able to help you. These are the things that bring us our reward.[2]

To a copy of this letter its recipient adds the following footnote:

I paid a visit to Freshfield and have lively recollections of a walk we had together over the sandhills, A.S.P. stumbling along not looking where he was going, being so absorbed in telling me all about the projected *Peake's Commentary*. It was characteristic of him to contrive this visit for me and spare me the time. He saw me off in the evening at Freshfield station, and I carried the memory with me through the war, of his figure on the platform waving his hand as long as he could see me, his face alight with friendly cheer.

The late Professor Victor Murray recalled in 1929 his indebtedness to Peake[3] with great feeling:

[1] *Memoir*, p. 319.
[2] A.S.P. to P. J. Fisher, 9 June 1915.
[3] *P.M.L.* 5 September 1929, under the *nom de plume* 'Oxoniensis'. Professor Murray, who died in 1967, was President Emeritus of Cheshunt College, Cambridge at the time of his death.

I wrote to him when I was a boy at school. It was a time of deep disappointment for I had tried for a scholarship at Oxford and had not got it. In a North of England colliery village to whom could I go for help and advice? A few days before I had bought for twopence the *Christian Endeavour Year Book*. There was an article in it on 'Reading' by a man of whom I had never heard—Professor Peake. Urged on by despair to take defeatist measures, I wrote to this distinguished stranger and told him all my hopes and woes. I carried the letter about for days not daring to post it. Then I did post it. Curiously enough, only a few hours before, I learnt that I had got a scholarship after all. But it was too late then to recall it. Ten days later a reply came, beginning 'Dear Friend'. In the meantime he had been thinking it all over and had practical suggestions to make and an offer of help from himself.

That was how it all began. He saw me through Oxford. I had no resources but his on which to draw and he let me draw upon them without stint. I had no claim on him whatever, yet he always acted as if I had. He treated me like a father, encouraged me in reading, helped me out of difficulties, invited me to his house, introduced me to interesting people. Through him I got to know Deissman in Berlin and Sanday in Oxford, and was associated with Mansfield from my very first term. In all this I was simply a raw undergraduate, just like hundreds of others, and yet having all these opportunities because I had *him*, and he created them for me.

Peake's kindness of spirit inevitably manifested itself in a never failing courtesy, which indeed had its source in his deep Christian experience. His secretary tells of an occasion which illustrates this innate quality in him. A poor man had called at the house asking for work, and Peake had given him something to do in the garden, and told him to come again the following day. Thinking that his regular gardener might pass that way and feel upset at seeing someone else at work there, he sent a note to him explaining the situation. Again, as an example, the Rev. Thomas Nightingale, Secretary of the National Free Church Council, relates a simple incident which occurred during one of Peake's visits to the office during his year as President of the Council. On leaving, Mr Nightingale had accompanied him along the passage talking to him on some subject of importance. As he was waiting for the lift one of the office girls passed him, but Peake was so engrossed in the matter of the conversation that he scarcely noticed the girl. Presently he became aware that she had passed, and immediately he retraced his steps to the office to shake her hand and apologize for his apparent discourtesy.

As the wider circle of those who knew him bear testimony, this ministry of kindness was fulfilled again and again in the letters he wrote. His friend of the early years, William Meredith, declared: 'As iron sharpeneth iron so do your letters give a brightness to the day in which they come, especially when they are so full of happiness as the last'. 'It sweetens life and makes the world seem brighter to get a letter like yours', was the word of another of his correspondents. He had a genius for putting forth the right word graciously, 'as apples of gold in baskets of silver'. Thus one whom he had known from her childhood received on the morning of her wedding day the following letter written when Peake was in the Tyrol at the time of the Lausanne Conference in 1927:

My dear Dorothy,

I am sending this letter which will, I hope, reach you before you take 'the nuptial flight', as the entomologists describe the similar adventure of the soaring lady-ants on their wedding-day! This will reassure you that I have not forgotten next Wednesday, and indeed you have been often in my mind during these days of absence from England. I am very sorry that I can be with you only in spirit: from anywhere in our own land I would have come to take whatever share in the rites you had chosen to allot to me.

The Baptist deacon who followed an announcement of the approaching wedding of two members of the church with the further announcement of the hymn 'Mistaken souls who dream of heaven' was not exemplary for tactfulness: but his indiscretion is a useful reminder that heaven on earth is not achieved by dreaming, but by resolute effort directed to its attainment: and that where there are present in full measure self-renouncing love and sympathetic imagination—that highest virtue and all too rare in its perfection—there will be much inevitable sorrow and strain. But this will draw you into more intimate fellowship and understanding of each other and give a depth and intensity to your affection such as unalloyed bliss cannot give.

Yet I do not wish, on this day of all days, to do more than touch this tragic note, which I cannot miss as my mind travels down the years. And I touch it now simply to assure you that even this discordant note will bring with it an otherwise unattainable harmony. My dominant thought and desire for you is that your happiness in each other may never diminish, and that the sorrow needed for its ripening, for its richness and depth, will always come from without and not from within. And underneath all sorrow—even the ultimate sorrow—may there be the peace which passeth all understanding.

So with full confidence in both of you, radiant expectation and deep affection —faith, hope, love—I bid you God-speed in your new life.

With much love, my dear Dorothy, and many tender, wistful thoughts
Ever yours affectionately
Arthur S. Peake

One of Peake's friends refers to 'the many to whom you have shown the kindness of God'. It was to a friend that Professor Deissman of Berlin wrote in a letter of 'the kind eyes of Dr Peake'. Throughout his life Peake possessed in a profound measure this ineffable quality of character —*anima naturaliter Christiana*.

III

It is not surprising that the depth and extent of Peake's influence is something beyond our power to measure or even trace. The influence has been felt in so many ways, public and private, that it is difficult to evaluate it; it was an influence quietly and pervasively, and indeed unconsciously, exercised. Very early was it exerted. A master at New College, Eastbourne, who had been a fellow student of Peake's at Oxford, wrote in 1892:

> I cannot say how much I am indebted to you for the *tone* you imparted to my life in Oxford. I may have an opportunity some day of publicly acknowledging that next to my own beloved father, you have exercised more influence over me than any one else.[1]

Following one of his visits to Woodbrooke, Selly Oak, Birmingham to give a course of lectures one who was present wrote to Peake:

> Your visit has left behind something that has enabled me to go rejoicing on my way ever since. I am afraid of trying to say how much you do for me, but I should seem to claim a clearness of sight and a constancy of purpose which I am still very far from having reached—but this much at least is true that I never see you without thanking God and taking courage.[2]

And again, following a visit to Manchester, the same writer adds:

> Especially am I grateful for the opportunity my visit offered for a long talk with you. It did indeed uplift me and sent me on my way with a gladder heart than I have had for a long time.[3]

Amongst his colleagues at the University the diffusion of his fragrant personality was noted:

> His work was so fine, his character and influence was so noble and his modesty and charm were so great, that few men have exercised a finer and wider influence.... To us here he was so wise and kind a colleague, so fine and helpful a scholar and so gifted a teacher that we feel he cannot be replaced.... He had so much affection and admiration from us all.[4]

We have already indicated to some measure the wide influence which he exerted through his writings, not least through the circulation of his *Commentary*. The extent is shown when we find that it was used in American and Australian Colleges and adopted as a text-book by the Education Committee of Natal for use in school. His *Commentary* was quoted in Rumania in the theological lectures of a Greek Archimandrite. Meeting the Archdean of the Orthodox Churches in Cyprus, Peake himself was gratified to learn that he had the *Commentary*, and 'had learnt much from it'. A correspondent overseas writes: 'You have a very grateful and appreciative audience out here in New Zealand'; from an African correspondent comes this observation: 'The life and culture and outlook of the African Church will be the richer through all generations for his life and labours.'[5] A distinguished Welsh preacher finishes his letter: 'I cannot

---
[1] D. Herridge to A.S.P., 17 June 1892.
[2] Mabel Frith to A.S.P., 18 February 1904.
[3] Ibid., 18 September 1907.
[4] H. P. Turner to Mrs Peake, August 1929.
[5] F. W. Dodds to Mrs Peake, 1929.

close without a word of thanks to you for all the help you are giving to the ministers in Wales by your books'.[1] A senior chaplain to the Forces, who was one of Peake's former students wrote:[2]

I have travelled to Salonica with an R.C. Chaplain who joined from St Bede's,[3] and who had heard a great deal about you and had read your books. I have met scores of chaplains of all denominations who have read your books. At the present moment in my division there is a Wesleyan Chaplain who is using your book *Christianity: Its Nature and Truth* as a text-book for his theological class for ministerial candidates. I have also had some of your books sent out to me by the Red Cross Book Committee, and there are several active-service libraries where your books have a prominent place. So you have helped a good deal in many ways during this great war, and I wanted to tell you about it.

It was most natural that amongst his students, alike in their College days and later, in their varied spheres of ministry, Peake's influence should be deep and widespread. His influence upon their minds was lasting—'it was the method of a living mind that strove to conduct the student to where he could "see", knowing that till each saw for himself he must for ever go unillumined'.

Rarely did one catch the note of dogmatism in this master's teaching. Sometimes the immature, in their ardour for finality, wished that the dogmatic note were more often present. He knew better. The overpowering weight of his amazing learning, the ungainsayableness of his acknowledged authority—these he might well have twisted to our mental destruction. But whether from respect for intelligences which he desired should ever be free and strong in this freedom, or from humility in the face of mysteries no man fully understood and quite possibly most men misunderstood, or out of regard for the principle that for a pupil the adoption of a right method of study and point of view is much more important than the gift of any number of correct answers to most points, he most fastidiously refrained from venturing his own conclusions upon his students' attention. It was fine gesture; it was supreme wisdom.... What did concern him was that, under unobtrusive guidance, every man should acquire a habit of mind that rendered it ceaselessly hospitable to truth from whatever quarter it might come.... Methods of critical analysis: scrupulous fairness to one's own documents; exegesis as veracious as study and thought and prayer can make it; refusal to surrender any position till that position is untenable, and then ungrudging surrender at whatever cost of personal pain, and the moving to the new position indicated and offered as sound—all these habits of mind were formed under the same influence, or if already formed, were immeasurably strengthened by that same influence.[4]

The ultimate source of Peake's influence lay in his own personal spiritual quality, interpretative of his own personal experience. This was discerned, for example, on the occasion of a communion service in the

---

[1] T. Charles Williams to A.S.P., 2 June 1915.
[2] George Kendall to A.S.P., 6 January 1919.
[3] St Bede's is a Roman Catholic School near to Hartley College, Manchester.
[4] J. E. Storey in *H.R.* January 1930, pp. 23-4.

College chapel, which was attended by members of another College, one of whom wrote long afterwards about the occasion:

The senior men will never forget how the Doctor read the lesson at the sacramental services in Hartley College Chapel twelve months ago. He read the closing verses of the eighth chapter of Romans: 'For I am persuaded ... shall separate us from the love of God'. The verses were read in the Doctor's customary quiet way, but we all felt it to be a declaration of his own faith.

Wherever his former students met the conversation would very soon converge on the debt they owed to him and the affection with which he was universally held—and this is still true regarding those of his 'Peake's men' who, forty years after his death, still survive.

Here is a tribute to his influence felt by a small company of missionaries in the heart of Nigeria:

Was ever any man more highly regarded, more warmly valued, more unfeignedly loved by our church. Wherever his old students assembled for an hour or two together, though they were but two or three, it would be a marvellous thing if his name were not mentioned, in terms of deepest reverence and plainest gratitude. Many, is the evening that has passed pleasantly for three or four lonely fellows in the tropical bush as they reviewed old Hartley days, recounted some one or more of the Doctor's famous stories, or some incident showing his deep understanding of men. Perhaps it was this last that so greatly endeared him to us. We felt he knew us all so well, could lay his finger on this foible or that, and could use just the right way to get from us our best. . . .

As we talk of him out here in Nigeria, one thing always arises in our conversation—our admiration of his simple godliness. In all our church we know no man liker Christ—with all reverence I say it. He taught men from the abundance of his knowledge, but he also taught men by the example of his gracious soul.[1]

And it was likewise for men working, often in difficult places, in the homeland for the gospel's sake. Here is a word from one toiling in a slum area of Manchester:

Living as I am in this district in the very centre of gambling, drunkenness and wickedness of every description, confronted at times with these ugly demons I feel the awful power of evil. But when I think of your devoted character, my faith is strengthened, my difficulties overcome: and it is impossible to resist the overwhelming gratitude of my heart to one who has helped me so many times to surmount and subdue wickedness.

Such illustration of Peake's influence could be multiplied again and again. Let one further example be set down as an illustration of the saving power of his unconscious ministry. One of his students, a man from a mining town, suffered a spinal injury just before coming to College. This darkened

---

[1] F. W. Dodds to Mrs Peake. From the letter of another missionary in South Central Africa comes the following sentence: 'I never look at your portrait—which is before me on my study wall as I write—without being conscious of an earnest desire to live a pure and faithful life in the service of the Master, and without feeling inspired to scorn all cheap ambition and sordid aims.'

the early part of his time of training. Some years later he wrote the following letter:

My first year in College was a terribly grim one for me. I could not join in the pleasures and pastimes of my comrades; with the greatest difficulty I sat listening to the lectures, and spent my afternoons often in bed. Then day by day I witnessed my cherished ideas of the Scriptures and Divine things torn to shreds and theologically I was soon in the deepest bewildering darkness, knowing neither 'What' nor 'Why'.

And yet the problems of Job and other similar problems were simple compared with the problems of my own life. Why should I be so stricken? Was God all-wise, all-loving too? Did all things work together for good?

But, Sir, when I could not see my God and but dimly see my Saviour, when black darkness surrounded me on every hand I knew not whither, I remembered how you had walked through the valley of the shadow, had also fought with the grim monsters, pain and mystery and doubt, and yet withal had held on to God through his Son Jesus Christ. I marked—especially in the prayer meetings at Western Street—your magnificent faith in a loving Father, and if you don't mind my saying what is in my heart—I held on to you, Sir, while you held on to Jesus. For I said within myself, here is one who has trod the path before me, let me follow him and maybe I shall yet endure. I thank God, Sir, that you led me, by force of your own faith, and your devoted instruction from time to time, in various ways and manners, at last to an understanding of the sacred Book and to an intelligent and firm faith in God through Jesus Christ.

Faith is vindicated. I am now quite well again and I feel that, though I have passed through the fires, the process has been refining, for I am conscious of a mellowness of soul and a sympathy with suffering that otherwise I could not have possessed. And every day is adding proof that 'the All-great were the All-loving too'.

Peake was profoundly moved by this letter and fortunately his acknowledgement of it, written by his own hand, has survived.

I meant to have answered your letter earlier, but I mislaid it and have only just found it again. It gave me great pleasure: the sense that quite unconsciously to myself I had helped you through so critical a period was a great encouragement to me. I was glad indeed to have been counted worthy of such a privilege. I cannot feel sorry that you have passed through so bitter an experience, for I feel that it was worth while as part of your equipment. It is very good of you to have written to tell me so. Whether one knows the results of one's work or not must make no difference to the finality with which one does it, but it is always a help to be assured that it has not been in vain.
      With kindest regards,
       Yours faithfully,
        A. S. Peake.

Of Peake it can be truly declared that, throughout his life and work the did 'breathe perpetual benediction'

IV

Any attempt to summarize Peake's achievement may well begin by recalling the words of an eminent biblical scholar written at the time of his death: 'We have lost the greatest biblical scholar of his generation, a man whose international reputation was as enviable in the field of New Testament studies as it was outstanding in the ranks of Old Testament scholars'.[1]

In the foregoing pages we have suggested something of Peake's contribution: a careful survey will show that two factors lay at the foundation of his achievement.

The first of these was his profound religious experience. *Pectus fecit theologum*—religious experience makes the theologian; this saying of Neander was eminently true of Peake. In his early experience he had consciously undergone a radical transformation in the attitude of his personal will—'from the self-centredness of the natural man to the God-centredness of the new man in Christ', after the type of Paul's own conversion, the classical example in history. This explains why 'Paulinism' became his favourite study—'the field in which he most showed originality and mastery of grasp from first to last'. To Peake, Paulinism was not 'an excrescence on the original stock', as some suggest, but in fact the key to the secret of Christianity. It was not to be regarded as forming a rigid and enclosed system but a singularly living and flexible body of principles. To him the central thought in the theology of Paul was that of the mystical union of the believer with Christ—an emphasis which lifted much of the current exposition of Paul's thought away from a mere forensic interpretation; this must be distinguished as a secondary doctrine, not the primary one, in the theology of Paul. Peake was really speaking of himself when he wrote: 'The secret of the spell which the theology of Paul has cast on such multitudes is to be found in the illumination which it has brought to their own spiritual history'.[2] Peake's special and permanent distinction lay in his interpretation of the Pauline type of Christianity, and he may still be regarded as the most competent modern exponent of the mind of the Apostle.

The second factor which was contributory to Peake's achievement was a personal quality—his soundness of judgement. We have already noted his amazing wealth of knowledge; aided by an exceptional memory, he gathered to his storehouse material from the work of scholars far and wide, and because of this secured a great comprehensiveness. It would seem that he read everything within the field of biblical learning that was printed in English, French and German at least, and it was his own careful judgement of this vast field that he gave to the world. He had a remarkable power of discovering the truth as he weighed the evidence on all sides; in addition he had an immense facility in the presentation of the subject

---

[1] W. F. Howard in the *British Weekly*, 22 August 1929.
[2] A.S.P., *The Quintessence of Paulinism* p. 31

with which he dealt. It is significant that throughout the innumerable reviews of his books and articles and the massive correspondence appreciative of his writings, the word 'lucid' is the most frequent in estimating his work. This soundness of judgement is illustrated in the almost uncanny faculty by which, with great foresight, he recognized the opportunity of the moment and closed with it. His realization that the acceptance of the call to Manchester would prove the opening of a door to the fashioning of a whole ministry within his own Church and perhaps beyond; his keen insight into the foundations for the first interdenominational theological faculty with teaching and examining functions in a modern British university, so that in a very real sense the achievement in the unsectarian recognition of theology in a modern university became his own creation; his seizing of the opportunities, afforded respectively by the Lambeth Appeal of 1920 and the beginnings of the movement towards Methodist Union, to enlarge Christian understanding and forward the cause of Christian unity—all these were situations the significance of which he at once recognized and then stepped forth to meet the opportunity.

Likewise the writings which came forth from his prolific pen were in a large part the response to an intellectual and spiritual need which he recognized as calling for fulfilment. His earliest book, *A Guide to Biblical Study* (1897), was published in days when 'criticism' was still widely thought of as something that had arisen out of Germany to destroy the faith, a mistaken view that needed positive correction. Beginning about 1887 there had been a widespread agitation on the question of 'higher criticism'; it was in this year that W. Robertson Nicoll wrote an article in the *British Weekly*[1] entitled 'The Coming Battle', in which he tried to indicate the seriousness of the situation. By the middle of the 1890s the battle had been largely won by the critics, for by this time the impact upon the leadership of the chief English denominations had become accepted. Nevertheless there remained a large number of lay-folk, and indeed some ministers, who refused to accept the new critical position even in principle. These did not constitute a well-defined block of traditionalist conviction, but it could not be ignored. The years of the greatest crisis were already passed before Peake's influence became widely felt, but he recognized the importance of bringing this widespread traditionalist opinion to an understanding of the critical approach to the Scriptures, and seized the occasion for so doing. As we have seen, it was in 1897 that he published his first book. During the years that followed, however, there were further occasions when there was a resurgence of the traditional emphasis, and this became the reason for his writing *The Bible: Its Origin, Its Significance and Its Abiding Worth* (1913),—'to prove helpful in the present perplexity'—and also the editing of the *Commentary*, planned in 1913, though unavoidably delayed for publication until 1919. His *Nature of Scripture* (1922) was published because 'the advocates of

[1] *H.R.* January 1926.

traditional theories on the Bible have been stirred up to new efforts' . . . 'the recent course of discussion has suggested that the publication of this volume might serve a useful purpose'. This recognition of the opportunity and his closure with it could be illustrated in regard to other of his writings, but one more example will suffice. *Christianity: Its Nature and Truth* (1908), as an exposition of Christian theology, was written against a background of a wave of secularism: 'the task is especially urgent for the sake of the young people in our churches, who are drifting away from the faith because they had been trained neither to understand nor defend it'.

It would be a mistake, however, if we were to assume that Peake's chief concern was to secure an acceptance of the critical view of the Bible. A rather pathetic interest attaches to some words which he wrote in January 1926.

People have often disappointed me by putting the emphasis of my work where I should never have dreamed of putting it myself. It is something no doubt to be grateful for, that we have come through the difficulties raised by biblical criticism so well. But criticism for myself has never been anything more than a means to an end. It is not merely that critical problems attract me much less than some other biblical problems, but that I regard them as far less fundamental. My own mind has always been far more concerned with the history of religion than with the analysis and dating of documents, though it is indispensible to get your documents in their right order if the history of the religion is to be reconstituted. But I do not regard the problem of the Pentateuch or the Synoptic Problem as intrinsically more interesting that the Homeric problem . . . But if I am remembered by anything after I am dead, I hope it will not be as a student of biblical criticism, but as an interpreter of the great personalities of Scripture and their contributions to religious thought.[1]

Fundamentally Peake was a student of the Word of God to men, and no investigation of the minutiae of scholarship—though no one could examine those points more accurately than he could—was allowed to interfere with or obscure his main purpose—that of making clear the message of the Living God to his readers. His study of the Scriptures led him to the declaration that the key to an understanding of the Bible was a recognition of its essential nature as the written record of the progressive revelation of the character and purposes of God in history and in experience. This truth concerning the nature of Scripture he never ceased to expound and it is here that we can begin to discern the greatness of his achievement. He strove unceasingly to spread this truth far and wide to ordinary, intelligent folk, by his many books, by his innumerable articles and reviews, and by his lectures and by the sermons he preached. Looking back upon Peake's work taken as a whole it becomes clear that its most important feature was the power of mediating to the plain man this truth as the means by which, in the light of modern research, the Bible must be read in true perspective: using his own discoveries he laid down a sound

[1] Ibid.

foundation of historical fact upon which the Christian affirmations rested. Peake's supreme achievement lay in his commitment to popularization. He was himself accustomed to say that his mission was that of 'the middleman'. So his distinctive accomplishment lay in the diffusion of the methods and results of sound biblical learning. He lifted a generation of Christian laity, brought up in the old tradition, to the making of the difficult transition to a modern outlook without loss of balance, and his work did much to save (in particular) the Free Churches of Great Britain from the baneful effects of Fundamentalist controversies, though his influence extended far beyond that sphere.[1] We may well summarize his achievement in the following words:

Throughout that long and heroic life, he remained true to his great task of bringing down the close study of the Word of God from heaven to men.... Like a true musician, he made others share what his own ear could detect, the most delicate harmonies and the broad sweeping effects; while, as those who knew him best were aware, he could frame out of three sounds not a fourth, but a star.[2]

V

As we have noted, the approach of Peake's sixtieth birthday in 1925, made it evident that his physical condition was bending more and more under the immense burden which, by virtue of his vast commitment, he was carrying. In 1926, when invited to deliver the Cole Lectures at Vanderbilt University in the United States it was the condition of his health which was the basic factor, not only in the proposed postponement of acceptance, but subsequently the final ground on which he declined the invitation, being forbidden by his medical advisers. In 1927 when he was approached as to his becoming President of the National Free Church Council it was only on condition of a most strictly limited programme of duties, that he finally accepted the invitation, and even then this left a deep concern regarding him in the minds of his friends. It was an amazing achievement that in 1928 he carried through to the end of his presidential year without disaster.

It was in the early spring of 1929 that Peake embarked upon a holiday tour to the Mediterranean and Palestine. The party included old and congenial friends—the Rev. J. Harryman Taylor, whom he had known at Oxford, the Rev. Dr George Jackson and the Rev. Harry Bisseker, Head Master of the Leys School, Cambridge. Travelling overland to Genoa, they embarked on the *Ausonia* calling at Naples, where they visited the ruins of Pompei, then sailing on to Alexandria. They spent some time in

---

[1] *D.N.B.*, C. H. Dodd. Cf. *The Times*, 20 August 1929. G. Jackson, the *Manchester Guardian*, 19 August 1929.
[2] W. F. Lofthouse, *London Quarterly Review*, January 1930.

Cairo, from whence they visited the Pyramids; then across the Suez Canal and on to Jerusalem. In Palestine they saw 'the most essential things', visiting Bethlehem and Nazareth, which country they found interesting despite 'the rank growth of ecclesiastical legend'. Peake made a personal journey to Anathoth, the birthplace of Jeremiah. They came eventually to Haifa on the coast where they embarked on the *Italia* for the return journey. Calling at Cyprus they went on through the Dardanelles to Constantinople, where a large quantity of letters awaited him. They moved on through the islands of the Aegean Sea, and came to Athens. They reached Marseilles and finally arrived in London on April 25. The tour had brought some renewal of strength and refreshment of mind.

On his return Peake found an invitation asking him to write a long article on 'The History and Religion of Israel' for the new *Dictionaire Encyclopedique de la Bible*, which Professor Westphal of Paris was editing. The invitation was accepted, and it was to prove the last piece of work he was to undertake. This was in June 1929.

In July he attended the meetings of the Society for Old Testament Study at Oxford. On his return the following day he developed what seemed to be influenza, with an obstinately high temperature. Ten days later, on the advice of Dr Burgess, the newly-elected President of the British Medical Association, he was removed to a private ward in the Manchester Royal Infirmary. On 6 August an operation was performed for the removal of a hydatid cyst, and during the following thirteen days his life hung as by a thread. In the early morning of 19 August the end came.

Three days later the funeral service took place in the Chapel of the College to which he had given so much of his life's work, and throughout it was marked by the note of Christian triumph. Afterwards, all that could die of Arthur Samuel Peake was laid to rest in the Southern Cemetery, Manchester.

The tributes in the press far and wide and the letters of sympathy received by the family were almost without number, all of which revealed true greatness. One letter, written to Mrs Peake we may quote:

Dear Mrs Peake,
We have the news here this morning of the migration of our beloved friend. How they will be ringing the bells of Paradise over the arrival, and how they will throng around him, and ask how it was he was so long in coming. We could tell them, because we know how much he was wanted here, however they may crown him otherwise. I will try to come over, but am not very certain of my movements.
    Thy friend,
    Rendel Harris.

Arthur Samuel Peake left behind him a stainless name and the memory of a quiet and universally effective service.

On 2 June 1933, in the presence of a widely representative company, a bronze memorial tablet was unveiled in the College Chapel by the President of Conference, Dr J. Scott Lidgett. It bears this sentence:

> He gave counsel by his understanding
> Wise were his words in their instruction.

APPENDIX

SELECT BIBLIOGRAPHY
of Dr A. S. Peake's Printed Works

THE following bibliography is necessarily incomplete. Some of the material is elusive, for sometimes review articles are unsigned; also the amount of material is so vast that time has not allowed for complete search, and in any case space would forbid the printing of a full record, even if such could be made. Selection has therefore been necessary.

This bibliography takes no account of the enormous number of reviews to be found in the pages of the *Holborn Review* (during the years 1919–29); in the *Times Literary Supplement*, some fifty of which fortunately survive amongst the Peake papers, and which, although they bear no printed indication as to the writer, yet have Peake's written signature, but form only part of his contribution (1919–1929) to that periodical; in the *Primitive Methodist Leader*, the *Methodist Recorder*, the *Methodist Times*, the *British Weekly*, the *British Friend*; and in numerous other periodicals. Neither does it include his large correspondence in the press.

Nor are all the articles which have been traced recorded here, again owing to the restriction of space. Those set down, however, may be regarded as representative, and the following list will serve at least to indicate something of Peake's enormous literary output, and will reveal in particular his deep concern to mediate the truth of Christianity and the methods and results of biblical scholarship to the ordinary person.

Abbreviations:

        P.M.Q.R. : *Primitive Methodist Quarterly Review*
        H.R. : *Holborn Review*
        P.M.L. : *Primitive Methodist Leader*
        B.J.R.L. : *Bulletin of John Rylands Library*

1891
'The Synoptic Problem' in *P.M.Q.R.*

1892
'The Textual Criticism of the Old and New Testaments' in *P.M.Q.R.*
'Mansfield College and Nonconformity' in *P.M.Q.R.*

1893
'The Higher Criticism and the Old Testament' in *P.M.Q.R.*
'The Place of Christ in Modern Theology' in *P.M.Q.R.*

1894
'Biblical Study' (four articles) in *P.M.Q.R.*
'Thomas Kelly Cheyne' in *Expository Times*. Vol VI

1895
'Professor W. Robertson Smith' in *P.M.Q.R.*
'Wellhausen and Dr Baxter' in *Expository Times*. Vol VII
'A Reply to Dr Baxter' in *Expository Times*. Vol VIII

1896
'The International Commentary' in *P.M.Q.R.*
'The Life of Cardinal Manning' in *P.M.Q.R.*
'Woman under Monasticism' in *P.M.Q.R.*

1897
A Guide to Biblical Study
'Dr Hort' in *P.M.Q.R.*
'Archbishop Benson's *Cyprian*' in *P.M.Q.R.*

1898
'Recent Literature on the New Testament' in *P.M.Q.R.*
'The Evolution of the Idea of God' in *P.M.Q.R.*

1899
'Recent Anthropology' in *P.M.Q.R.*

1900
'The *Encyclopaedia Britannica*' in *P.M.Q.R.*
'Gospel Problems' in *P.M.Q.R.*

1902
'Professor A. B. Davidson' in *P.M.Q.R.*
The Epistle to the Hebrews in 'The Century Bible'.

1903
The Epistle to the Colossians in *The Expositor's Greek Testament*. Vol III

1904
Articles in Hastings's *Dictionary of the Bible*:
Ahaz, Baal, Beelzebub, Benjamin, Dan, Dionsyia, Ecclesiastes, First Fruits, Issachar, Josiah, Judah, Manasseh, Uncleanness, Vow.

The Problem of Suffering in the Old Testament (Hartley Lecture, 1904; reprinted 1952)
'A Reply to Dr Denney' in *The Expositor*

1905

The Book of Job in 'The Century Bible'.
(ed.) *Inaugural Lectures delivered by Members of the Faculty of Theology* (1904-5) (University of Manchester). Chapter on 'The Recent Movement of Biblical Science'.
'Some Recent New Testament Criticism' in *P.M.Q.R.*
Articles in *P.M.L.*
  'What is Religion?'
  'The Permanence of Religion'.
  'Religion and Morality' (two articles).
  'Religion and Theology'.
  'The Construction of Theology' (two articles).
  'Religious Persecution' (two articles).
  'Reminiscences of a Book-Buyer' (two articles).
  'Social Law in the Spiritual World'.
  'John Wilhelm Rowntree'.

1906

Reform in Sunday School Teaching.
Articles in Hastings's *Dictionary of Christ and the Gospels*. Vol II Immanuel, Law.
'Some Recent New Testament Literature' (two articles) in *P.M.Q.R.*
Articles in *P.M.L.*
  'Jesus and Paul' (three articles).
  'Our Responsibility to Inferior Races'.
  'The Policy of Silence' (five articles).
  'The Old Version'.
  'The Distrust of Criticism' (four articles).
  'The Argument from Prophecy' (six articles).
  'Some Exegetical Commonplaces' (three articles).
  'Plain Truths for my Critics' (six articles).
  'A New System of Doctrine'.

1907

'The Problem of the Old Testament' in *Contemporary Review*.
'The Oxford Hebrew Lexicon' in *P.M.Q.R.*
'Messianic Prophecy' in *Lux Hominum: Studies in the Living Christ in the World of Today* (ed. T. Orde Ward).
Articles in *P.M.L.* (a series dealing with Scripture texts usually misunderstood and misapplied). Those marked with an asterisk are reprinted in *Plain Thoughts on Great Subjects*:

*'I have trodden the wine-press alone'.
*'Fools shall err elsewhere'.
'A peculiar people'.
*'Not with water only'.
'My Spirit shall not always strive'.
'How art thou fallen from heaven!'
*'Ye search the Scriptures'.
*'Christ's suffering in our flesh'.
'The heart of the Gospel'.

Also:
'The Presentation of Jesus in the Gospel of Mark'.
'Yahweh or Jehovah'.
'What is the meaning of Yahweh?'
'Books for Preachers' (two articles).
'Wrede on Paul' (two articles).
'The New Testament' in *The Year's Work in Classical Studies*.

1908

The Religion of Israel
Christianity: It's Nature and Truth
The Christian Race
Election and Service
Faded Myths
Articles in *P.M.L.*
'The Incarnation and Recent Criticism'.
'Studies in the Inner Life of Jesus' (two articles).
'The Doctrine of the Trinity'.
'The New Gospel Fragments' (Oxyrhynchus)
'The Cities of St Paul'.
'Books for Ministers' (three articles).
'The Cry of Desertion': A Sermon preached at Wesley's Chapel, London, January 21, 1908.
'The New Testament' in *The Year's Work in Classical Studies*.

1909

A Critical Introduction to the New Testament.
Articles in Hastings's *Encyclopaedia of Religion and Ethics*: Basilides, Cerinthus, Corinthians.
Articles in *P.M.L.*
'The Faith of the Prophets' (three articles)
'The Place of the Evangel in the Preaching of Today'.
'The Bible in the Light of Modern Research'.
'The Son of Perdition'.
'Studies in Mystical Religion' (two articles).
'The Christian Doctrine of God'.

'The Discipline of Inaction' (three articles).
'The New Testament' in *The Year's Work in Classical Studies*.
'The Verification of Religious Experience'. Paper read at the Methodist Assembly, Wesley's Chapel, 5 October 1909.
'The Cambridge Biblical Essays'.

1910

Heroes and Martyrs of Faith.
The Book of Jeremiah (Vol I) in 'The Century Bible'.
'Some Recent New Testament Literature' in *H.R.*
Articles in *P.M.L.*
   'The Gospels as Historical Documents'.
   'The Person and Place of Jesus Christ'.
   'Telling the Truth as a Fine Art'.
   'The Revised Version with Fuller References'.
   'The Perennial Fountain and the Broken Cistern'.
   'The Jungle of Jordan'.
   'The Inspiration of Prophecy'.
   'The Tercentenary of the Authorised Version'.
   'The Record of Revelation' (two articles). Official Sermon for the British and Foreign Bible Society.
   'Changing Conditions and Unchanging Realities'. Official Sermon preached before the Primitive Methodist Conference.
'The New Testament' in *The Year's Work in Classical Studies*.

1911

'Recent Literature on the New Testament' (two articles) in *H.R.*
'Dr Moffatt's *Introduction to the New Testament*' in *H.R.*
'The Methodist Church' in *Evangelical Christianity* by W. B. Selbie.
Articles in *P.M.L.*
   'The Tercentenary of the Authorised Version'.
   'Some Tercentenary Literature'.
   'The English Church in the Nineteenth Century'.
   'The Transcendance of God and the Authority of the Church'.
   'The Permanent Results of Biblical Criticism': Paper read at the Conference of the Methodist Episcopal Church, Toronto. 9 October 1911.
'The New Testament' in *The Year's Work in Classical Studies*.

1912

The Book of Jeremiah (Vol II) in 'The Century Bible'.
'Some Recent Work in Anthropology and Religion' in *H.R.*
Articles in *P.M.L.*
   'The Modern Criticism of the Bible'.
   'Professor Lake on The Earlier Pauline Epistles'.

'Time in the Light of Eternity'.
'Robertson Smith' (two articles).
'Principal A. M. Fairbairn' in *The Expositor*.

1913

The Bible: Its Origin, Its Significance and Its Abiding Worth.
'Some Recent Literature on the New Testament' in *H.R.*
Articles in Hastings's *Dictionary of Christ and the Gospels* (Vol II) Mockery, Parable of the Talents.
Articles in *P.M.L.*
   'Light on the Gospel from an Ancient Poet' (The Odes of Solomon).
   'A Study in Social and Religious History' (Review of Deissman's *St Paul*).
   'A Critical Introduction to the Old Testament' (Review of G. B. Gray's book).
   'Comparative Religion and Christian Missions'.
'The New Testament' in *The Year's Work in Classical Studies*.

1914

'Bibliographical Notes for Students of the Old and New Testaments' in *B.J.R.L.*
'Professor S. R. Driver' in *The Expositor*.
Articles in *P.M.L.*
   'Paul and Other Theologians'.
   'The late Professor Driver'.
'Samuel Rolles Driver: An Appreciation' in Manchester Egyptian and Oriental Society's Journal.
'The New Testament' in *The Year's Work in Classical Studies*.

1915

The History of German Theology during the Nineteenth Century.
'The Life of Dr Fairbairn' in *H.R.*
Articles in Hastings's *Dictionary of the Apostolic Church*. Cainites, Jude the Lord's Brother, Epistle of Jude.
Article in *P.M.L.*
   'The Heavenly Vision and the Missionary Vocation'. Sermon preached for the Missionary Society at the Reading Conference of the Primitive Methodist Church.

1916

Article in *P.M.L.*
   'Good Friday in War Time'.

1917

The Quintessence of Paulinism in *B.J.R.L.*

'A Record of Professor J. H. Moulton's Work with some Explanation of its Significance' in *James Hope Moulton (1863–1917)* in *B.J.R.L.*
Articles in *P.M.L.*
  'James Hope Moulton'.
  'Who is Offended and I burn not?' (eleven articles).

1918

Prisoners of Hope: The Problem of the Conscientious Objector.
'Universal Priesthood' in *Towards Reunion.*
'The Old Testament' in *Reunion in Eternity* by W. Robertson Nicoll.

1919

Peake's Commentary on the Bible (edited), including the following articles written by A. S. Peake:
  The Development of Old Testament Literature.
  The Chronology of the Old Testament.
  Genesis.
  The Poetical and Wisdom Literature.
  The Prophetic Literature.
  Isaiah 1–39.
  Jonah.
  Organisation, Church Meetings, Discipline, Social and Ethical Problems.
  The Pauline Epistles.
  1 Corinthians.
  General Bibliographies.
'The Person of Christ in the Revelation of John' in *Mansfield College Essays presented to A. M. Fairbairn.*
The Revelation of John (Hartley Lecture).
'In Memoriam: H. E. Kendall and J. Day Thompson' in *H.R.*
'Professor Saintsbury on The French Novel' in *H.R.*

1920

The Roots of Jewish Prophecy and Jewish Apocalyptic in *B.J.R.L.* (reprinted in *H.R.*) 1924.
'Some Recent New Testament Literature' in *H.R.*
'Dr Sanday' in *The Expositor.*
'In League with the Stones of the Field' in the *Expository Times.* Vol XXXIV.
Articles in *P.M.L.*
  'The Union of the Methodist Churches' (two articles).
  'Methodist Union: The Doctrinal Statement'.
  'Methodist Union: Why remain separate?'

1921

'The Intellectual Influences of the Age in their bearing on Personal Evangelism' in *Evangelism: A Re-interpretation* (ed. E. Aldom French).
'I believe in Jesus Christ' in *Our Common Faith* (a Sermon preached in St Ann's Church, Manchester) (ed. D. Dorrity).
Articles in *P.M.L.*
  'Methodist Union: The Ministerial Office Defined'.
  'The Victorian Attitude'.
  'The New Situation'.
  'The Army and Religion'.
  'The Average Soldier'.
  'The Defect in Religious Knowledge'.

1922

'Some Recent New Testament Literature' (two articles) in *H.R.*
'The Significance of the Book of Job' in *The Book of Job: A Metrical Version* by A. H. Mumford.
'The New Testament Record' in *The Christian Faith* (ed. C. F. Nolloth).
'The Social Mission of the Church'.
'The Bible and Social Reform' in *The Social Mission of the Church* (ed. National Free Church Council).
Articles in *P.M.L.*
  'The Indictment of the Churches' (five articles).
  'Christianity and War'.
  'Has the War raised New Problems in Theology?'
  'The War and German Theology'.
  'Commending Christianity'.
  'A Standard Christianity'.
  'Methodist Union Proposals: The Ministerial Session'.
  'Methodist Union: The Official Proposals'.
  'Methodist Union Opposition: Indictment of the Manifesto'.
  'The Reunion of Christendom': An address delivered at the Wesleyan Conference Unity Meeting at Sheffield on 25 July.

1923

Brotherhood in the Old Testament (The John Clifford Lecture for 1923).
Articles in *P.M.L.*
  'The Old Testament in the Sunday School' (two articles).
  'Sir William Robertson Nicoll'.
  'Memories of Dr Clifford'.
Bibliography in *Prophecy and the Prophets of Ancient Israel* (Theodore H. Robinson).

1924

The Messiah and the Son of Man in *B.J.R.L.*

'The Supernatural Birth of Jesus' in *Methodist Quarterly Review* (Methodist Episcopal Church, U.S.A.).
Articles in *P.M.L.*
  'Methodist Union and Doctrinal Standards'.
  'Methodist Union and the Sacraments'.
  'The Methodist Pulpit and Modern Thought'.
  'Christ's Unsearchable Riches' (a sermon preached at the Missionary Society meeting at the Primitive Methodist Conference).
  'Methodist Union: Reasons for acceptance of the Scheme'.

1925

Life of Sir William P. Hartley.
(Editor) *The People and the Book*. Chapter by A. S. Peake on 'The Religion of Israel from David to the Return from Exile'.
'Theology and Classical Scholarship' in *H.R.*
(Co-Editor) *An Outline of Christianity* (five volumes).
Chapters by A. S. Peake on:
  The Preparation for Christianity in Israel. (Vol I).
  The New Testament Assembled. (Vol I).
  The Genius of Methodism (Vol III).
  The Criticism of the Old Testament (Vol IV).

1926

'Some Recent Biblical Literature' in *H.R.*
'Sir William Robertson Nicoll' in *H.R.*
'Introduction and a Bibliography for English Readers' in *Introduction to the Old Testament* (E. Sellin, trans. W. Montgomery).
'Introduction to *Jonah*' by A. D. Martin.
Articles in *New Standard Bible Dictionary* (ed. by M. W. Jacobus, E. E. Nourse and A. C. Zenos) Isaiah; The Religion of Israel; Jeremiah.
Article *P.M.L.*
  'Our Approach to the Bible'.

1927

'Some Notes on Recent Biblical Literature' in *H.R.*
Elijah and Jezebel in *B.J.R.L.* Vol XI.
Commentaries on the Old and New Testaments (four articles) in the *Expository Times*, Vol XXXIX.
Introduction to *The Apocrypha: Its Story and Message* by S. H. Mellone.
'The Problem of the Suffering Servant' in *The Bible and Modern Religious Thought* (March 1927).

1928

Paul the Apostle: His Personality and Achievement in *B.J.R.L.*
Recent Development in Old Testament Criticism in *B.J.R.L.*

Pray for the Peace of Jerusalem: Presidential Address to the National Free Church Council, Bridlington Assembly.

'The Nature and Authority of Scripture' in *The Future of Christianity* (ed.) Sir James Marchant.

1929

Paul and the Jewish Christians in *B.J.R.L.*

'The Scholar and Theologian: Work on the Old and New Testaments' Ch. V. in *Joseph Estlin Carpenter: A Memorial Volume* ed. C. H. Herford.

'The Revelation of John' in *The Study Bible*.

1931

The Servant of Yahweh: Three Lectures delivered at King's College, London, during 1926, together with the Rylands Lectures on Old Testament and New Testament Subjects. Prefaced with Memorial Tribute by Dr Henry Guppy, Librarian of the John Rylands Library, Manchester.

BOOKS ON DR PEAKE

Arthur Samuel Peake, A Memoir by Leslie S. Peake (1930).
Plain Thoughts on Great Subjects, ed. L. S. Peake (n.d.).
Recollections and Appreciations, ed. W. F. Howard (1938).
Arthur Samuel Peake, 1865–1929: Essays in Commemoration. (ed. John T. Wilkinson, 1958).

INDEX

Aberdeen, University of, 75–6
Aberystwyth, University College of, 78
Abrahams, Dr Israel, 100n
Acton Scott, Shropshire, 9–10
Adeney, Dr W.F., 66
Anathoth, 101
Andrews, Prof. H. T., 112
Antliff, Dr Samuel, 45, 141
Antliff, Dr William, 45
Apocalyptic, 102, 106–7, 112–3
Arch, Joseph, 148
Arnold, Matthew, 173–4
Ashida, Prof., 129
Australian Methodist Conference, 131

Bartlet, Prof. Vernon, 35, 42
Baxter, Richard, 166
Bell, Anning (R.A.), 61
Bell, (Miss) Dorothy, 73–4, 187
Berry, Rev. Charles A., 91n
Bertholet, Prof. A., 104
Birkenhead, Cheshire, 9
Birmingham, University of, 79
Birtley, Radnorshire, 2n
Bitter Cry of Outcast London, The, 29, 147–148
Black, Dr Matthew, 128n
Blue Ribbon Movement, 150–1
Bolton, Lancashire, 78
Booth, William (General), 149
Bradley, A. C., 33
Brecon, Breconshire, 65
Brewis, Rev. J. T., 56, 178
British Weekly, 36, 88n, 90n
Bromsgrove, Worcs., 9–10
Brotherhood Movement, 106, 118
Browning, Robert, 22, 56, 175
Brucker, Raymond, 104
Buckley, Rev. E. R., 41–3
Bunyan, John, 10, 95, 185
Burgon, Dr (Dean), 34

Burkitt, F. C., 72
Burnet, J., 33

Cadoux, Dr. C. J., 77
Cairns, Dr D. S., 108
Campbell, Rev. R. J., 115
Cann (Miss) Elsie, ix, xi, 62–3, 127, 175, 185
Carpenter, Dr J. Estlin, 112, 155
Cheyne, T. K., 24, 100
Christian Ambassador, The, 45, 133
Church, R. W., 26
Church Stretton, Shropshire, 9, 11, 182
Classical Association, The, 78
Cole Lectures, 79, 195
Colenso, Bishop, 6
Comparative Religion, 69, 71
Contemporary Review, 97n
Congregationalism, 35
Congregational Quarterly, The, 136, 183
Conway, Prof. R. S., 112n, 114
Cooper, Prof. James, 76n
Coventry, 14, 29–30
Crompton, Rev. James, 16, 138–9, 144–5
Currie, R., 170n

Dale, Sir Alfred, 119–20
Dale, Dr R. W., 35, 94
Dante Society, 78
Davidson, Dr A. B., 25n, 98
Delitzsch, E., 26
Denney, Dr James, 119–20
Dodd, Prof. C. H., 72n, 195n
Dodds, Rev. F. W., 190
Dods, Dr Marcus, 88, 110, 111n
Driver, Prof. S. R., 18, 24–5, 89, 91, 97
Drummond, Dr Henry, 23
Duhm, 97, 100, 104n
Dummelow, Rev. J. R., 131–2
Dyke, Thomas, 13, 111

Edinburgh Theological Society, 78

INDEX

Egyptian and Oriental Society, 25n, 78
Elijah, 107–8
Elmfield College, York, 45
English Church Union, 132–3
Escott, Mr, 14, 21, 31
Essays and Reviews, 91, 93, 95n
Essenism, 109
Expositor, The, 25n, 36, 123
Expositor's Greek Testament, The, 109, 110

Fairbairn, Dr A. M., 26–7, 30, 35–6, 46–8, 52–3, 69–70, 74–5, 81n, 86, 103, 111, 119n
Farndale, Rev. W. E., 56n
Farr, James, 3n, 48
Farrar, Archdeacon F. W., 23
Findlay, Dr G. G., 168
Fletcher, Rev. John, 1
Fletcher, (Mrs) Mary, 1
Free Church Federal Council, 156, 162–3
Free Churches, National Council of, 151, 156–7, 179, 186, 195

Geden, Prof. A. S., 109
German Theology, 120–1
Giesebrecht, 100
Glasgow Theological College, 78, 120
Glover, W. B., 91n
Gnosticism, 23, 109
Gore, Bishop Charles, 132
Goudge, Dr H. L., 132
Grafian Theory, 97, 100
Gray, G. Buchanan, 36, 87n
Greenwood, B. J., 130
Grieve, Dr A. J., 127
Griffith-Jones, Dr E., 126–7
Guillaume, Prof. A., 132
Guppy, Dr Henry, 82–3

Hacking, Rev. Thomas, 3n
Hackney College, London, 143
Hadnall, Shropshire, 9
Harnack, Prof. A., 111
Hartley College, 45–67
  curriculum, 53
  extensions, 58
  library, 54–5
Hartley Lectures, 103, 112
Hartley, W. P., 37, 46, 48, 57–9, 61, 73, 77, 84, 119, 122
Harris, Dr J. Rendel, 155, 196
Hatch, Dr E., 26
Headlam, Dr A. C., 26n
Heidelberg, 38, 49–51, 108
Herford, Prof. C. H., 76, 82n, 99n, 103n, 155
Herman (Mrs) E., 135
Herridge, D., 40–1
Hird, Rev. Arthur, 182
Hobhouse, L. T., 33
Hobhouse, Stephen, 154–5

Hogg, Prof., 67, 71, 82
Holborn Review, 45, 134–6, 177
Holmes, Rev. Frank, 55n
Hölscher, 97
Hopkinson, Sir Alfred, 69
Horwill, H. W., 34
Howard, Dr W. F., 79n, 114, 126n, 135, 171, 192n
Humphries, Rev. A. L., 57, 60

Ingham, Rev. E. E., 3n, 11
International Critical Commentary, 26n
International Lessons, 145–6

Jackson, Dr George, 195
Japan, 135–6
Jewish Chronicle, 100n, 125n
Jewish Community, 78
Joachim, H. H., 33
Johnson, Dr Hewlett, 28n, 182
John Rylands Library, 81
John Rylands Library Bulletin, 82–3, 97, 106n, 113–4
Jones, Rev. Richard, 79
Jowett, Benjamin (Master of Balliol), 91, 93n, 95
Jowett, Dr J. H., 143

Kendall, Rev. George, 189
Kendall, Rev. H. B., 134
Kennedy, Dr H. A. A., 89
Keswick, Cumberland, 142
King's College, London, 80, 105
Knox, Bishop E. A., 68
Kuenen, 115

Lambeth Appeal, 163–4
Lancashire Independent College, 65, 68n, 69, 71, 111
Lang, Archbishop, 165
Lausanne Conference, 164
Lawley, Joseph, 34
Lawrence, J. J., 34
Lee, Atkinson, 60
Leintwardine, Shropshire, 2n, 11–13
Lewis, Rev. T., 65
Liddon, Canon H. P., 26
Lidgett, Dr J. Scott, 172, 197
Life of Faith, 131n.
Lightfoot, Bishop J. B., 18
Liverpool, University of, 78
Lofthouse, Dr W. F., 43, 79, 195n
Louvain, University of, 82
Ludlow, Shropshire, 11

Mackintosh, Dr Robert, 57, 65, 75
Macpherson, Rev. James, 45–6
Magdalen College, Oxford, 32
Manchester Guardian, 76, 111n, 117n, 164n, 195n

Manchester, University of, 68–84
Manicheism, 23
Mansfield College, Oxford, 26–7, 39
Manson, Prof. T. W., 71–2, 91n
Marti, 97
Matsumoto, Dr Tokio, 135–6
McFadyen, Dr J. E., 92, 113, 173
McGill University, 79
McKechnie, Rev. C. C., 36–7
McLachlan, Dr H., 177n
McLaren, Dr Alexander, 69
Meredith, George, 56
Meredith, William, 13, 19, 23, 29–30, 186
Merton College, Oxford, 33–4
Methodism Divided, 170n
Methodism, Primitive, 1, 6–8, 33, 35, 45–6, 134, 163, 167, 169–70
Methodism, United, 66, 170
Methodism, Wesleyan, 166–7
Methodist Union, 165–71
  doctrinal standards, 167
  opposition to, 167–9
  pastoral session, 167
  Enabling Bill, 171
Milligan, Dr George, 108
Ministerial Training, 45–6, 48–9, 53
Modern Churchman, The, 125n
Moffatt, Dr James, 83
Moorhouse, Bishop James, 68
Moulton, Dr J. Hope, 57, 75, 76, 78, 85, 98n, 101n, 102, 111n, 118, 121, 177
Murray, A. Victor, 185–6
Murray, Prof. Gilbert, 89, 99n. 151n, 152
Murray, H. J. A., 33

Natal, 188
Neilson, Rev. Daniel, 59
New Brighton, Cheshire, 9
New College, Oxford, 32
New Commentary of Holy Scripture, 132–3
New *Peake's Commentary*, x, 128n
Newman, John Henry (Cardinal), 19
Newton, Herefordshire, 1
New Zealand, 128
Nicoll, Dr William Robertson, 36, 47, 109, 117n, 120, 121n
Nigeria 190
Nightingale, Rev. Thomas, 186
North Rev. C. R., 81, 125n
Nott, Humphrey, 13, 37–8
Nowell, A. T., 61

Oldham, Lancashire, 78
Orr, Dr James, 78n
Owens College, 68–9
Oxford, 18–44
Oxford, Socialists', 40, 147
Oxford, University of, 18

Parkin, Rev. George, 59

Parsons, Dr R. G., 125
Paulinism, 23, 87–8, 114–5, 120
Peake, Annetta (cousin), 29, 140–1, 148
  Benjamin (grandfather), 1
  Emily Margaret (sister), 4
  George (uncle), 1
  George Newton (brother), 3–4, 11
  Harriet Mary (wife) *et passim*, 37–8, 149
  Irene (neice), 76
  Leslie Sillman (son), ix, *et passim*
  Margaretta (aunt), 3
  Rosabella (mother), 1, 2
  Rosabella Alice (sister), 4
  Samuel (father), 1, *et passim*
  William (brother), 3n
PEAKE, ARTHUR SAMUEL,
Biographical main sequence chronologically arranged
  birth and parentage, 1–4
  schooldays, 12, 14–15
  early reading, 9–10
  begins study of Greek, 14
  early friendships, 13–14
  death of mother, 14
  early academic successes, 14–15
  scholar of St John's, Oxford, 15–17
  award of Coventry Exhibition, 15, 17
  early Oxford days, 16–17, 19–24
  Third Class in Classical Moderations, 21
  enters Honours School of Theology, 21
  contributed theological papers, 23
  attends Bampton Lectures, 23
  his Oxford Tutors, 24–8
  first meeting with Dr A. M. Fairbairn, 26
  studying German theology, 28
  influence of W. Robertson Smith, 28
  discovers vocation, 29
  considers entering Congregational ministry, 30
  decides to remain a layman, 31
  award of Casberd Scholarship, 31
  First Class in Honours School of Theology, 31
  gains B.A., 31
  awarded Denyer and Johnson Scholarship, 31
  gains Ellerton Essay Prize, 32
  elected Fellow of Merton College, 32–4, 150
  becomes Lecturer at Mansfield College, 36
  guest of Dr Robertson Nicoll, 36
  becomes Book-Editor for the *P.M.Q.R.*, 37
  proceeds to M.A., 37
  interview with Mr W. P. Hartley, 37
  marriage to Miss Sillman of Oxford, 37–8
  two months at Heidelberg, 38–9
  leaves Mansfield College, 39
  church activity at Coventry, 15
  recreations at Oxford, 40
  influence of Oxford, 43–4

INDEX

PEAKE, ARTHUR SAMUEL,—*cont.*
  appointed tutor at Hartley College, 46–50
  account of first lecture, 55
  college curriculum, 53
  first enlargement of the College, 58
  further extensions, 58
  accepts lectureships at Lancashire and Victoria Park Colleges, 65–6
  removal to Freshfield, xii, 60
  students' presentation to, 57
  majority celebrations, 61, 183
  presentation of portrait, 61
  criticism of college curriculum, 63–4
  amalgamation of Hartley College and Victoria Park College, 64
  creation of Faculty of Theology at Manchester University, 68–9
  first John Rylands Professor of Biblical Exegesis, 69
  appointed Dean of the Faculty of Theology, 70, 124
  resigns lectureships at Lancashire and Victoria Park Colleges, 67
  return to Manchester, 64
  becomes Pro-Vice-Chancellor, 72
  President of the P.M.U.U., 73
  presents Dr Fairbairn for first Honorary D.D. of the University, 74–5
  receives Honorary D.D. of Aberdeen University, 75
  receives Honorary D.D. of Oxford University, 76–7
  extra-mural lectures, 78, 117
  illness, 80, 196–7
  membership of learned societies, 78
  President of Society of Old Testament Study, 80, 125
  Governor of John Rylands Library, 81
  approach to return to Oxford, 83–4
  accepts editorship of *Holborn Review*, 134
  attends Lausanne Conference, 164
  member of Reunion Conversations Committee, 163
  accepts Presidency of National Free Church Council, 156, 195
  Palestine tour, 101, 195–6
  final illness and death, 55*n*, 196–7
Selective References
  administration, skill in, 71–2
  appearance, 41, 55, 187
  biblical criticism, attitude to, 42, 194–5
  book-reviewer, 36, 134
  children, understanding of, 180–1, 183*n*
  Church and State, views on, 157–60
  classical scholar, 21, 78
  conscientious objector, defence of, 152–5
  courtesy, 62, 130, 186, 188
  detective stories, love of, 42, 182
  editorial qualifications, 124
  family relationships, 3*n*, 4, 180–1

Free Churchman, 30, 33, 156–61
friendship, power of, 40–1, 73–4
generosity, 185
German scholarship, valuation of, 28*n*, 82, 108, 120–1
health, 8, 16, 20–1, 65, 178–9
holidays, 11, 178–9
humour, sense of, 42, 74*n*, 184–5
industry, 85, 173–4
judgement, power of, 81, 96, 192–3
kindness, 185–6
library, 176
memory, 175
ordination, views on, 159–60, 162–3
Peake's Commentary, 126–33
  origin of, 126–8
  criticism of, 130–3
  influence of, 188
political views, 40, 148
prayers of, 180, 190–1
first sermon of, 138
preaching, features of, 141–3
  influence of, 141–3
prose style, 86
reading, range of, 65, 173, 183
rectitude, 19, 57, 188
religious experience, 8, 192
Roman Catholicism, attitude to, 17, 161–2
Shropshire, love of, 10*n*, 181
sacraments, view of, 157–8, 169–70
secret of influence, 54, 65, 187–91, 195
self-criticism, 183
serenity, 176, 191
social reform, interest in, 147–52
Sunday Schools, views on, 8, 40, 145–7
sympathy, 62–3
teaching, method of, 55–7
temperance movement, work for, 150–1
teller of stories, 42, 181
theological position, 115–6
uniqueness, 182–4, 187
unwritten works, 106
work, method and hours of, 175–6
Pearson, Rev. Samuel, 111
Peel, Dr Albert, 136, 183
Petty, Rev. John, 45
Pinchard, Rev. Arnold, 132–3
Presbyterianism, 159
Primitive Methodist Quarterly, 37, 119, 123
Primitive Methodist University Union, 73–4

Rees, Dr T. Hopkyn, 118
Rhys Davies, Prof. T., 68
Ritchie, Dr D. L., 79
Robinson, John (Pilgrim Father), 96
Robinson, E. B., 53–4
Robinson, Dr Theodore H., 80–1, 138*n*, 173
Roman Catholicism, 17, 161–2
Rowley, Prof. H. H., 128*n*
Rylands, Mrs, 68, 81–2

St John's College, Oxford, 17, 41
Sanday, Prof. W., 18, 25–6, 32–3, 69, 129
Scott, Dr Caleb, 69
Selbie, Dr W. B., 35, 69n, 83, 108
Servant Songs, 104–6
Sherwood, Rev. Thomas, 66
Shillito, Rev. George, 66
Simon, Dr D. W., 35
Skinner, Dr John, 76n, 77, 104n, 155, 173
Smith, Rev E. W., 123
Smith, Prof. George Adam, 76n, 77, 99n
Smith, W. Robertson, 28, 29n
Snow, T. C., 21–2, 129
Society for Old Testament Study, 80, 124–5, 196
Stead, W. T., 29n
Strand Magazine, 117
Stratford-upon-Avon, 14
Stringer, Charles, 16
Sunday Schools, 8, 144–7
Sunderland Institute, 45

Taylor, Rev. J. Harryman, 32, 37, 47n, 195
Taylor, Dr Vincent, 28n
Temple, William (Bishop of Manchester), 82
Thackeray, Dr H. St John, 76n
Thomson, Dr Alexander, 65
Torr, Dr W. G., 41, 131

Times, The, 88n, 132n
Times Literary Supplement, 123, 130n, 177
Tout, Prof. T. F., 70
Turner, Prof. H. P., 188

Unitarianism, 57, 68n

Vanderbilt University, U.S.A., 79, 195
von Hoonacker, Prof. A., 82
Victoria Park College, 64, 68n, 71
von Hügel, Baron, 76–7

Wales, University of, 79–80
Wardle, Rev. W. Lansdell, 60, 100n
Watson, Dr John, 59
Watts-Dunton, Theodore, 100n
Weatherhead, Rev. Leslie D., 173
Welldon, Bishop J. E. C., 164
Wellhausen, 18, 100, 115
Welsh Outlook, The, 79
Wesley Bible Union, 130n
Wesley, John, 1, 167
Wheaton Ashton, Staffs, 2
Whichcote, Benjamin, 92, 93n
Williams, Rev. T. Charles, 189
Wood, Dr Joseph, 46, 59
Woodbrooke Lectures, 78, 188
Whyte, Dr Alexander, 114